OS X® Mavericks

PORTABLE GENIUS

OS X® Mavericks

PORTABLE GENIUS

by Dwight Spivey

WILEY

OS X® Mavericks Portable Genius

Published by
John Wiley & Sons, Inc.
10475 Crosspoint Blvd.
Indianapolis, IN 46256
www.wiley.com

ISBN: 978-1-118-68322-4

Manufactured in the United States of America

10 9 8 7 6 5 4 3 2 1

For general information on our other products and services or to obtain technical support, please contact our Customer Care Department within the U.S. at (877) 762-2974, outside the U.S. at (317) 572-3993 or fax (317) 572-4002.

Wiley publishes in a variety of print and electronic formats and by print-on-demand. Some material included with standard print versions of this book may not be included in e-books or in print-on-demand. If this book refers to media such as a CD or DVD that is not included in the version you purchased, you may download this material at http://booksupport.wiley.com. For more information about Wiley products, visit www.wiley.com.

Library of Congress Control Number: 2013941605

Credits

Acquisitions Editor
Aaron Black

Project Editor
Martin V. Minner

Technical Editor
Paul Sihvonen-Binder

Copy Editor
Gwenette Gaddis

Editorial Director
Robyn Siesky

Business Manager
Amy Knies

Senior Marketing Manager
Sandy Smith

**Vice President and Executive
Group Publisher**
Richard Swadley

Vice President and Executive Publisher
Barry Pruett

Project Coordinator
Patrick Redmond

Graphics and Production Specialists
Jennifer Goldsmith
Christin Swinford

Quality Control Technician
Jessica Kramer

Proofreading and Indexing
BIM Indexing & Proofreading Services
Wordsmith Editorial

About the Author

Dwight Spivey is the author of several Mac books, including OS X Mountain Lion Portable Genius and Mac OS X Lion Portable Genius. He has specialized in working with Mac operating systems, applications, and hardware, as well as color and monochrome laser printers, for more than 15 years. He teaches classes on Mac usage and is a member of the Apple Developer Program. Dwight lives on the Gulf Coast of Alabama with his beautiful wife Cindy and their four amazing children: Victoria, Devyn, Emi, and Reid. He studies theology, draws comic strips, and roots for the Auburn Tigers ("War Eagle!") in his ever-decreasing spare time.

For my wife and children: I do what I do for love of you.

Acknowledgments

Thanks to my family (especially my wife and children) and friends for putting up with my many absences during the writing of this book. Much love, y'all!

Many thanks to my agent, Carole Jelen McClendon, for keeping me rolling!

I am very grateful to Aaron Black and Martin V. Minner. Aaron put this whole thing together, while Marty kept the ship afloat and on course.

Very special thanks to my technical editor, Paul Sihvonen-Binder (this is our second go-round in this series). The man continues to know his stuff.

Another special thank-you goes to Gwenette Gaddis for being my copy editor, which is just another way of saying that she made me sound much smarter than I could ever really hope to be.

To everyone else who has had a hand in getting this book from raw manuscript to the beautiful publication that it is, I cannot thank you enough. You make my work so much better than I deserve. I sincerely thank you for all your hard work and dedication to this book.

Contents

chapter 4

How Do I Manage User Accounts? 80

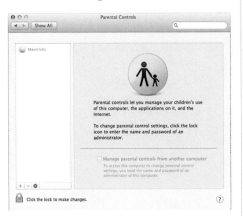

chapter 5

What Can I Do with Applications? 100

chapter 6

What Can I Do with Utilities? 138

chapter 9

How Do I Master the Web with Safari?   206

chapter 10

How Do I Stay Connected with Mail?   228

chapter 14

How Can I Automate My Mac? 346

chapter 15

How Do I Install Microsoft's
Windows Operating System
on My Mac? 366

appendix a

appendix b

chapter 16

Do You Have Any
Troubleshooting Tips?   380

Introduction

Thanks yet again, Apple! Again, you've raised the bar for your competitors and knocked the socks off the rest of us. Mavericks is not only the best-looking operating system around, it's also the most functional and easy to use.

Some of you may be rolling your eyes right now; all computers use the file and folder concept and some sort of colorful user interface, so there couldn't be that much difference between OS X and its competitors, right? Wrong! I don't say this just because of some blind devotion to all things Apple. I've actually used different flavors of Windows and Linux for more than 17 years, right alongside my trusty Mac, so experience has been my teacher. If I have any devotion to Apple, there are plenty of good reasons why, the subject of this book being the first.

Readers of this book who are already Mac users understand exactly what I'm talking about. For those of you moving from other computing platforms, it's my desire that by the end of this book you have a new perspective on computing and see what it means to have fun while working with your computer.

With OS X Mavericks Portable Genius you learn much more than the basics. You learn the subtle nuances and little tips and tricks that make using your Mac that much easier. I cover the gamut, from printing files, surfing the Internet, and using e-mail, to partitioning your hard drive, automating repetitive tasks, and troubleshooting pesky problems (with a little bit of geeky humor thrown in for good measure).

I hope this book does justice to OS X Mavericks, which isn't just a computer operating system, but an art form.

How Do I Get Started with Mavericks?

You are about to embark on the world's most advanced operating system experience, courtesy of Apple. In this chapter, I show you how to get OS X Mavericks up and running, as well as how to navigate Mavericks using the Finder application, which helps you find just about anything on your Mac. I also cover how to view a file without opening its parent application, how to find items on your Mac, easy ways to manipulate numerous open windows, and the latest and greatest method for launching your applications.

System Requirements for Installing Mavericks

As eager as you probably are to get started, make sure that your Mac meets all the necessary hardware requirements for properly installing and running Mavericks. Table 1.1 lists the requirements.

Table 1.1 Requirements for Installing Mavericks

Requirement	Minimum Specifications
Processor	Intel Core 2 Duo processor or better.
Memory	2GB is needed to run all the bells and whistles at a decent speed.
Media	Internet access is required to upgrade your Mac to Mavericks. You also must be running Mac OS X Snow Leopard 10.6.8 or higher to install Mavericks from the Mac App Store.
Hard drive or solid-state storage	At least 8GB of free space.

What's New in Mavericks?

Apple has been busy: Mavericks adds more than 200 new features to OS X! But it's not the quantity of features that impresses — it's the quality. Check out some of the more prominent Mavericks goodies:

- **Finder.** Apple has made a few improvements to the Finder that enhance what's already a sturdy staple of every Mac user's experience. Mavericks adds the convenience of tabs to Finder windows, along with an enhanced tagging system to better organize files.

- **iCloud Keychain.** iCloud Keychain keeps all your passwords, and even credit card information, current and protected across all devices that you authorize for its use. This makes it a breeze to keep up with the multiple passwords and card numbers that most of us have.

- **Safari.** Safari has experienced significant improvements, particularly in terms of speed and simplicity. Even features we're familiar with have been streamlined for greater functionality; see Top Sites in Chapter 9, for example.

- **Calendar.** Calendar has been given a new look and a simpler interface, along with the ability to make changes to events in a snap. Find more on Calendar in Chapter 8.

- **Notifications.** When you receive something new on your Mac (e-mail messages, reminders, and so on), Notifications now allows you to respond to them from within the notification pop-up, without having to leave the app you're currently in. Also, this new version of Notifications allows you to receive alerts from websites without needing Safari.

- **Maps.** If you're familiar with Apple's iPhone or iPad, you've most likely used the Maps app. Well, Mavericks brings the Maps app to OS X. Find out more in Chapter 5.

- **iBooks.** iBooks has been everybody's favorite e-reader on the iPhone and iPad for quite a while, and now Mavericks brings its magic to Macs everywhere.

- **Lots of under-the-hood enhancements.** Mavericks has numerous features that average users don't want to read about, but they're thankful when these features positively affect the daily use of their Mac. Technologies such as Compressed Memory, App Nap, and Timer Coalescing team up to make your Mac much speedier and more efficient, which we all can appreciate.

Upgrading to Mavericks

Let's get started with your upgrade to the latest from Apple. Follow these steps:

1. **Make sure you are connected to the Internet.**

Caution Back up your files before performing the upgrade to Mavericks! Years of experience have taught me not to make a major leap (such as an operating system upgrade) without backing up first. If you don't, Murphy's Law dictates that something will erase Grandma's recipes that have been passed down for generations.

2. **Check the version of OS X you currently have installed by choosing Apple menu ⇨ About This Mac in the upper-left corner of your screen.** You must have at least Mac OS X 10.6.8 to install Mavericks (10.9).

3. **Open the App Store, and type** Mavericks **into the search field in the upper-right corner.**

4. **Select and buy Mavericks from the App Store.** You must have an Apple ID to do so. If you don't have one, click the Create an Apple ID button when prompted.

5. **After Mavericks downloads, it begins the installation process.** Follow the on-screen instructions to complete your upgrade. You are now fully Mavericksized!

Working with the Finder

After your Mac boots or when you first log in, look at that smiley-face guy grinning at you near the bottom-left corner of your screen. That's the Finder, as shown in Figure 1.1, and it's one of the most important items in OS X Mavericks.

The Finder is an application that always runs in Mavericks, and it has been a part of Mac OS since its inception. The Finder is what Mac fans have used for decades to browse their computer drives and discs.

It has evolved into a great tool that I can't imagine not having (especially because you can't view the contents of your hard drive without it). For Windows converts, think of the Finder as the OS X equivalent to Windows Explorer. In this section, I show you how to use the basic features in Finder, and I give you tips to make it even easier and more productive to use.

1.1 The Finder icon.

The Mavericks desktop at a glance

The desktop is what you see when you first start up or log in to your Mac. This is where all the action in your applications takes place. The desktop is a major part (and actually, the starting point) of the Finder.

Figure 1.2 should mirror your own Mac screen very closely after you log in. It shows the major parts that you see when the Finder first comes up.

Now that you know the names of the items you see in the Finder, you can use Table 1.2 to decipher what functionality they provide.

Table 1.2 Finder Items

Item	Function
Apple menu	This menu provides quick access to functions, such as Sleep, Restart, Shut Down, Recent Items, and System Preferences. Windows users find that it functions similarly to the Start menu.
Menu bar	Use the menu bar in the Finder and in other applications to print, copy and paste, and change application preferences.
Desktop	This functions like the desktop on your desk. It's where everything else (such as documents and applications) sits while you are working. You can easily change the desktop picture; see Chapter 2 for more details.
WiFi Status	This displays the signal strength of your wireless network connection.
Volume	This adjusts the Mac volume.
Clock	This displays the current date and time.
Users menu	This shows the user currently logged in, as well as a list of other users.
Spotlight	This searches your Mac for files and folders. I discuss this more later in the chapter.

Item	Function
Notification Center	View new and pending notifications by clicking this icon.
Dock	This houses icons that link to applications and other items that you use most frequently. You can modify the Dock, as explained later in this chapter.
Trash	This contains files and folders that you want to remove from your Mac. Former Windows users will find it similar to the Recycle Bin.
Downloads stack	This provides fast access to items in your home folder's Downloads folder.

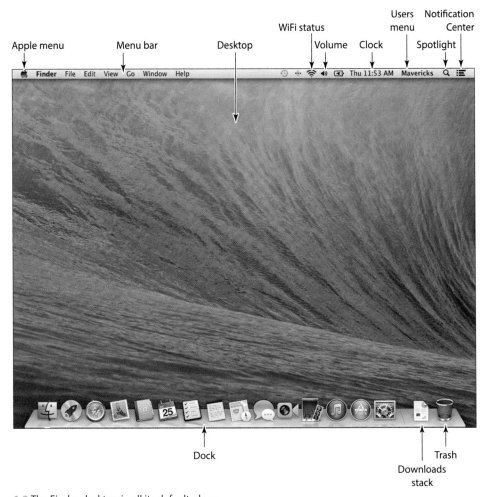

1.2 The Finder desktop in all its default glory.

Now that you are more familiar with the features of the desktop, you can examine a Finder window, which is the mechanism you need to view files and folders on your drives. Figure 1.3 shows a default Finder window.

Table 1.3 gives a brief breakdown of each noteworthy item in the Finder window.

1.3 Finder windows are used for browsing your drives, files, and folders.

Table 1.3 Finder Window Components

Component	Description
Folders	These store files and other subfolders.
Toolbar	This contains tools for accessing files and folders.
Sidebar	This provides quick links to drives, favorite folders, shared folders, and pre-configured searches.
Search	Type a search term to look for it in the current folder.
Share	Click the Share button to share a selected item.
Full screen	This icon toggles between windowed and full-screen viewing modes.
Results window	This shows the files and subfolders that reside in a folder and displays search results.

Setting the Finder preferences

You'll notice throughout this book that you can modify most things in Mavericks to match your personal preferences and tastes (to one degree or another), and that's the way I like it. The Finder is no exception; see Chapter 2 for lots of Finder customization tips. To access its preferences, choose Finder ⇨ Preferences or press ⌘+,. Let's look at the preferences that the Finder allows you to control.

General

The options listed in the General tab of the Finder Preferences window, as shown in Figure 1.4, are fairly self-explanatory, with the exception of spring-loaded folders and windows, which are so cool that they get their own sidebar.

The available options allow you to do the following:

1.4 Options available in the General tab.

- **Show certain items (such as hard or external disks, CDs, DVDs, iPods, or servers) on the desktop.**

- **Choose which folder automatically opens when you open a new Finder window.**

- **Decide whether to always open folders in tabs or new (separate) windows.** I discuss tabs a bit more later in this chapter.

Spring-Loaded Folders and Windows

Spring-loaded folders and windows are a neat feature of the Finder, but they're foreign to many Mac users, especially new recruits. Enabling spring-loaded folders and windows allows you to move items between folders and drives with minimal effort.

With this feature enabled, you can drag an item over any folder, hold it there for just a split second, and the folder automatically opens. Continue to hold the mouse button down while you position the item over each subfolder, and they all behave accordingly— automatically opening and allowing you to drill down into the subfolders as far as you need to. Finally, drop the item into the folder you want to move it to by releasing the mouse button. Reading a description of this feature can be pretty boring, so give it a try on your own to master this nifty little trick.

Tags and Sidebar

The Tags tab of the Finder Preferences window allows you to assign color and/or label tags to categories that you determine. You can decide which tags appear in the Finder sidebar from here, as shown in Figure 1.5, as well as delete and rename tags.

The Sidebar tab of the Finder Preferences window simply lets you choose which types of items to display in the sidebar of every Finder window.

Advanced

Table 1.4 explains the options available in the Advanced tab of the Finder Preferences window.

1.5 Determine which tags are available in the Finder's sidebar.

Genius You can securely empty the Trash on a case-by-case basis instead of enabling it all the time. To do so, place the item you want to permanently delete in the Trash, and then choose Finder ➪ Secure Empty Trash.

Table 1.4 Advanced Tab Options

Option	Function
Show all filename extensions	Each file has an extension at the end of its name that is hidden by default. This extension helps Mavericks know what type of document it is and with which application it is associated. Unless you understand these extensions, it is best to leave this option deselected.
Show warning before changing an extension	Mavericks warns you that you are about to change the extension of a file. This warning is beneficial so that you don't accidentally change an extension, which could cause your document to open in a different application than intended, or not open at all.
Show warning before emptying the Trash	Mavericks prompts you to confirm that you mean to empty the Trash before allowing you to do so. This option is designed to help prevent accidental deletions of important info.

Option	Function
Empty Trash securely	Select this option to make certain that all traces of a file are removed from the hard drive when you empty the Trash. This is a feature security nuts love, but it prevents you from ever recovering any files you may have accidentally deleted. Use this option with caution.
When performing a search	Determine the default location for searches by selecting an option from this pop-up menu.

Moving around in Finder

OS X employs the same basic navigation techniques as any other graphical operating system. Double-clicking opens files and folders, while right-clicking (or Control-clicking) items opens contextual menus with which you can alter or perform an action on an item. You can also click and drag items to move them to and fro. I'm sure you're experienced at the basics of mouse operations, so I'll move on to more Finder-centric tasks and options.

Utilizing Finder tabs

Tabs have become the norm in web browsers, but they are making their debut as a Finder navigation and organization tool in Mavericks. Tabs, shown in Figure 1.6, allow you to have multiple folders open at once, without the clutter of open window after open window mucking up your screen—not to mention confusing your eyes. Tabs allow you to keep a team of folders open within one neat, uncluttered window, all while freeing up tons of screen real estate. Here's how to utilize tabs within a Finder window:

- Press ⌘+T to open a new tab.
- Right-click or Control-click a folder to open it in a new tab.
- Rearrange tabs by simply clicking and dragging a tab from its current location to the preferred one in the tab bar.
- Close a tab by hovering your mouse pointer over the left corner of it and clicking the X that appears. You can do this whether or not you're viewing the contents of the tab.
- You can use any view you like within tabs. One tab can be in Cover Flow, another can use columns, and so on.
- Move items from one tab to another by simply dragging it from its current tab and dropping it onto the new one. If you want to place the item into a folder within another tab, use spring-loaded folders to do the job: Hold the item you're moving over the new tab until it opens, and then drop the item onto the folder you want it to occupy (drill as far down into the subfolders as you need to go).

1.6 Tabs keep your desktop from getting cluttered with multiple windows.

Organizing files with tags

Tags allow you to organize your files and folders by assigning them labels and colors of like items. For example, if you're working on a personal financial plan, you may have several documents (such as budgets and bank account records) that you use to put together and administer your plan. Tagging these documents with the same tags will make it simple to find and bring them all together, whether on your Mac or using iCloud.

To assign a tag to a file or folder:

1. **Right-click or Control-click a file or folder to open the contextual menu.**

2. **Select Tags from within the menu.**

3. **When the Tags pop-up opens, as shown in Figure 1.7, select the tags you want to assign to the file or folder.** You can choose as many as you deem appropriate.

Genius

You can create your own tags instead of relying on the few supplied by Mavericks. When the Tags pop-up menu appears, simply type the custom text for your new tag. If you want this new tag to appear in the Finder sidebar, don't forget to make that change in the Finder Preferences.

1.7 Assigning tags to like files and folders keeps them organized and easy to find.

You can quickly find items by clicking the appropriate tag in the Finder sidebar or by typing the tag name in the Search field of the Finder window.

Finder viewing options

You can change the way files and folders are displayed in Finder windows by choosing one of the four View options in the toolbar: icon, list, columns, or Cover Flow. Let's look at how each option displays the contents of the same folder so that you can clearly see the differences between the views.

Quickly Open Commonly Used Folders

I can't speak for other Mac users, but the Finder menu that I most wish I had discovered years ago is the Go menu, which you see in the menu bar when the Finder is active. The Go menu gives you instant access to the most commonly used folders in Mavericks, but I overlooked it for years. Click the Go menu to quickly go to the Applications or Utilities folders, your Network, and more.

Better yet, familiarize yourself with the keyboard shortcuts (listed to the right of each command in the Go menu) used to access those items. If an item you want to jump to isn't in the Go menu, press ⌘+Shift+G to open the Go to Folder window, type the path of the folder you want, and then click Go to jump over to it.

Icon view

Icon view shows each file and folder as large icons in the window, as shown in Figure 1.8.

1.8 A folder in icon view.

List view

List view does just what it says: It displays the files and folders in a list. You can arrange the list by filenames, the date the files were modified, the size of the file or folder, and the kind of item it is.

Columns view

My personal favorite is columns view. This view arranges the contents of a folder into columns, with each column displaying the contents of the subsequent folder. The final column shows a preview of any item you have selected.

Cover Flow view

Cover Flow is hands down the coolest viewing option at your disposal. As shown in Figure 1.9, files and folders are displayed as they really appear when opened in an application, which can be a great help when searching for a particular document or picture.

1.9 Click and drag the slider back and forth in Cover Flow view to see how effortlessly the Finder zooms through the files in the folder.

Getting Information on Files and Folders

You can never have too much information, and OS X is happy to provide you with what you need to know about the files and folders on your computer. To find out what there is to know about an item, click the file or folder you want information about, and then press ⌘+I, or choose File ➪ Get Info. Figure 1.10 shows a typical Info window.

To quickly get information on multiple items without having to open separate Info windows for each one, you can use the Inspector, which is a floating version of the Info window. To do this, follow these steps:

1. **Open a folder that contains the items about which you want to see information.**

2. **Press ⌘+Option+I to open the Inspector window. It looks just like a standard Info window.**

3. **Click each file in the folder to see its information in the Inspector window.** The Inspector changes information for each file you select. You can move between files by using the arrow keys on the keyboard.

Table 1.5 explains the categories that are available in the Info window.

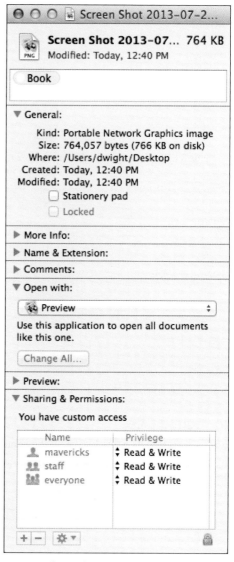

1.10 An Info window with several categories expanded.

16

Table 1.5 Information Categories

Category	Information Displayed
Tags field	This lists the tags assigned to the file or folder.
General	This tells you information such as what kind of item you're viewing, its size, where it's located, and when it was created and/or modified.
More Info	The information shown here varies depending on the type of item this is. If the file is an image, you might see its dimensions and color space.
Name & Extension	This allows you to change the name and extension of the file, and to hide the extension.
Comments field	Type information about the file that helps you find it using a Spotlight or Finder search. I discuss this more later in the chapter.
Open with	Select the default application that you want to use to open this type of file. This option displays only when getting info about a file.
Preview	This shows a small thumbnail version of the file.
Sharing & Permissions	This allows you to change access permissions for the item. Click the lock icon in the bottom-right corner to change the permissions. Click the plus (+) or minus (–) sign to add or remove users from the permissions list.

Using Quick Look

Quick Look is one of the best features in Mavericks. It allows you to see the contents of a file without actually opening it in its native application. For example, you can see every page of a Word document without having to open Word itself. This makes it really easy to find a document if you've forgotten its name but know the content that you're looking for, or when you're looking for just the right image but don't want to wait for Photoshop to load. To use Quick Look, follow these steps:

1. **Find the file you want to view, and click it once to highlight it.**

2. **Press the spacebar to open the file in Quick Look view, an example of which is shown in Figure 1.11.**

3. **To see the item in Full Screen mode, click the diagonal arrows at the top right of the window.** To exit Full Screen mode, click the arrows again.

4. **To open the item in its default application, click the Open button in the upper-right corner of the window.** In Figure 1.11, it says Open with Preview.

5. **Click the Share button to instantly share the file with friends, family, and colleagues.**

6. **If the file contains multiple pages, you can scroll through them by using the sidebar on the right side of the window.**

7. **Close the Quick Look window by clicking the X in the upper-left corner or by pressing the spacebar again.**

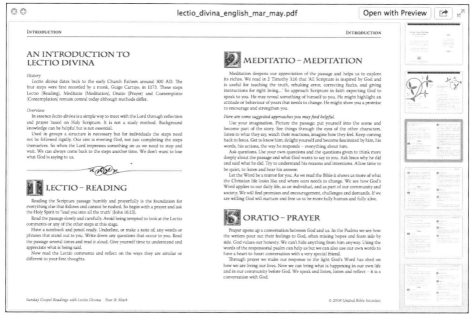

1.11 A file being viewed in Quick Look.

Working with Removable Media

When you insert or connect removable media, such as CDs, DVDs, external hard drives, and USB flash drives, Mavericks automatically mounts and makes them immediately available for use. The media icon appears on your desktop, in a Finder window, or both, depending on how you configure your Finder preferences. Figure 1.12 shows a flash drive (KINGSTON) and a DVD (RETURN_OF_THE_KING) in the sidebar of the Finder window under Devices. You can also double-click the icon on the desktop to see the media contents, just as you would any other drive or folder.

1.12 A DVD and a flash drive appear on the desktop and in the sidebar of the Finder window.

Perform one of the following actions to disconnect or eject removable media:

● **Click the Eject icon to the right of the media in the sidebar of the Finder window.**

● **Click and drag the media icon from the desktop, and drop it on the Trash icon in the Dock.**

● **Right-click (or Control-click) the media icon on the desktop or in the sidebar, and then select Eject from the contextual menu.**

● **Click the icon for the media once to highlight it, and press ⌘+E.**

Searching for Items

Apple introduced Spotlight in Mac OS X Tiger and instantly changed the way Mac users look for items on their computers. Spotlight finds things on your Mac much faster than you could if you were poking around every file and folder. In fact, it's the quickest way I've ever seen to find things on a computer.

When you first log in to your Mac, OS X creates an index of every file and folder it contains. Mavericks knows everything there is to know about every single thing that occupies your Mac, whether or not the item is visible. Mavericks stores this information, or metadata, and Spotlight uses the information, along with filenames and content, to find what you are looking for. Every time you add or remove an item, or add or remove something within that item (like text within a document), Mavericks updates its index files, thereby keeping all your searches up-to-the-minute accurate.

With all this information to look through, you might think a search could take forever, but that's not true. Spotlight can find items containing your search words almost as quickly as you can type them.

Searching with Spotlight

Chances are good that no matter how long it's been since you've seen the file you're looking for, Spotlight can dig it up for you. Here's how to use this amazing feature:

1. **Click the Spotlight icon (the magnifying glass) in the upper-right corner of the Mac window to reveal the Search text field, as shown in Figure 1.13.**

1.13 Type your search words into Spotlight.

2. **Type your search criteria in the text field.** Some applications have Spotlight Search fields in their toolbars, which you can use to type search words when specifically searching for items within that application (for example, when searching for an e-mail within Mail).

3. **Spotlight immediately begins searching your Mac and displays the information it finds that matches the criteria you typed in Step 2.**

4. **Scan the list for the item you want, and click it to open it in its default application.** Spotlight shows only the top matches in each category. To see all the matches, click Show All at the top of the list.

Genius

Did you notice that Spotlight doesn't show you only items such as documents and folders that contain your search words? Spotlight literally searches every file on your Mac for your search criteria, including e-mails, web pages you've visited, contacts, music, movies, images, and PDF files. Spotlight can even search other Macs on your network if they have file sharing enabled.

You can easily modify Spotlight to search where and how you want it to, using its preferences. Choose Apple menu ⇨ System Preferences, and then click the Spotlight icon to access the Spotlight preferences pane, as shown in Figure 1.14.

Figure 1.14 shows the Search Results section of the preferences pane. This section lists the categories of files that appear in the search results window. Select the check box next to those categories you want Spotlight to search, and deselect those you want it to leave alone.

For example, if you don't want Spotlight to check your e-mail when performing a search, simply deselect the Mail & Messages check box. You can also click and drag the categories into the order in which you prefer the results to be displayed.

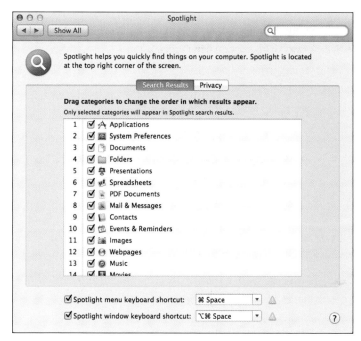

1.14 The Spotlight preferences let you search the way you want.

Click the Privacy tab at the top of the preferences pane to reveal the Privacy list. This section allows you to specify directories (folders) on your Mac that you want to exclude from any searches.

To modify the Privacy list, follow these steps:

1. **Click the plus sign (+) under the bottom-left corner of the list.**

2. **Browse your Mac for the folder you want to exclude from searches, highlight it, and click Choose.** The folder is now shown in the Privacy list.

3. **You can remove a folder from the list by highlighting it and clicking the minus sign (–) under the bottom-left corner of the list.**

The two check boxes at the bottom of the preferences pane allow you to enable Spotlight keyboard shortcuts for opening a Spotlight menu or window with the stroke of a couple of keys, as shown in Table 1.6. You can also select which keys perform these functions by choosing a key combination from the pop-up menus next to each option.

Searching with the Spotlight menu is certainly fast and easy, but it doesn't always yield the best results. In fact, it may give you so many results that you could never realistically review them all in a reasonable amount of time. To remedy this situation, Spotlight brings in your trusty friend, the Finder.

Table 1.6 Spotlight Keyboard Shortcuts

Function	Keys
Open the Spotlight menu	⌘+spacebar
Open the Spotlight (Finder) window	⌘+Option+spacebar
Jump to the first item in the next heading	⌘+Down arrow
Jump to the first item in the prior heading	⌘+Up arrow
Show an item in the Finder	Click the item while holding down ⌘.

Searching within a Finder window

The Finder gives you much more leverage to enhance your search beyond the Spotlight menu's capabilities.

To perform a basic Spotlight search within a Finder window, follow these steps:

1. **Open a Finder window by pressing ⌘+N while the Finder is activated.** If the Finder isn't the activated (or foremost) application, click the Finder icon on the left side of the Dock.

2. **Browse your Mac for the folder that includes the files you are looking for (or through), and click it to highlight it.**

3. **Type the search criteria into the Search text field in the upper-right corner of the Finder window.** Your results are displayed in the Finder.

Any search utility worth using allows lots of flexibility to narrow searches, and Spotlight is as flexible as they come.

Figure 1.15 shows a Finder search window that has been assigned several search attributes to act as filters for your search results. These attributes allow you to specify the type of file you want, including its name, when it was last opened, and many other specifications.

1.15 Customize your searches in Spotlight.

To add attributes to a search, follow these steps:

1. **Click the plus sign (+) next to Save in the upper-right area of the Finder window to add the first attribute.**

2. **Choose the type of attribute to use by clicking the pop-up menu (refer to Figure 1.15).** There are many more attributes preconfigured by Apple that you can access by choosing Other from the attribute list. You can also add other conditions (specifically, the All, Any, or None of the following are true criteria) to the search by holding down the Option key while clicking the plus sign (+). Also, some attributes have several pop-up menus that you can change to customize them.

3. **Make any setting changes to the attribute to narrow your search. Your new filtered search results are displayed almost instantly after you add an attribute.**

4. **Continue to add or remove (by clicking the minus sign) as many attributes as necessary.**

Genius

Use Boolean operators such as AND, OR, and NOT to logically narrow your search. You may also use quotes around text to specify that the words in the quotes must be found in the exact order you typed them.

Managing Windows with Mission Control

Mission Control is a feature that allows you to see every open window, Dashboard, and all your Spaces (more on those later in this chapter). Individual windows are grouped according to the application to which they belong. Figure 1.16 shows Mission Control in action.

1.16 Mission Control shows every open window and other items, such as Dashboard, all in one location.

Manipulating open windows

You can launch Mission Control in several ways:

- **Swipe up on your trackpad or Magic Mouse using three fingers.**
- **Click the Mission Control icon in the Dock.**
- **Press the Mission Control key on your keyboard, or press F9 (or fn+F9 for laptops) if you don't have a Mission Control key.** Consult the documentation for your Mac to find out if you have a Mission Control key.

Now that Mission Control is running, you can use it to move or copy files from location to location.

Moving a file from a folder to the desktop

You can easily move files from a folder to the desktop using Mission Control. Follow these steps:

1. **Find the file you want to move to your desktop, and click to select it.**

2. **Start dragging the file while simultaneously pressing ⌘+Mission Control (use F11 if you don't have a Mission Control key or fn+F11 on a laptop) to hide all windows.**

3. **To move the file, just drop it onto the desktop.**

    To copy the file to the desktop, press Option before dropping it.

    To create an alias for the file, press ⌘+Option before dropping it onto the desktop.

Copying text and graphics to the desktop

You can use Mission Control to quickly copy text or graphics from another item, such as a document or website. To do so:

1. **In the window that you want to copy from, select the text or graphics you want to copy to the desktop.**

2. **Start dragging the text or graphics, and press ⌘+Mission Control at the same time.**
   If you don't have a Mission Control key, use F11 (or fn+F11 on a laptop).

3. **Drop the text or graphics onto the desktop by releasing the mouse or trackpad button.**

Copying text and graphics from one window to another

Mission Control affords the flexibility to copy text and graphics from one open window to another. The window could be a folder, a website, or a document. To copy from one window to another, follow these steps:

1. **Open the window containing the text or graphics you want to copy, and then select the material.**

2. **Start dragging the text or graphics by performing one of these options:**

    - **If copying the text or graphic into another window in the same application, press Control+Mission Control (F10 if you don't have a Mission Control key, or fn+F10 for laptops).**

    - **If copying the text or graphics into a window from another application, press Mission Control (F9 if you don't have a Mission Control key, or fn+F9 on a laptop).**

25

3. **Hold the text or graphics over the window to which you want to copy them, and press the same keys you used in Step 2.**

4. **Copy the text or graphics to the other window by releasing the mouse or trackpad button.**

Setting Mission Control preferences

You can control several behaviors of Mission Control through the use of preferences. I'm big on preferences because they let you control more of the action.

Open the Mission Control preferences, shown in Figure 1.17, by choosing Apple menu⇨ System Preferences and selecting the Mission Control icon.

1.17 Configure the Mission Control preferences to suit your needs and work habits.

The preferences allow you to do the following:

- **Determine whether to show the Dashboard as a space**
- **Arrange spaces automatically according to which ones you used most recently**
- **Switch to a space automatically when choosing an application that has a window open within it**
- **Configure keyboard and mouse shortcuts for launching Mission Control, switching to application windows, showing the desktop, or showing Dashboard**

Managing Windows with Exposé

Exposé is a great feature for helping clear up the jumbled mess of windows that can grind your productivity to a halt. Exposé arranges your windows in one of three ways, using three of the function keys at the top of your keyboard: F9, F10, and F11. You've actually already used Exposé in conjunction with Mission Control if you performed any of the Mission Control tasks earlier in this chapter.

Note As with Mission Control, if you have a laptop you must press and hold the fn key in conjunction with the F9, F10, and F11 keys for them to function correctly with Exposé.

Press F9 to arrange the open windows so they can all be seen. Move the mouse pointer over the windows to see which applications they belong to. Click the window you want to bring to the forefront, or press F9 to return the Finder to its previous state.

Press F10 to bring all the open windows for the current application to the forefront. Press F11 to make all the open windows scram out of the way so you can see the desktop. To return the windows to their previous position, press F11 again.

Using Multiple Desktops with Spaces

Spaces is an organizational tool that lets you create multiple spaces for certain tasks. Spaces are essentially additional desktops. You could have a space for surfing the web and checking e-mail, another space to watch your stocks, a third space to work on a spreadsheet, and so on.

Adding and removing spaces

You can have as many as 16 spaces at one time. There's nothing magical about adding or removing spaces:

1. **Launch Mission Control.**

2. **Move your mouse pointer to the upper-right corner of the screen. A plus sign (+) appears, as shown in Figure 1.18.**

3. **Click the plus sign (+) to add a new space to the top of the Mission Control window.**

You can remove spaces just as easily as you add them:

1. **Launch Mission Control.**

2. **Move your mouse pointer to the upper-left corner of the space you want to remove. A small circle containing an X appears, as shown in Figure 1.19.**

3. **Click the X to remove the space.**

Moving between spaces

You can jump from space to space in several ways:

● **Launch Mission Control, and click the space to which you want to move.**

● **Press Control and the corresponding number key of the space to which you want to jump.** For example, if you want to move to the fourth space, press Control+4.

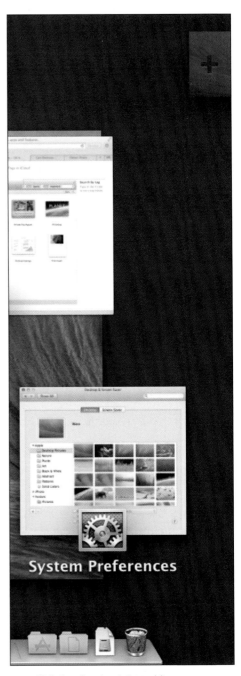

1.18 Click the plus sign (+) to add new spaces.

● **The coolest way is to swipe three fingers to the left or the right to scroll through your spaces.**

● **Press Control and the right or left arrow key to scroll from space to space.**

1.19 To remove a space, click the X.

Moving windows between spaces

You can easily move a window from one space to another:

● **Launch Mission Control from within the space that contains the window to which you want to move.** Drag and drop the window into the space you want it.

● **Place the mouse pointer over the window you want to move.** Press Control and the corresponding number key of the space to which you want to move the window, or press the right or left arrow key to find the desired space. Release the keys to drop the window into its new space.

● **Drag the window you desire to move all the way to the edge of the screen, and hold it there for a moment.** Mavericks detects that you want to move the window to another space and automatically switches to the next space. When you get to the space to which you want the window moved, release the mouse or trackpad button.

Assigning applications to spaces

One feature I love in Spaces is the ability to assign applications to always open in a specific space. To assign applications to spaces, click and hold the application icon in the Dock to open the shortcut menu. If you don't see the application icon, open it so the icon appears in the Dock.

Select one of the following options to assign an application to a space (or all spaces):

- **Assign the application to open in one assigned space.** Choose Options ⇨ This Desktop, as shown in Figure 1.20. The application now opens only in the assigned space.

- **Assign the application to open in all spaces.** Choose Options ⇨ All Desktops. When you open the application, it opens and is available across all the spaces you have in Mission Control.

1.20 Choose the space in which your applications are assigned to open.

- **Assign the application to open only in the space in which you are currently working.** Choose Options ⇨ None.

Managing Applications with Launchpad

Launchpad is an application launcher instantly familiar to folks who've used an iPhone, iPad, or iPod touch because of its obvious tie to iOS (the operating system used by those devices).

Launchpad displays all the apps installed on your Mac in full-screen mode, as shown in Figure 1.21.

Launching installed applications

Launching an application in Launchpad doesn't get much easier than this: Simply click the icon of the application you want to open. That's it!

If you don't see the application you want to open in the initial Launchpad window, it may be because you have so many applications installed that they cannot all fit into one window. If that's the case, notice the dots at the bottom of the Launchpad window (refer to Figure 1.21); these indicate that there is more than one Launchpad window. Swipe the trackpad or Magic Mouse with two fingers to see the contents of the other Launchpad windows. You can also type the name of the application you're looking for in the Search window at the top of the Launchpad screen to quickly find it.

1.21 Launchpad affords a quick, easy solution to finding and launching applications.

Grouping applications with folders

You can group applications according to their type to help you organize them in the Launchpad window. For example, Launchpad automatically groups your utilities in a Utilities folder, as shown in Figure 1.22.

To group apps into folders, follow these steps:

1. **Click and drag the application you want to add to a folder on top of another application that you want to add to the same folder.**

2. **Drop the first application onto the icon of the second to create a new folder.**

3. **Click the name of the folder once to highlight it, and type a descriptive name.**

To access the applications in a folder, click the folder and then click the app icon to launch it. To remove applications from a folder, click the folder and drag the app icon from the folder to the Launchpad window.

1.22 In Launchpad, you can group similar applications into folders.

How Can I Customize Mavericks?

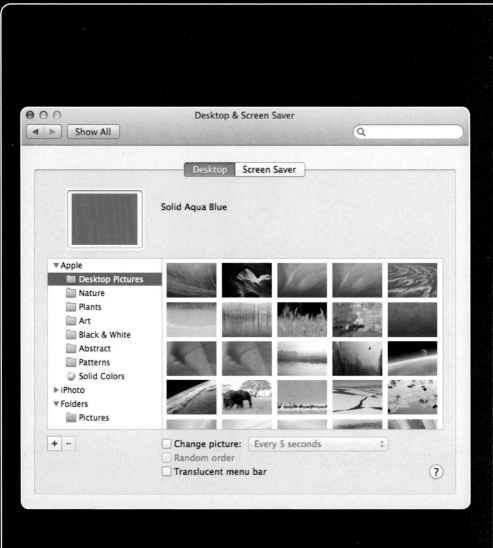

As attractive as Mavericks already is, you can also customize your Mac to match your personality and preferences. Customizing creates a more enjoyable work and play environment. One of the slickest ways to customize Mavericks is with Dashboard and its widgets. These miniature applications can help you do a multitude of things, such as keep up with the weather or get flight information. This chapter explores the numerous ways you can tweak Mavericks so you feel as comfortable in front of your computer as you do in your living room.

The General Preferences Pane

The General preferences pane, shown in Figure 2.1, is your first stop on the Mac customization tour. Here, you can modify the basic color and textual elements of your Finder windows. To open this pane, click the System Preferences icon in the Dock, or choose Apple menu⇨System Preferences. Next, click the General icon in the Personal category of the System Preferences window.

2.1 The General preferences pane.

Sidebar icon size

If the icons in Finder's sidebar are too large or too small for your preference, you can adjust them by using the options in the Sidebar icon size pop-up menu. Be sure to open a Finder window and watch it as you make the size selection.

Color modifications

The Appearance menu lets you choose the color you prefer for your system-wide menus and buttons. I hope either blue or graphite suits your taste because those are your only options.

You can change the default color used to highlight text with the Highlight color menu. Thankfully, there's a lengthy list of color choices available here.

Scrolling options

You have several options for viewing information that doesn't fit your screen. For example, scroll bars usually appear when they are needed and the area they reside in is moused over, as shown in Figure 2.2.

2.2 Scroll bars appear when the information in the window is too large to fit.

The options shown in Table 2.1 allow you to control how your Mac scrolls through documents or web pages that are too large for the screen.

Table 2.1 Scrolling Options

Option	Description
Show scroll bars	Scroll bars typically appear in a window only when the items within it don't quite fit and you are using a mouse or trackpad to maneuver within the window. This behavior is the Automatically based on mouse or trackpad option, which is the default. Choose the When scrolling option to have the scroll bars appear only when scrolling or Always to always display the scroll bars in windows.
Click in the scroll bar to	Select the Jump to the next page option for each click in the scroll bar to advance you one page in the document. The Jump to the spot that's clicked option moves you to the spot in the document that you are clicking. If you click the top of the scroll bar, you jump to the first page of the document.

Genius

You can switch between the Jump to the next page and Jump to the spot that's clicked options by holding down the Option key while clicking in the scroll bar.

Keeping changes to documents

By default, Mavericks automatically saves changes you've made to a document when you close it. If you prefer to be asked whether changes should be kept, select the box labeled Ask to keep changes when closing documents. The latter approach is most useful because you may not mean to keep changes to a document, and if you accidentally close it, those changes are saved anyway.

Closing windows when quitting an app

When you quit an app, Mavericks closes its windows and doesn't reopen them upon relaunch of the app. If you would rather Mavericks reopen the windows that were open before you last quit an app, deselect the box called Close windows when quitting an app.

Accessing recently used items

There's a very handy way to see and quickly access applications, documents, and servers that you've used recently. Simply click the Apple menu, and hold your mouse over Recent Items, as shown in Figure 2.3. The Number of Recent Items pop-up menus in the General preferences pane let you choose how many of each item type you want to list.

Viewing fonts

OS X uses a technique called anti-aliasing (or font smoothing) to help fonts appear without jagged edges. To enable or disable font smoothing in Mavericks, select the check box for Use LCD font smoothing when available (refer to Figure 2.1).

Changing the Desktop

No two things personalize your Mac quite as much as great desktop pictures and really cool screen savers. From photos of the kids to fantastic paintings of faraway space battles, desktop pictures and screen savers can be very personal displays of individual taste and style.

2.3 Looking at items that you've recently used.

Choosing a desktop picture

Open System Preferences by clicking its icon in the Dock or by choosing Apple menu ➪ System Preferences. Click the Desktop & Screen Saver icon in the Personal category, and then click the Desktop tab at the top of the pane.

The left side of the Desktop tab, shown in Figure 2.4, lists the desktop pictures available on your system. Apple has taken the liberty of supplying you with lots of pictures and has even arranged them into subject folders.

2.4 The Desktop tab of the Desktop & Screen Saver preferences pane.

You can also add your personal collection of desktop pictures to this list by following these steps:

1. **Click the + (plus sign) below the list.**
2. **Browse the hard drive for the folder that contains the pictures you want to use.**
3. **Click Choose.**

To remove folders from the list, simply highlight the folder to be removed and click the minus sign (–) below the list. To set an image as your default desktop picture, browse the list for the picture you want to use and click it.

Finding Desktop Pictures on the Web

The Internet is chock-full of great websites for downloading desktop pictures. You can find a desktop picture to suit just about any mood or taste by performing a search for "desktop picture" or "wallpaper." If you want to find Mac-specific desktop pictures, simply add "OS X" or "Mac" to your search criteria.

Here are a few sites you may want to check out:

- www.macdesktops.com
- www.theapplecollection.com/desktop/
- http://interfacelift.com/wallpaper/downloads/date/any/
- www.pixelgirlpresents.com/desktops.php
- http://browse.deviantart.com/customization/wallpaper/

If you get bored with your choice of desktop picture, or if it's just too hard to decide which one you like best, select the Change picture check box at the bottom of the pane. Use the pop-up menu next to this check box to determine how often you want your Mac to change its desktop background. To add even more spice, select the Random order check box. This allows your Mac to use its own discretion when choosing a desktop picture.

Selecting a screen saver

Screen savers look really great on a Mac screen, and they're somewhat useful for security purposes, but if not for these factors, screen savers would be obsolete in today's computing world. At one time, screen savers were a necessary tool to prevent burn-in from occurring on CRT-based monitors. Burn-in happens when a latent image appears on a monitor after it is turned off. New monitors are typically LCD or plasma, and burn-in is no longer as much of a concern.

To choose a screen saver that meets your personal standards of coolness, do the following:

1. **Open the Desktop & Screen Saver pane in System Preferences (Apple menu ⇨ System Preferences ⇨ Desktop & Screen Saver), and click the Screen Saver tab.**

2. **Browse the list of screen savers on the left side of the pane, and find the one that grabs your attention. Select the Random screen saver check box to allow OS X to choose the screen saver it uses.**

3. **Select the Show with clock check box if you want a digital clock displayed on-screen with the screen saver.**

4. **Choose an option within the Start after pop-up menu to set the amount of time that your Mac is idle before the screen saver starts.**

5. **Finalize your selection, and close System Preferences.**

Note   OS X comes loaded with several really neat screen savers, but plenty of screen savers can be downloaded from the web, so you can personalize to your heart's content. Open Safari, and search for "OS X screen savers" to find more screen savers than you can shake a stick at.

Setting the screen saver options

Some screen savers allow you to change the way they behave by supplying a Screen Saver Options button below the Preview window, as shown in Figure 2.5. Click Screen Saver Options to make adjustments to the look of the chosen screen saver. For example, select the Flurry screen saver from the Screen Savers list on the left of the pane. Click Screen Saver Options, and you see the options that are specific to that screen saver.

Using hot corners

Have you noticed the Hot Corners button in the bottom-left corner of the pane? Click it to see the Hot Corners preferences sheet, similar to the one shown in Figure 2.6. Here, you can set actions for your Mac to take when you move the mouse pointer to one of the four corners of your screen.

2.5 The Screen Saver tab of the Desktop & Screen Saver preferences pane.

41

Click one of the four pop-up menus to select an action for the corresponding screen corner. Table 2.2 lists actions you can select for hot corners.

2.6 The Hot Corners preferences sheet, also known as Active Screen Corners.

Table 2.2 Hot Corner Actions

Action	Result
Start Screen Saver and Disable Screen Saver	These two options speak, quite clearly, for themselves.
Mission Control	All open windows are arranged in the screen so they can be seen.
Application Windows	All open windows for the currently active application are neatly arranged so each of their contents can be displayed at once. This is also achieved with the F10 key and Mission Control, as discussed in Chapter 1.
Desktop	This is another feature of Mission Control, which causes all open windows to zoom off the screen so the desktop can clearly be seen. On current keyboards, this feature is mapped to ⌘+F3; on laptops, it's fn+F11.
Dashboard	The Dashboard opens when the mouse is moved to the hot corner. See sections later in this chapter for more information on Dashboard.
Notification Center	This opens the Notification Center.
Launchpad	This instantly brings up Launchpad.
Put Display to Sleep	This causes the monitor to go into sleep mode.
- (Minus sign)	This disables the hot corner.

Customizing the Finder

The Finder is the application you use most often on your Mac, so you may as well customize it to suit your needs and preferences. OS X gives you lots of latitude when it comes to customizing the Finder, and I show you a few of my favorite tweaks to this quintessential Mac OS standby in this section. Chapter 1 covers the ins and outs of using the Finder; in this chapter, you can discover how to give it that personal touch.

Finder windows

The Finder is a great tool for navigating your Mac, and I like to take full advantage of the available customization to make the Finder work for me.

Figure 2.7 shows an example of the Finder modified to my specs. One of the differences between my customized Finder window and the default configuration is that the toolbar and sidebar have been changed significantly. This gives me quick access to the tools and folders I use the most. I've also changed my view from Icons to Columns, and there are two new additions to the bottom of the window: the path and status bars.

In the rest of this section, I show you how I customized Finder. Of course, you don't have to make the same changes. In fact, I encourage you to experiment with all the options the Finder affords, including those I don't touch on, so you can find the combination that works best for you.

2.7 The Finder done my way.

Note   The path bar is an easy way to see where you've been and to quickly get back there. To enable it, open a new Finder window and choose View ➪ Show Path Bar. It then appears in the bottom of the Finder window, as shown in Figure 2.7. The folders in the path bar change as you browse your hard drive. Double-click one of the folders in the path bar to zoom back to it. It's sort of like taking a tiny step back in time!

Modifying the toolbar

The toolbar gives you fast access to common tasks and actions, and it helps you navigate your Mac more efficiently. You can change the default set of tools in the toolbar by adding items that you use more than others and removing those you don't need. All this is done in the Customize Toolbar sheet, shown in Figure 2.8.

Follow these steps to customize the Finder toolbar:

1. **Activate the Finder by clicking its icon on the left side of the Dock.**

2. **Choose View ⇨ Customize Toolbar to open the Customize Toolbar sheet.**

3. **To add an item to the toolbar, drag and drop it from the sheet to the position in the toolbar where you want it to appear.**

4. **To remove an item from the toolbar, simply drag and drop its icon anywhere outside of the Finder window, and it disappears.**

5. **If the arrangement of the icons in the toolbar doesn't suit you, just click and drag them to the spot where they work best.** As you drag an icon, the other icons move automatically to make room for it.

6. **After you have everything just right, click Done to close the sheet.**

2.8 The Customize Toolbar sheet allows you to edit the tools available in the toolbar.

Table 2.3 gives an overview of the function of each item in the Customize Toolbar Sheet to help you make informed decisions about those you want to include.

Genius

The fastest way to alter items already on the toolbar (or even the toolbar itself) is by using the trusty ⌘ key. To quickly rearrange items on the toolbar, hold down the ⌘ key, and click and drag the item to its new location. To remove an item, simply press ⌘+click and drag it out of the toolbar, and then drop it.

Table 2.3 Customize Toolbar Sheet Items

Item	Description/Action
Back	Navigate forward or backward in the folder path.
Path	Click to see the current folder path.
Arrange	Select a method for organizing items in the Finder window. Select from Name, Kind, Application, Date Last Opened, Date Added, Date Last Modified, Date Created, Size, Label, or None to return to the default arrangement.
View	Quickly change the view for the current Finder window.
Action	Choose from a list of common actions, such as creating a new folder or getting information on an item.
Eject	Eject a disc or other removable media.
Burn	Burn a CD or DVD.
Space and Flexible Space	Use this to separate items and groups of items.
New Folder	Create a new folder within the current one.
Delete	Move the selected file or folder to the Trash.
Connect	Open the Connect to Server window, which allows you to quickly connect to other computers.
Get Info	Show all information relative to the selected file or folder.
Search	Type the name of the item(s) you need to find on your hard drive.
Quick Look	This provides a glance at the contents of a file without having to open the application that created it.
Share	This affords a quick way to share items via e-mail, instant message, Twitter, or Flickr. The options for sharing vary depending on the file type of the item selected.
Label	Add a color-coded label to a file or folder. Select the item in the Finder window, and then click and hold the Label button to select a color.

Changing the sidebar

The sidebar contains links (or shortcuts) to folders, discs, and servers to which you often need access. You can modify the contents of the sidebar in a number of ways:

- **To remove an item you don't use, right-click (or Control-click) the item and select Remove from Sidebar.**

- **Add your favorite folders by dragging their icons into the sidebar under the Favorites section, as shown in Figure 2.9.** The other items in the sidebar shift as necessary to make room for their new neighbor.

- **Adjust the size of the sidebar by clicking and dragging the divider bar.**

● **Hide the sidebar from view altogether by choosing View ⇨ Hide Sidebar from the menu or by pressing ⌘+Option+S.**

● **Rearrange items in the sidebar by clicking and dragging them to their new location.**

Note See Chapter 1 to discover how to choose which Devices, Shared, Places, and Search For items are displayed by default in your sidebar.

2.9 Make the sidebar conform to your needs.

Adding a background image or color

One trick that adds a touch of class and functionality to your Finder windows is to add a background picture or color to them. These can be used for simple decoration or to differentiate the contents of each folder. For example, if you keep records of your children's homework on your

Mac, you could assign a picture of each child to the folder containing her homework. When you then open one of these folders in a Finder window, a light background picture of your little darling instantly identifies whose homework you're checking. This option is especially helpful if you have multiple windows open. To add a background image or color to your Finder windows, do the following:

1. **Open the folder to which you want to add the image or color.**

2. **Choose View ⇨ Show View Options, or press ⌘+J.**

3. **Select the Color option in the Background section to add a color to the window, or select the Picture option to place an image in the background, as shown in Figure 2.10.**

   ○ **If you choose to use a color, click inside the white square to the right of the option button to open the Colors palette.** Select the color that you want to use for the background, and close the Colors palette.

   ○ **If you select Picture, drag an image into the Drag image here box next to the Picture option button.**

2.10 Make changes to a folder's window background by using the Background section of the View Options window.

47

Note You must be in Icon view in order to use a background or color image in the Finder window. To do so, simply click the Icon view icon in the toolbar of the Finder window.

Caution A potential "oops" when using an image is that if the image is too large to fit in the window, you see only the part of it that does fit. The Preview application that is loaded with OS X Mavericks is a great tool for easily resizing images. See Chapter 12 for step-by-step instructions.

Changing icons

A popular method for redecorating your Mac is using custom icons for applications, folders, and files. You can change a plain folder icon into something more suitable for its contents. For example, you might use a football icon for the folder in which you keep your child's practice and game schedules. I've seen many a Mac on which icons were changed system-wide, from top to bottom!

Here's how to change any icon in OS X Mavericks:

1. **Highlight the icon you want to use, and press ⌘+I (Get Info) to open its Info window.**

2. **Click the icon picture in the upper-left corner of the Info window, as shown in Figure 2.11, and copy the icon by pressing ⌘+C or choosing Edit ⇨ Copy.**

3. **Close the Info window.**

4. **Highlight the item with the icon you want to change, and open its Info window by pressing ⌘+I.**

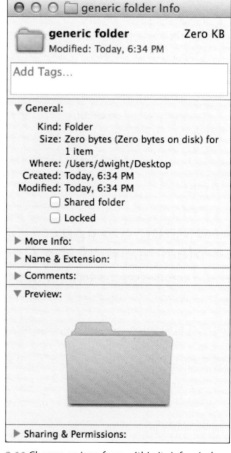

2.11 Change an icon from within its Info window.

5. **Click the icon in the upper-left corner of the Info window, and paste the new icon there by pressing ⌘+V or choosing Edit⇨Paste.**

6. **Close the changed item's Info window.**

Adding and removing items in the Dock

You can add and remove items to and from the Dock as you please, and it's easy to do:

- **To add an item to the Dock, simply drag its icon to the Dock and drop it where you want it.** You can also reposition an item in the Dock by simply dragging and dropping it in its new location.

- **If you have an application open that you want to keep in the Dock, click and hold its icon, hold your pointer over Options, and select Keep in Dock from the contextual menu that appears, as shown in Figure 2.12.**

- **To remove an item, drag its icon from the Dock and let go of the mouse button.** The icon disappears in a puff of smoke! Don't worry: The original item is still in its location; you've just removed its alias.

2.12 Keep an icon in the Dock if you use it often.

Changing the appearance or placement of the Dock

You can tame the Dock by setting its preferences to meet your needs. Open the Dock preferences by right-clicking (or Control-clicking) the divider line and selecting Dock Preferences.

The Dock preferences window lets you make several changes:

- **Increase or decrease the size of the Dock by moving the Size slider.**

- **If your icons are too small to see clearly, select the Magnification check box and adjust the slider to increase or decrease the amount of magnification.** Magnification of the icons occurs when you hold the mouse pointer over the Dock.

- **The Dock can be positioned on the left or right side of the window or at the bottom (the default setting).**

- **The Minimize windows using option lets you choose the special effect that occurs when you minimize a window into the Dock.** To minimize a window, click the yellow button in its upper-left corner.

- **Select the Double-click a window's title bar to minimize check box to enable the feature it describes.**

- **To save tons of space in the Dock, select the check box called Minimize windows into application icon.** To access minimized windows using this method, click and hold the icon for the application that owns the window, and you see the window in the contextual menu; click to maximize it.

- **Select the Animate opening applications check box to cause the icon of an item you are opening to bounce up and down in the Dock.** I leave this option deselected; the bouncing annoys the heck out of me.

- **If you don't like the Dock cramping your style—or your desktop space—you can hide it by selecting the check box next to Automatically hide and show the Dock.** When you inevitably have to use the Dock again, hold your mouse pointer at the bottom of your window for just a second. The Dock temporarily pops back into view, only to go back into hiding when you finish.

- **Select the Show indicator lights for open applications check box if you want bright white dots to appear beneath the icons of applications that are open.**

Working with Widgets

Mavericks includes an application called Dashboard that affords you another fun way to customize your Mac. With Dashboard, you can access and manage a multitude of widgets to track packages, get driving directions, browse the Yellow Pages, check stocks, see the latest weather forecasts, find out what movies are playing at your local multiplex, play Sudoku, and so on. Widgets are one of those rare things that make your life easier and are cool to use at the same time. In the next few sections, I show you how to access, use, customize, and even create your own widgets.

Genius

If you have a Mac laptop with a multi-touch trackpad, or if you have the Magic Trackpad for your desktop Mac, simply swipe three fingers from left to right to flick over to the Dashboard screen!

To open Dashboard and see the default set of running widgets, do one of the following:

- **Click the Dashboard icon in your Dock.**

- **Press F4 if you have a newer keyboard or F12 if your keyboard is a bit older.**

Note Newer Mac keyboards, including those on newer laptops, may use F4 instead of F12. However, on laptops, you can use fn+F12 to achieve the same functionality. Consult the documentation that came with your keyboard or laptop for more information.

In the main body of the screen, you see the four widgets that Mavericks runs out of the gate: Calculator, Calendar, Weather, and World Clock. These are very basic widgets that you can use to get your feet wet in the world of widgetry (yes, I just coined that term). To get a quick feel for using a widget, click the Calculator to bring it to the forefront, and use your mouse to perform calculations on the widget's virtual keypad or use your keyboard to type information.

Genius Don't like the placement of the widgets on the screen? Move them wherever you want by clicking anywhere on a widget and dragging it to the preferred location.

Notice the plus sign (+) in the small circle that appears in the lower-left corner of the screen when you activate Dashboard. Click it to open the widget launchpad. This grants access to all the widgets that Mavericks so graciously includes. It also allows you to change those you have running.

Peruse the widget launchpad until you see a widget that strikes your fancy, and then click to open it. When you click the widget you want to open, Dashboard drops it on your screen.

To close any widget, click the minus sign (–) in the lower-left corner of the screen and then click the X in the upper-left corner of the widget. Dashboard even has a neat effect for this action: The widget is sucked into the X until it disappears. If that's not cool enough for you, hold down the Shift key while clicking the X to watch it disappear in slow motion.

The Mavericks preinstalled widgets

Because quite a few widgets come preinstalled on Mavericks, I want to give you a quick description of what's available and what each one can do. Table 2.4 spells out the details.

Table 2.4 Mavericks Widgets

Widget	Function
Calendar	This displays your schedule for the day selected.
Contacts	This lets you quickly search your Contacts and displays information for the contact.

continued

Table 2.4 continued

Web site	Description
Calculator	This performs basic mathematical computations.
Dictionary	This is a fast way to look up definitions, and it doubles as a thesaurus.
ESPN	Find all the latest scores and sports news.
Flight Tracker	When you type a flight number, Flight Tracker details its status.
Movies	This gives you the movie show times for local theaters. You can also view trailers or buy tickets online.
Ski Report	You can type the name of your favorite ski resort to get the latest information on skiing conditions.
Stickies	You can use them just like you would the real thing—to keep little notes all over your Mac!
Stocks	Keep up with all the latest Wall Street comings and goings for stocks that you specify.
Tile Game	This keeps a really, really bored person occupied for awhile.
Translation	Instantly translate words or phrases from one language to another.
Unit Converter	Convert units for several different measurements, such as time, length, currency, and pressure.
Weather	This provides the latest weather prognostications for your neck of the woods, and it's covered in detail later in this chapter.
Web Clip	This lets you create your own widgets. You find more on this feature later in this chapter.
World Clock	This displays an analog clock that can give you the time of day for hundreds of locations around the world.

Setting preferences in widgets

Many widgets require a bit of customization to effectively utilize them. For example, Movies doesn't do you much good if you live in Auburn, Alabama, and it only gives you show times and theaters in Cupertino, California. Stocks won't be of much assistance either, if you want to see what a hot new stock is doing but all you get are the default stocks set up in the widget.

Let's use Weather to illustrate how to edit the preferences of a widget:

1. **Press F4 (or F12 on an older keyboard) to open Dashboard.**

2. **Position your mouse pointer over the lower-right corner of the Weather widget to see the Information button, which is a lowercase "I" (i), as shown in Figure 2.13.**

3. **Click the Information button to flip the widget over to see its available preferences.** Make the preference changes you desire, and click Done.

4. **The widget should now reflect the changes you made to its preferences.**

2.13 Click the Information button to open a widget's preferences, if available.

Note

Not all widgets give you the option of adjusting their preferences, so don't beat yourself up if you can't seem to find the elusive Information button.

Finding more cool widgets

So far, the only widgets you've been privy to are those that come with Mavericks, but I'm about to change that. Hundreds of widgets have been developed, and some of them may be exactly what you're looking for.

One of my favorite places to find new widgets is the Apple website (more on that in a moment), but you can also find widgets by simply performing a web search for OS X widgets.

To get new widgets the quick and easy way, do the following:

1. **Press F4 (or F12 on an older keyboard) to open Dashboard.**

2. **Click the plus sign (+) in the lower-left corner of your screen to open the widget launchpad.**

3. **Click More Widgets at the bottom of the window.** Safari automatically whisks you away to the Apple Dashboard Widgets website, shown in Figure 2.14. Here, you can browse massive numbers of available widgets created by developers and regular users alike.

4. **Use the Widget Browser to find one you want to try.** You may need to scroll down slightly on the page to see the browser.

5. **Click Download to have Safari download the widget.**

6. **Click Install when prompted to open your new widget in Dashboard.** If Mavericks tells you that the widget can't be opened because it's from an unidentified developer, click OK, find the downloaded widget file (Safari puts them in the Downloads folder by default), and hold down the Option key while clicking the widget icon to open it. Click the Open button when prompted, enter an admin username and password, click Modify Settings, and finally click the Install button to install the widget. That security stuff is a barrel of fun, isn't it?

2.14 The Apple website is a one-stop shop for your Dashboard widget needs.

Creating your own widgets using Web Clips

A neat feature in Dashboard is the ability to create your own widgets using clips of web pages. This is a great feature for tracking information from a website without having to constantly navigate to it to check its status. For example, you can see the most popular available widgets on the Apple Dashboard Widgets website without browsing to the site. You can simply view the list in Dashboard, as shown in Figure 2.15, by pressing F4 (or F12 on an older keyboard).

To create a widget using Web Clips, do the following:

1. **Press F4 (or F12) to open Dashboard.**

2. **Click the plus sign (+) in the lower-left corner of the screen, and then click the Web Clip icon in the widget bar.**

3. **Click the Safari icon in the Web Clip Widget window to open Safari.** If Safari's window doesn't open, simply press F4 to exit Dashboard and select Safari's icon in the Dock.

4. **Type the address of the website you want to use to create your widget.** In this example, I use www.apple.com/downloads/dashboard/.

5. **Choose File⇨Open in Dashboard.** The web page darkens, and you are presented with a selection box, as shown in Figure 2.15.

6. **Position the selection box over the section of the web page you want to use for your widget, and click to select the area.** You can drag the handles that appear around the selection box to adjust the selected area.

7. **Click Add in the upper-right corner of the Safari window (in the purple bar).** Safari passes the selection on to Dashboard, where your new widget is created.

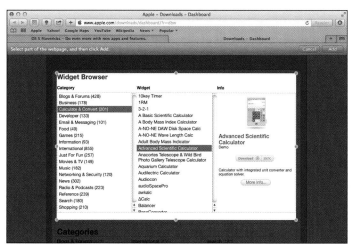

2.15 Place the selection box over the part of the web page that you want to use for your widget.

Uninstalling third-party widgets

Mavericks comes fully stocked with a great set of widgets, but there are many of them. Those you never use may just take up real estate on your screen. If you install other widgets, as discussed earlier in this chapter, you must browse through many icons in the widget launchpad. Dashboard provides a handy way to uninstall third-party widgets:

1. **Press F4 or F12 to open Dashboard.**

2. **Click the plus sign (+) in the lower-left corner of your screen to open the widget launchpad.**

3. **Click the minus sign (–) in the lower-left corner of your screen.** The widget icons begin to jiggle about like jumping beans, and a small X appears in the upper-left corner of the icons of third-party widgets, as shown in Figure 2.16.

4. **Click the small X in the upper-left corner of the third-party widget you want to uninstall, and click the Delete button when asked to confirm the deletion.**

By this point, you are familiar with my affinity for making your Mac behave as you want. No other place in Mavericks gives you more control over your Mac than System Preferences. This is where you can assert yourself as the alpha user and firmly establish yourself as the ruler of your computing domain. In System Preferences, you can make local and system-wide changes to networking, security, software, hardware, sound, and the appearance of Mavericks. This chapter explains what preferences are available to help you tame Mavericks and how to change them if you need or want to.

Personal

The Personal section of the System Preferences, as I prefer to still call it, is where you can customize the way your Mac looks and behaves. I cover only the Language & Region, Security & Privacy, Spotlight, and Notifications preferences here because the others are covered in detail in Chapters 1 and 2.

Note

For the first time since OS X's inception, the System Preferences have lost their section titles (Personal, Hardware, and so on). The section titles were what I used to delineate the different parts of this chapter in the past, and because the preferences still fall under these general ideas, I continue to use the old section titles for this chapter's various section headings. If it ain't broke, don't fix it, Apple.

Open System Preferences before reading any further in this chapter by choosing Apple menu ⇨ System Preferences. You are rewarded with the System Preferences window, as shown in Figure 3.1.

3.1 Click the preference you want to view or change from within the System Preferences window.

Note Some preferences panes are unlocked, while others need to be unlocked in order to access their contents. Click the Lock icon in the lower left of the window, and enter the username and password of an administrator account.

Language & Region

Mavericks is quite the international sensation and can speak more languages than I ever knew existed! The Language & Region preferences pane helps your Mac flex its multilingual muscles.

Preferred language settings

The Preferred languages section of the Language & Region preferences pane allows you to decide the order in which languages are used for application menus, for sorting items, and for dialog windows.

Mavericks is fluent in more than 165 languages (about 33 are fully supported), so the list of available languages is quite lengthy. To add those you think might come in handy, click the + button under the Preferred languages list and select the ones you need, as shown in Figure 3.2.

3.2 Your Mac can be very cosmopolitan using the Language & Region preferences pane.

Regional settings

You can use the regional settings in the Language & Region preferences pane to decide how items such as dates, time, monetary increments, and measurements display on your Mac by default. Figure 3.3 shows the options that are available for localizing Mavericks.

3.3 Choose how best to display regional items with the Region tab.

Click the Advanced button to further customize the layout of dates, time, and other general items.

Security & Privacy

Even a Mac needs to be secured from outside troublemakers, so Mavericks comes packaged with some very nice security features that you can access through the Security & Privacy preferences pane in System Preferences.

General

Figure 3.4 shows the options available under the General tab.

These are fairly self-explanatory, but some aren't quite as intuitive as others. The General tab options are as follows:

- **Require password after sleep or screen saver begins.** Select this check box to lock your Mac from any user who doesn't know your account password after it goes to sleep or a screen saver activates. Use the pop-up menu to determine when the password is required.

- **Show a message when the screen is locked.** Select this check box and type in the text box provided. This text can be anything you want, from stern warnings to leave your precious Mac untouched, to helpful information for those authorized to log in to the system.

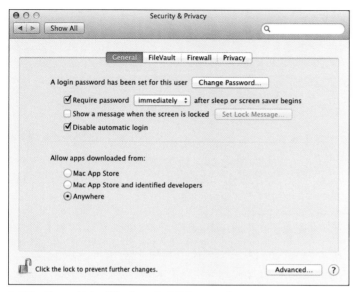

3.4 The General tab of the Security & Privacy preferences.

● **Disable automatic login.** If this check box is not selected, your Mac simply boots up into the default account without any prompt for a password.

Note If most of the options in the General tab of the Security & Privacy preferences pane are grayed out, click the lock icon in the lower-left corner of the window and type the username and password of an administrator account on your Mac.

● **Allow applications downloaded from.** Mavericks provides this new feature to help prevent you from installing software that may cause problems. You have three choices:

   ● **Mac App Store.** This option allows you to install only apps downloaded from the App Store.

   ● **Mac App Store and identified developers.** You can install apps that are downloaded via the App Store and from developers who have identified themselves with Apple.

   ● **Anywhere.** You can install any app in Mavericks, regardless of whom it came from.

Genius

Sometimes, you may install a perfectly legitimate app, but for some reason the developer may not have identified himself with Apple. You can still install these apps; Apple isn't trying to be the heavy-handed app police, preventing you from installing apps they don't like or trust. If you trust the developer, that's all you need to know. Hold down the Option key while double-clicking the downloaded installer file. When the warning dialog appears, click Open to access the installer.

Click the Advanced button at the lower-right corner of the Security & Privacy preferences pane to view these additional options:

- **Log out after X minutes of inactivity.** Select this option to have your Mac automatically log out of your account after the specified time of inactivity.

- **Require an administrator password to access system preferences with lock icons.** There is a lock icon in the bottom-left corner of each preferences pane. If you select this check box, the icon remains in the locked position for every pane in System Preferences and unlocks only with an administrator password.

- **Disable remote control infrared receiver.** Some Macs have infrared receivers that they use to receive commands from an Apple remote control for viewing movies, listening to music, and other activities. Select this check box if you want to disable your infrared receiver so that other Mac owners can't control your Mac using their remote. You also may click the Pair button to link your Mac to a remote, eliminating the need to disable the option altogether.

Caution

I highly recommend that you use both the Require password after sleep or screen saver begins and Disable automatic login options. Not selecting these allows unfettered access to anyone who turns on, restarts, or wakes up your Mac. At that point, the fate of your Mac and all the files it holds is entirely in the hands of the trespasser.

FileVault

The FileVault tab lets you enable the Mavericks FileVault feature, which I do not recommend unless you are a very savvy and security-minded computer user. FileVault encrypts your entire home folder, which prevents anyone else from seeing its contents. Although this sounds great, the big downfall for someone who is not used to such high security is that if you forget your user account password or recovery key, then all content in the home folder is lost. Yikes!

If you want to turn on FileVault protection for your account, click the FileVault tab in the Security & Privacy preferences pane and click Turn On FileVault. Your Mac must have enough space available on its hard drive to store an encrypted version of your home folder.

Firewall

A firewall prevents unauthorized users from accessing your Mac through the Internet or your network. These bothersome folks are up to no good, but a firewall may keep them at bay. To select firewall settings, click the Firewall tab in the Security & Privacy preferences pane. Enable the firewall for your Mac by clicking Start. You can then configure the following settings, shown in Figure 3.5, by clicking the Firewall Options button on the right side of the pane:

3.5 Configure your firewall to customize incoming connections.

- **Block all incoming connections.** This option prevents all incoming connections from touching your Mac, except the most basic types needed for Internet access, such as DHCP and Bonjour.

- **The allowed applications box lists applications from which you want to receive incoming connections.** Click the plus sign (+) under the lower-left corner of the box to add an application to the list, and use the pop-up menu to allow or restrict incoming connections for it. Click the minus sign (–) to remove applications from the list. This box also shows you other sharing functions you've enabled in the Sharing preferences pane, such as file and printer sharing.

● **Automatically allow signed software to receive incoming connections.** If you select this option, an application or service signed by a valid certificate authority automatically appears in the allowed applications box.

● **Enable stealth mode.** Stealth mode allows your Mac to hide from network probing requests, such as ping.

Note   If you are connecting to the Internet through a router, you probably won't need to enable the Mavericks firewall because the router is most likely running one. Check your router documentation to be certain of its firewall settings. However, if you are on a large network you may want to enable the firewall to prevent uninvited guests from entering your Mac via your network.

Privacy

Your Mac can make certain information available to those seeking it, such as its physical location for a map service. The Privacy tab of the Security & Privacy preferences helps you to keep tabs on apps that request access to certain items on your Mac, as well as helping Apple improve their products by anonymously sending them diagnostics and usage information from your Mac.

Hardware

The hardware-centric portion of System Preferences lets Mavericks know how you want it to interact with the various hardware components of your Mac. For information on the Printers & Scanners preferences, see Chapter 13.

CDs & DVDs

When you insert a CD or DVD into the Mac disc drive, something's going to happen; what that is, however, is entirely up to you. The CDs & DVDs preferences pane lets you tell Mavericks how it should behave when you insert a disc, as shown in Figure 3.6.

3.6 Tell Mavericks how to handle CDs and DVDs from here.

Displays

The Displays preferences help you set the resolution of the Mac monitor or screen. The options in both tabs of the pane, Display (shown in Figure 3.7) and Color, are standard on any computer. A third tab called Arrangement appears if you connect a second display to your Mac. Follow the instructions in the Arrangement tab to set up an extra display.

3.7 Adjust the monitor settings under the Display tab in the Display preferences pane.

The Display tab allows you to change these settings (some settings may not appear, depending on what type of display you are using):

● **Resolutions.** This setting lets you choose the amount of detail your screen shows. The higher the resolution, the smaller the items are on your screen; the lower the resolution, the larger the items are.

● **Refresh rate.** This setting determines how often the display is redrawn. If you aren't using a Mac with a built-in display, such as a laptop or an iMac, consult the documenta-tion that came with your monitor for appropriate refresh rates.

● **Gather windows.** Click this button to move all Display preferences panes to the display the button is available on. You must be using multiple displays to see this button.

● **Rotation.** This option allows you to rotate the images on your display by the amount you select.

● **Brightness.** Drag the slider to increase or decrease the brightness of your display.

● **Show displays in menu bar.** Select this check box to place a shortcut to the Display preferences in the menu bar.

● **Show mirroring options in menu bar.** Select this check box to place a shortcut to the mirroring options (when using multiple monitors) in the menu bar.

● **Overscan.** If you are using a TV as a display, you may not be able to see the menu bar at the top of the screen. If this is the case, simply enable this option to see the menu bar.

The Color tab is where you can set your display to use color profiles so it can represent colors more accurately. Deselect the Show profiles for this display only check box to see all profiles installed on your Mac.

Genius

Sometimes, the best color is what suits your eye, rather than what Mavericks automatically chooses for your monitor. You can create a custom profile for your monitor to use by clicking Calibrate and following the instructions. If color matching is old hat to you, select the Expert Mode check box in the Display Calibrator Assistant Introduction screen to gain access to a more finely tuned process.

Energy Saver

Everyone's trying to be a bit greener these days, and Mavericks is no exception. The Energy Saver preferences provide settings for your computer, hard drive, and display to sleep when they are inactive for the period of time that you set by dragging the sliders, as shown in Figure 3.8.

3.8 Save energy by having your display and computer go to sleep when not in use.

66

Note

The Energy Saver preferences differ slightly depending on whether you are on a notebook or desktop.

Click the Battery, Power Adapter, or UPS tab in the Energy Saver preferences pane to set these options (options may differ depending on the type of Mac you have):

- **Put the hard disk(s) to sleep when possible.** This puts the hard drive to sleep whenever it's inactive.

- **Slightly dim the display when using this power source.** This lowers the brightness when the power source is switched to the battery.

- **Wake for network access.** This wakes your Mac up when a network administrator is trying to access it through the network.

- **Automatically reduce brightness before display goes to sleep.** The brightness on your display decreases a couple of minutes before it goes to sleep when it's not in use.

- **Start up automatically after a power failure.** Select this option to have your Mac restart on its own after an interruption in power.

- **Restart automatically if the computer "freezes."** Selecting this option causes your Mac to restart automatically should it experience a freeze (become totally unresponsive).

- **Show battery status in menu bar.** This places a battery icon in the menu bar on a laptop, allowing you to easily monitor the amount of remaining charge.

- **Schedule.** The Schedule options let you set up a daily schedule for turning your Mac on and off or putting it to sleep.

Keyboard

The Keyboard preferences pane gives you four tabs—Keyboard, Text, Shortcuts, and Input Sources—to configure how your keyboard interacts with Mavericks. You can also set up a wireless keyboard using Bluetooth and create your own keyboard shortcuts.

Click the Keyboard tab to modify how quickly the keyboard responds to a key press or whether to automatically illuminate your keyboard in low-light settings. The available options are self-explanatory, but if you need further help, click the Help button (the question mark) in the lower-right corner of the window.

Text

The Text tab of the Keyboard preferences pane, shown in Figure 3.9, allows you to customize substitution features, spell-checking, and more text magic.

3.9 In the Text tab, you can customize text substitution and more.

Options available in the Text tab include:

- **Use symbol and text substitution.** Applications in Mavericks can substitute text you don't want for text you do want. (This is especially helpful in Messages.) For example, if you type "omw," it is replaced by "On my way!" Click the plus sign (+) in the lower-left corner to add your own custom symbol and text substitutions.

- **Spelling.** Mavericks can check spelling for you automatically if you select the Correct spelling automatically check box, and you can use the Spelling pop-up menu to customize the languages used.

- **Smart Quotes.** Modify how double and single quotes display around your text using the pop-up menus.

Shortcuts

I love the fact that Apple gives you the opportunity to make your own keyboard shortcuts for applications under the App Shortcuts section of the Shortcuts tab, shown in Figure 3.10. Click the plus sign (+) in the lower-left corner to create a new one, or highlight a shortcut in the list and click the minus sign (–) to delete it. To disable a shortcut, simply deselect the check box next to it. You can also enable or disable shortcuts for the other sections in the Shortcuts tab, such as Services and Spotlight.

3.10 Create and modify your own keyboard shortcuts.

Input Sources

Some languages use more characters than there are keys on the keyboard. In these cases, input methods provide a way for you to access those characters. The Input Sources tab, shown in Figure 3.11, allows you to choose from among the multitude of input methods that ship with Mavericks. Many of these input sources are different keyboard layouts. The keyboard layout used by English speakers is called the QWERTY layout. Click the + button in the lower-left corner to add keyboard layouts for other languages.

For more information, click the Help button (?) in the lower-right corner of the tab.

Mouse

The Mouse preferences pane gives you the ability to configure how your mouse behaves with Mavericks. You can also set up a wireless mouse using Bluetooth. Mavericks determines the kind of mouse you have and gives you the options necessary for configuring its operation, but you see something similar to what is shown in Figure 3.12.

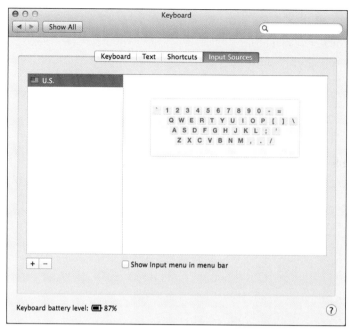

3.11 You can use the Input Sources tab to access characters that aren't available on a standard keyboard.

3.12 Mavericks lets you configure your mouse according to its capabilities.

Trackpad

The Trackpad preferences pane, shown in Figure 3.13, appears only if you are using a laptop or have a Magic Trackpad connected to your desktop Mac.

The Multi-Touch trackpads on Mac laptops provide some amazingly cool features that you can modify to your liking with the options in the Trackpad pane (the look of this pane differs if you're using a laptop trackpad or the Magic Trackpad):

- **Adjust tracking, double-click, and scrolling speeds using their respective sliders.**

- **Customize trackpad gestures for scrolling, zooming, dragging, rotating, swiping, pinching, and clicking.** Apple has provided a great visual help with the gestures by using short video clips that illustrate each type.

3.13 Tweak the trackpad settings to reflect the way you work.

Sound

Configure the Mac sound in the Sound preferences pane, as shown in Figure 3.14.

Table 3.1 gives a brief overview of each tab in the pane.

71

3.14 Change your Mac sounds using the Sound preferences.

Table 3.1 Sound Preference Pane Options

Tab	Options
Sound Effects	Select which sounds to use for system alerts, adjust their volume, and set the system-wide output volume.
Output	Choose output devices (such as external speakers) to broadcast Mac sounds and adjust the sound balance.
Input	Select a sound input device (such as an external microphone) and adjust the volume. You can also filter unwanted background noise on devices by selecting the Use ambient noise reduction check box.

Ink

Ink is available only if you have a graphics tablet connected to your Mac. It allows you to use the graphics tablet as an alternative input method. Ink recognizes your handwriting and translates it into text, as an alternative to typing.

Internet and network

The Internet- and network-centric preferences are where you tell your Mac how to communicate with the rest of the world through its network connections. The Bluetooth and Sharing preferences are covered in depth in Chapter 13.

iCloud

iCloud is Apple's cloud computing service that allows you to synchronize information across your devices, such as your iPad, iPhone, and Mac. iCloud handles the same services as MobileMe and much more, including the ability to push files to every device. For example, if you take a picture with your iPhone, iCloud automatically copies it to your other devices registered to iCloud, such as a Mac or iPad. iCloud handles these types of information:

- Music
- Photos
- Calendars
- Contacts
- Documents
- E-mail
- Apps
- Books

iCloud can also help you find lost devices or friends on the go. The iCloud preferences pane, shown in Figure 3.15, allows you to log in to your iCloud account from your Mac, as well as enable the various services it affords.

3.15 Enable the iCloud services you want to use.

Internet Accounts

The Internet Accounts preferences pane greatly simplifies the process of setting up service provider accounts that you might use for e-mail, calendars, and the like, such as Microsoft Exchange or Google accounts. To set up one or more of these accounts, simply click the plus sign (+) on the left, choose from one of the popular account types listed, and then type the information necessary to access the account. If you don't see what you need, click Add Other Account and select an account type from the list provided, as shown in Figure 3.16.

3.16 Manage accounts with service providers that you use for e-mail, calendars, and other items.

Network

The Network preferences pane, shown in Figure 3.17, is where you configure settings for your various network connection types. The list on the left side of the pane shows the network connections that your Mac supports. This list varies, depending on the network hardware available on your Mac.

● **Wi-Fi.** This contains settings for using the built-in AirPort card on your Mac or a third-party wireless adapter to access the network wirelessly.

● **Bluetooth.** Your Mac can use its Bluetooth adapter to share your cellular phone's Internet access (assuming the phone has a Bluetooth adapter, as well).

● **Ethernet.** This contains settings for connecting to a network using the built-in Ethernet port on your Mac.

● **FireWire.** Mavericks allows you to connect two Macs with a FireWire cable so you can share files or Internet connections between them.

Click one of the network connections to gain access to its innermost workings. Click Advanced in the lower-right corner, shown in Figure 3.17, to inspect or manually set the network connections for that particular method, as shown for Wi-Fi in Figure 3.18.

3.17 The Network preferences pane is where all your network settings are configured.

3.18 Advanced settings let you fine-tune the network options.

Detailed information on the options available for each of the connection types can be found by clicking the Help button (the question mark).

System

System Preferences contains panes for configuring the accounts on your Mac, updating software, choosing a startup disk, and many more system-wide options. For information about the Users & Groups and Parental Controls preferences, see Chapter 4. Time Machine is covered in Chapter 14.

App Store

Mavericks uses the App Store application to check for updates to the operating system and apps you've installed.

You can instantly check the Apple servers for new updates by choosing Apple menu ➪ Software Update. You can also schedule update checks by selecting the Automatically check for updates option. If you've purchased apps on other Macs, you can select the Automatically download apps purchased on other Macs option to have them installed on your current Mac.

Genius

There are several schools of thought when it comes to upgrading to the latest and greatest software. In my opinion, if an update is available for your operating system or an application, go ahead and get it. The vast majority of the time, updates don't cause any problems; on the contrary, they usually end up fixing or preventing them.

Dictation & Speech

Mavericks is so intelligent that it can talk to you and even respond to spoken commands. Dictation allows you to literally dictate to your Mac. Your Mac passes your dictation to Apple, and Apple sends it back to your Mac as text. This section describes the available options.

Dictation

The Dictation tab, shown in Figure 3.19, lets you turn Dictation on or off, as well as select the microphone with which your Mac should listen to you. You can also select a listening key using the Shortcut pop-up menu, which is the key you press to make your Mac listen to your dictation. Tell your Mac what language you will be dictating in using the Language pop-up menu.

To use Dictation, just open any app that contains a text field, make sure the cursor is in the text field, press your listening key, and begin speaking.

3.19 The options available in the Dictation tab.

Text to Speech

This section of the Dictation & Speech preferences lets you choose which voice your Mac uses when it speaks to you. Select from several pre-installed voices, and modify the rate at which your Mac says the words. You can also have Mavericks announce system alerts, announce when an application needs to be looked after, or speak text that you've highlighted in a document.

Date & Time

Adjust the Mac time settings with the Date & Time preferences pane, shown in Figure 3.20.

The tabs provide the following options:

- **Date & Time.** Select the Set date and time automatically check box to have your Mac get the correct date and time from an Internet time server, and then select a time server from the list provided. You can choose to make manual settings by deselecting this option and adjusting the date and time to your preference.

- **Time Zone.** Select the time zone you are in by choosing an area on the map.

- **Clock.** Decide whether and how to display the date and time in the menu bar, and allow your Mac to speak the time to you at the specified intervals.

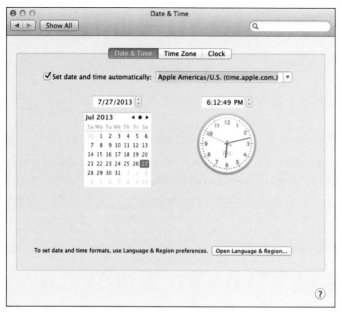

3.20 Set the date and time using the Date & Time preferences pane.

Startup Disk

This preference pane allows you to choose to start your Mac from any drive that contains a valid OS X or Windows installation. If you have multiple partitions or external drives containing operating systems on the Mac hard drive, the Startup Disk preferences is where you tell your Mac from which partition or drive you want it to start up. When you first open these preferences, you are presented with a list of drives that are considered to be valid startup devices. Select the drive with which you want to boot up, and then click Restart.

Accessibility

The Accessibility options help those of us who have hearing, vision, or mobility difficulties. Explore settings in the following categories to make using your Mac that much simpler and easier:

- Display
- Zoom
- VoiceOver
- Audio
- Captions
- Keyboard

- Mouse & Trackpad
- Switch Control
- Speakable Items

Adding an Archives preference pane

The most likely reason you would use the Mavericks Archive Utility is to compress files and folders. This makes them easier to send via e-mail and reduces the amount of space they take up on a drive. From time to time, you may desire to change the way Mavericks compresses files, depending on the tasks you are trying to perform, but there is no visible way to do so by default. Apple has a hidden preference pane that you can manually add to your System Preferences window. In this pane, you can change the way Archive Utility behaves. If you need to install it, follow these steps:

1. **Open a new Finder window by pressing ⌘+N from within the Finder.**

2. **Browse to the directory /System/Library/CoreServices, and locate the Archive Utility.**

3. **Right-click (or Control-click) the icon for Archive Utility, and select Show Package Contents.**

4. **Open the Contents folder, and then open the Resources folder.**

5. **Double-click the Archives.prefPane file.**

6. **Click Install when prompted to install the Archives preference pane for all user accounts on the computer.** Type the name and password of an administrator account when prompted, and click OK. The Archives preference pane, shown in Figure 3.21, can be found in the Other section at the bottom of the System Preferences window.

Other important preferences are covered throughout this book. Be sure to refer to the table of contents or the index if what you're looking for is not covered here.

3.21 Determine how Mavericks compresses files and folders.

◀ ▶   Show All   Q

Mavericks

Parental controls let you manage your children's use of this computer, the applications on it, and the Internet.

To change parental control settings, click the lock icon to enter the name and password of an administrator.

☐ Manage parental controls from another computer

To access this computer to change parental control settings, you need the name and password of an administrator of this computer.

+ − ✱

🔒 Click the lock to make changes.   �ⓘ

User accounts are the perfect way to ensure that multiple people can use your Mac without completely goofing up the whole thing. In this chapter, I show you how to create multiple user accounts and the types of accounts you can select. Individual accounts allow all users to configure certain settings to their liking while protecting the other accounts on the Mac. Mavericks also provides parental controls to help concerned moms and dads keep tabs on their prodigy's computer usage, protecting both their kids and their Mac.

Types of Accounts

Let's face it: Some computer users can be trusted more than others. Factors useful for assessing a user's trustworthiness may be age, maturity, responsibility, or prowess with a computer. Mavericks allows you to create user accounts with nearly complete access to every component of the operating system, accounts with strictly limited access, and anything in between.

Administrator

The administrator account is the big dogs of the user accounts world. It is the default account created when you first install Mavericks. An administrator can handle almost any task on your Mac, including:

- **Creating and removing (deleting) user accounts**
- **Changing settings for other user accounts**
- **Changing all system settings, including those that are locked in System Preferences**
- **Installing software and drivers that any user on the system can utilize (if you allow that, of course)**
- **Deciding whether to rule his Mac kingdom with an iron fist or to be a benevolent ruler, loved and adored by all his minions**

Standard

A standard account is adequate for most users. These accounts allow users enough freedom to customize without the power to alter other accounts. A standard account user:

- **Can install software in his own account, but only if he has access to that software**
- **Can customize her working environment with System Preferences; however, she cannot alter locked System Preferences**
- **Cannot modify, add, or delete other user accounts**

Managed with Parental Controls

Parental Controls are used to manage, or limit, these accounts and the privileges they have. I discuss Parental Controls in greater detail later in this chapter, so I won't deal with the particulars here.

Sharing Only

A Sharing Only account restricts a user to accessing the computer only through the network, just as he would a server. Sharing Only accounts are useful for sharing documents with others in your home or office, without giving them access to the rest of your home folder or Mac. The user cannot log on to the Mac with a Sharing Only account.

Guest User

The Guest User account allows a temporary user to log in to your Mac without you having to create an account for him. Guest users do not have access to any other user accounts, and their accounts can be limited by enabling parental controls for the Guest User account. Any files they create are deleted when they log out of the Guest User account. To enable the Guest User account:

1. **Choose Apple Menu ⇨ System Preferences, click the Users & Groups icon in the lower-left corner of the window, and then click the Lock icon in the lower left.** Enter an administrator username and password when prompted.

2. **Select Guest User from the accounts list on the left side of the Users & Groups preferences pane.**

3. **Check the Allow guests to log in to this computer box.**

4. **Check the Enable parental controls box and click the Open Parental Controls button to customize the Guest User accounts access to applications.**

5. **Check the Allow guests to connect to shared folders box to allow guest users to access the contents of shared folders in other accounts.**

Creating New User Accounts

Now that you understand the different account types, you can start to create some. To make a new user account, follow these steps:

1. **Choose Apple menu ⇨ System Preferences, and click the Users & Groups icon in the lower left of the window to open the Users & Groups preferences window, as shown in Figure 4.1.**

2. **If the lock icon in the bottom-left corner is in the locked position, click to unlock it.** Type an administrator account name and password when prompted.

3. **After you unlock the Users & Groups preferences, click the plus sign (+) in the lower-left corner of the Users & Groups window to add a new account.**

4.1 The Users & Groups preferences window is at your disposal.

4. **The new account window, shown in Figure 4.2, helps you set up the account.** Table 4.1 lists the new account fields and options, and explains how to configure them.

5. **When the account settings are in order, click Create User.**

4.2 The new account window is where you type the username and password information.

Table 4.1 New User Account Settings

Option	Function
New Account	Select the type of account you want to create: Administrator, Standard, Managed with Parental Controls, or Sharing Only.
Full Name	Type the name of the user to whom the account belongs.
Account name	Mavericks automatically trims the Full Name to provide an Account name, but you can edit it if you prefer.
Password	Create a password to allow access to the account.
Verify	Retype the password you created in the Password field.
Password hint	Type a hint that will help you to remember the password if you are unable to successfully enter it. Be careful, though: If you get too specific, your password will just be that much easier for others to figure out. For example, if your password is your mother's middle name and birthdate, you don't want your hint to be "mom's middle name and her birthdate."

Requesting password assistance

If you have difficulty coming up with a secure password, you can ask Mavericks for a little help. In the new account window, note the icon of a key next to the Password field; click it to open the Password Assistant window, shown in Figure 4.3.

Choose the password type you want to use from these options: Manual, Memorable, Letters & Numbers, Numbers Only, Random, and FIPS-181 compliant. Manual allows you to create your own password, while the other options let Mavericks choose a password for you, based on the type you select.

4.3 The Password Assistant can help you out of the password selection rut.

Modifying account settings

The new account is in the account list on the left side of the Users & Groups preferences window.

You can make a handful of modifications to the newly created account at this point (see Figure 4.1):

- **Reset Password.** Click to reset the account password. Only an administrator account can perform this action. Typically, you would use this feature only if the account user has forgotten his password, but obviously it can be abused by anyone who also has access to an administrator password.

- **Apple ID.** If the user has an Apple ID, enter the username and password here by clicking Set.

- **Allow user to reset password using Apple ID.** Selecting this option allows a user who may have forgotten his password to reset it after he successfully enters his Apple ID username and password.

- **Allow user to administer this computer.** Select this check box if you want to convert a standard account to one with full administrator rights.

- **Enable parental controls.** Change the account so it's managed with Parental Controls by selecting this check box. See more on Parental Controls later in this chapter.

- **Delete the account.** If you're an administrator, you can remove the account completely by clicking the account to highlight it and then clicking the minus sign (–) at the bottom of the Accounts window. Mavericks then gives you three options (four if you count the Cancel button): to save the home folder in a disk image, leave the home folder where it is (but delete the account), or delete the home folder entirely. Select your option and click the Delete User button.

- **Change the user account picture.** Click the user account picture to change it. The Edit Picture window opens, as shown in Figure 4.4. You can select one of the available pictures, or you can click Edit Picture and choose one from the Recent Pictures drop-down list, or you can click Choose to browse your Mac for a picture. If your Mac has an attached or built-in camera, you can click the Camera tab and then click the camera button to take a new photo. Drag the slider to alter the size of the picture, and then click and drag to center it. When finished, click Set in the Edit Picture window.

4.4 Edit the picture used for the account to match your preferences.

The Root Account

Until now, you thought that administrator accounts were the ultimate power trip, but now meet the real king of the accounts jungle: the root account! The root account is the only account in a UNIX-based operating system (which includes OS X Mavericks) that truly has full access to any and all files—visible or invisible—on the computer. Administrator accounts are limited in their ability to browse folders on other accounts (although, they can delete the other accounts). The root account isn't hindered from doing or accessing anything on the entire system, and that's why it's disabled by default in Mavericks. If you are logged in as the root user, one mistake could bring down the entire computer. There are good reasons for using the root account—for example, if you need to delete files owned by another user on the system—but I usually don't recommend enabling the root account for the typical user. However, if you want to, here's how (consider yourself duly warned):

1. **Choose Apple menu ⇨ System Preferences, and then click the Users & Groups icon.**

2. **Click the lock in the lower-left corner of the Users & Groups window, and then type an administrator username and password when prompted.**

3. **Select Login Options, and then click Join or Edit next to Network Account Server.**

4. **Click the Open Directory Utility button.**

5. **When Directory Utility opens, choose Edit ⇨ Enable Root User from the menu (if the lock icon in the lower left is locked, click it and enter your username and password to unlock, and then proceed to choose Edit ⇨ Enable Root User).** The root account is turned on at this point. Type a password for the root account when prompted. You certainly want to create a password; otherwise, your system is under an enormous security threat. To change the existing password, choose Edit ⇨ Change Root Password, type the current password, and then type the new one.

Caution

Enabling the root account can be bad for the health of your Mac if you aren't careful when logged in to it. As the root user you have complete autonomy and, as such, are given power to cause great good or great harm—especially the latter if you're a more inexperienced user. It's also a good idea to disable the root account once you're finished using it.

Logging In to Accounts

When you first start your Mac in the morning, or if you have to restart it at some point during the day, you most likely need to log in to the system using your account name and password. You can also log in to other accounts at the same time without having to restart the Mac or shut down your running applications. Now that's cool!

Login Options

Click Login Options at the bottom of the Users & Groups window to see what options you have, as shown in Figure 4.5.

4.5 Login Options allow you to configure how people log in to their accounts on your Mac.

Table 4.2 lists and explains each of these options.

Table 4.2 Login Options

Option	Function
Automatic login	If you enable this option, your Mac logs in to the default administrator account without prompting you for a password, which is most certainly not a good security decision. I recommend that you always set this option to Off.
Display login window as	Determine whether the login window at startup should show a list of all user accounts on the Mac or prompt for a username and password. If security is a concern, simply prompting for a username and password may be the best idea.

Option	Function
Show the Sleep, Restart, and Shut Down buttons	Select this option to have these buttons appear in the login window.
Show Input menu in login window	This displays the Input menu in the upper part of the login window. The Input menu is associated with the Input Sources tab of the Keyboard preferences pane, found in System Preferences. If some accounts use a different keyboard layout, they need access to the Input menu. Find out more about Input Sources in Chapter 3.
Show password hints	This option allows the password hints that you typed when creating the account to appear in the login window.
Show fast user switching menu as	This option allows multiple users to be logged in at the same time. After selecting the check box, determine how to show the account names in the fast user switching menu with the pop-up menu to the right. The name of the account to which the user is currently logged in is shown in the upper-right corner of the screen; click it to access other accounts.
Use VoiceOver in the login window	Select this option to have the contents of the login window spoken to you by the Mac.
Network Account Server	Click Join and type the name of the server to which you want to automatically connect when you log in to your account.

Login Items

Login Items are applications or utilities that you have slated to automatically start when you log in to your account. You must be logged in to an account to see its Login Items window, as shown in Figure 4.6.

4.6 You can add or remove Login Items here.

To change the Login Items for an account, follow these steps:

1. **Click the account you want to alter in the users list.**

2. **Click the Login Items tab near the top of the Users & Groups window.**

3. **To add items to the login list, click the plus sign (+) in the lower-left corner of the list and then browse your Mac for the items.**

4. **Remove items from the list by highlighting them and clicking the minus sign (–) in the lower-left corner of the list.**

5. **Select the Hide check box next to any item you want to be automatically hidden after login.** This prevents windows from open applications cluttering your Finder window when you first log in.

6. **Close Users & Groups window.**

Caution   Some applications or utilities may add items to your Login Items list that they need to perform tasks in the background. Be careful about removing Login Items for anti-virus software and other utilities that constantly monitor your Mac's activities.

Setting Up Simple Finder

Simple Finder is a Finder without the frills but with basic functionality for a managed user. Simple Finder allows the user to access only three folders in the Dock: My Applications, Documents, and Shared. Simple Finder doesn't allow access to the remainder of the Mac hard drive or System Preferences. This basic Finder is perfect for children or users who may be a bit uncomfortable with technology.

To use Simple Finder, follow these steps:

1. **Open the Parental Controls preferences by choosing Apple menu ⇨ System Preferences and then clicking the Parental Controls icon in the System section.**

2. **Choose the account you want to modify in the accounts list.** You may need to click Enable Parental Controls to access the Parental Controls features.

3. **Select the Use Simple Finder check box in the Apps tab.** The next time you log in to the account, it will use Simple Finder.

Figure 4.7 shows a typical Simple Finder desktop. The three folders in the Dock give the user access to the applications she has permission to use, as well as the Documents and Shared folders. To use the account with a full Finder, deselect the Use Simple Finder check box in the Parental Controls preferences.

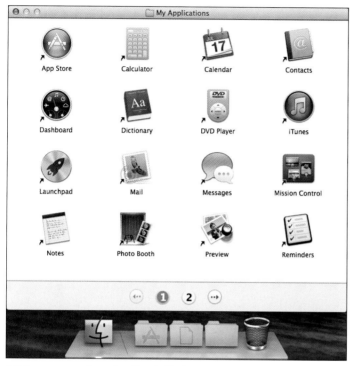

4.7 A user account running Simple Finder.

Changing Finder Preferences in Simple Finder

Simple Finder doesn't allow a user to change many settings. Therefore, if you do need to change settings, you must use an administrator account. In older versions of OS X, you must log out of the account using the Simple Finder, log in to an administrator account, disable Simple Finder in the managed account, and finally log back in to the managed account to change Finder settings. Whew! Thankfully, Mavericks changes all that. To change Finder settings while in Simple Finder:

1. **Choose Finder ⇨ Run Full Finder, and then type an administrator's username and password.**

2. **Choose Finder ⇨ Preferences to make the necessary changes.**

3. **Choose Finder ⇨ Return to Simple Finder when finished.** The Simple Finder window returns to normal.

Limiting Access with Parental Controls

A few of the most powerful societal influences on youngsters are the Internet, e-mail, and instant messaging. For all the wonderful content that's available on the Internet, there's an equal amount of horrifying content just waiting to be discovered and devoured by young eyes. The Parental Controls help protect our most impressionable citizens from some of the worst the world has to offer.

Take the time to investigate each of these settings to the fullest extent if you have children who use your computer to surf the Internet, receive e-mail, or send instant messages. As a parent, I completely understand the desire to protect your children from things that may be beyond their level of maturity and understanding.

Parental Controls is just as effective with adults as it is with children. If necessary, you can also manage the accounts of users who are inexperienced with computers, or those who, perhaps, haven't quite grown up in other ways.

Enabling Parental Controls

To use Parental Controls, you must either create an account managed by Parental Controls or enable Parental Controls for an existing Standard account. Follow the instructions earlier in this chapter for creating a new user account. To enable Parental Controls on a current account, follow these steps:

1. **Choose Apple menu ⇨ System Preferences, and click the Users & Groups icon.**

2. **If it is locked, click the lock icon in the lower-left corner and type an administrator username and password to unlock the Users & Groups preferences.**

3. **Select the account for which you want to enable Parental Controls in the accounts list.**

4. **Select the Enable Parental Controls check box.**

5. **Click the Open Parental Controls button to open the Parental Controls window.**

6. **Choose the Managed with Parental Controls account in the account list on the left side of the Parental Controls window, called Mavericks in Figure 4.8.** The account is ready for you to take control.

4.8 The Parental Controls window.

Setting application and function restrictions

An alternative to Simple Finder is to run the full Finder with limitations. Parental Controls allows an administrator to choose exactly which applications and utilities the managed account can use and what functions it can perform. To set these kinds of limitations, follow these steps:

1. **Open the Parental Controls preferences by choosing Apple menu ⇨ System Preferences and then clicking the Parental Controls icon. If the lock icon in the lower-left corner is locked, click it and type an administrator username and password to unlock the Parental Controls preferences.**

2. **Select the account you need to set limitations for from the list on the left.**

3. **In the Apps tab of the Parental Controls window (refer to Figure 4.8), select the Limit Applications check box.**

4. **Decide whether applications downloaded from the App Store can be used with this account by using the Allow App Store Apps pop-up menu.**

5. **In the Allowed Apps window, browse through the list of available applications and utilities.** Click the arrow on the left side of a category to expand it. When you find an application or utility that you want the user to be able to access, select the check box to its left.

6. **At the bottom of the window, select the check box next to Prevent the Dock from being modified (refer to Figure 4.8) if you want to restrict this kind of flexibility.**

Applying website restrictions

One of the most useful features in Parental Controls is the ability to control (for the most part) the websites that are accessible to a managed account. To start putting your foot down, click the Web tab in the Parental Controls window. Here, you can decide whether to allow unfettered access to the Internet, to filter websites based on their content, or to restrict access to certain websites.

Allow unrestricted access to websites

This works as advertised. If you don't want to restrict the Internet content that can be accessed through this managed account, select this option.

Try to limit access to adult websites automatically

This option enables website filtering, which scours the contents of a website for buzzwords that might alert the filter that the site is inappropriate for young and curious eyes. Click Customize to modify how the filter works, as shown in Figure 4.9.

4.9 Allow or restrict certain websites by customizing the website filter.

Mind you, the website filter isn't perfect. Sometimes, it may filter content that you consider safe for your children and may allow sites that you would normally curtail.

Click the plus sign (+) under the Always allow these websites section to type the addresses of sites you want the filter to allow, regardless of whether or not the site content conflicts with the filter.

Click the plus sign (+) under the Never allow these websites section to block access to websites that the filter might miss and that you do not want your children to see.

Allow access to only these websites

Select this option to allow access to only the specific sites you enter into the approved list, as shown in Figure 4.10.

Click the plus sign (+) beneath the list of approved sites to add websites, and then choose the Add bookmark option from the pop-up menu that appears. Highlight sites you don't want on the list, and click the minus sign (–) to remove them.

4.10 You can determine the specific websites to which the account user has access.

Setting Mail and Messages limitations

Controlling to whom your kids talk on the Internet is just as important as filtering website content. If you choose to allow the user of the managed account to have access to e-mail and instant messaging, the People tab of the Parental Controls preferences, shown in Figure 4.11, is right where you want to be.

95

To place restrictions on e-mail and instant messaging, select the check boxes next to Limit Mail to allowed contacts and Limit Messages to allowed contacts. Doing so allows you to add contacts to the Allowed Contacts list. Click the plus sign (+) under the list to add new names. To remove a name from the list, highlight it and click the minus sign (–).

Caution Note that these restrictions apply only to Mail and Messages, not third-party e-mail and instant messaging applications.

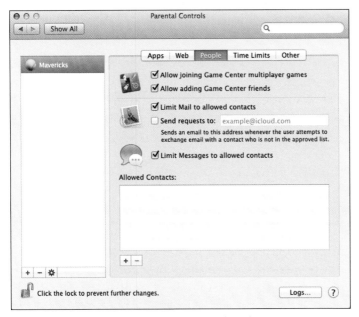

4.11 The People tab is where you control e-mails and instant messages for your managed accounts.

One of my favorite features in Parental Controls is the ability to have an e-mail sent to the address of your choice requesting your permission for a person to send e-mails or instant messages to the managed account. Select the Send requests to option and then type the preferred e-mail address to which these requests should be sent.

Setting time limits

Another great tool in Parental Controls allows you to limit the amount of time the user of the managed account can access the Mac. This is one that kids hate and parents love! Table 4.3 describes the options available in the Time Limits tab of the Parental Controls window.

Table 4.3 Time Limit Settings

Setting	Operation
Weekday time limits	Select the Limit computer use to check box, and then drag the slider to set the total amount of time the user of the managed account can be logged in for each weekday (Monday through Friday).
Weekend time limits	Again, select the Limit computer use to check box, and then drag the slider to set the total amount of time the user of the managed account can be logged in for a single weekend day (Saturday or Sunday).
Bedtime	Set the times of day for both school nights (Sunday through Thursday) and weekends (Friday and Saturday) that the user of the managed account cannot have access to the computer. This prevents any sneaking around in the middle of the night to check out those websites that you may have forgotten to restrict.

Other limitations

Table 4.4 lists the options found under the Other tab of the Parental Controls preferences pane. These options are functional in nature, and they allow or disallow the managed user to perform certain functions in Mavericks based on how you, the administrator, configure these settings.

Table 4.4 Functional Limitations

Option	Function
Disable built-in camera	Use this option to prevent a user from utilizing your Mac's built-in camera or a camera attached to a connected display. For example, this keeps users from making any unauthorized FaceTime or Skype calls.
Disable Dictation	This option keeps the user from using the Dictation feature in Mavericks.
Hide profanity in Dictionary	Select this check box if you prefer to hide profane words from prying eyes when your youngster uses the Dictionary application that is part of Mavericks.
Limit printer administration	Select this option if you want to keep the user from adding or removing printers or managing jobs in the printer queues.
Limit CD and DVD burning	This option prevents the user from burning music and data to CDs or DVDs.
Disable changing the password	Select this option to prevent managed users from changing the account password. This is a good idea if you want to make sure that you, as the administrator, can access the managed account at any time.

Keeping account activity logs

When all is said and done, there is simply no way for you to monitor your kid every second of every day. Apple thought of that when it designed Parental Controls. Mavericks can keep track of which websites your kids have checked out, which websites they are blocked from seeing, the applications they use while logged in, and with whom they are chatting. The Apps, Web, and People tabs of Parental Controls all feature a Logs button in the lower-right corner, as shown in Figure 4.12. This allows you to keep tabs on all the account activity so you're informed about what happens, even if you aren't there to see it.

4.12 Some may describe these logs as Big Brother gone awry; I call it responsible parenting.

Select the amount of time for which to show account activity in the Show activity for pop-up menu. Determine how the logs should be ordered by using the Group by pop-up menu and choosing either Application (depending on which collection you highlight in the Log Collections pane) or Date. If you find an objectionable site, application, or instant message, click it to highlight it in the Logs list and then click Restrict to block access to it.

Being diligent in browsing these logs only further protects your child.

What Can I Do with Applications?

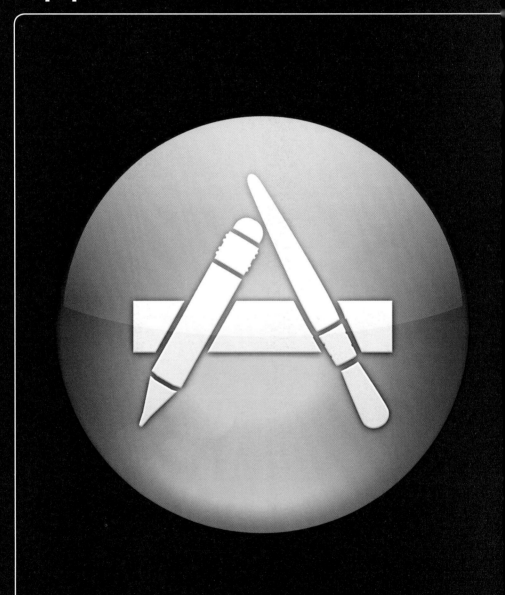

Mavericks is more than just an operating system; it's also full of applications designed to make your computing life as productive as possible, while being simple and fun to use. From word processing to buying music online, from surfing the web to taking photos with the Mac camera, OS X 10.9 comes in one flavor: fully loaded! This chapter introduces you to the myriad programs that come with Mavericks. I show you how to navigate most Mac applications, going in depth with TextEdit and Messages, as well as how to use common keyboard shortcuts.

Discovering Mavericks Applications

Mavericks ships with more than 25 applications, a.k.a. apps, each offering a unique way of handling various tasks. With so many applications, you may be wondering what they all do. I cover the lesser-known (or lesser-used) applications briefly in this chapter, but I go more in depth with the Mac word processor, TextEdit. Because I cover some of the more high-profile applications in other chapters, I give only short introductions to them here (see Table 5.3).

To see all the applications at your disposal, open the Applications folder, as shown in Figure 5.1.

5.1 The Applications folder in all its glory.

You can open the Applications folder in these ways:

- **Click the Go menu in the Finder, and select Applications.**
- **Click the Launchpad icon in the Dock.**
- **Press ⌘+Shift+A while in the Finder.**

Now, let's look at some of the hidden gems in Mavericks.

Calculator

Calculator, as shown in Figure 5.2, is not a basic run-of-the-mill addition, subtraction, multiplication, and division tool (although it can perform those basic functions with the best of them). Calculator has three modes: Basic, Scientific, and Programmer. Table 5.1 gives a brief description of each.

If you want to see a printout of your calculations, you can use the Paper Tape function. Choose Window ⇨ Show Paper Tape or press ⌘+T to open the Paper Tape window. Choose File ⇨ Print Tape to print your calculations and results.

5.2 Calculator can also convert units of measure such as area, currency, speed, and volume.

Table 5.1 Calculator Modes

Mode	Function
Basic	Performs the traditional tasks of addition, multiplication, subtraction, and division.
Scientific	Expands the Basic mode to perform advanced mathematical calculations, such as trigonometric functions, factorial functions, and square roots.
Programmer	Performs calculations that only a true geek could love (or, most likely, understand), including hexadecimal conversions, binary computations, and logical operations.

Chess

You may have noticed that OS X Mavericks doesn't come with Minesweeper and Hearts. No, the brainiacs at Apple prefer to include Chess instead, as shown in Figure 5.3. Chess is one of the world's most challenging games, making it ideal to include in such a sophisticated operating system.

To play a game of Chess, simply double-click the icon in the Applications folder. You can play against another person or test your wits against the Mac. To move the board, simply drag any corner of it to the position in which you want it.

Choose Chess ⇨ Preferences to change things, such as the look of the pieces and board or the difficulty level of the computer player, and to allow moves to be spoken aloud. Refer to the Chess Help section (choose Help ⇨ Chess Help) for more information about this great version of a classic game.

Note You can play against other opponents online by signing in to Game Center. When you start a new game in Chess, you are asked to sign in to Game Center, if you aren't already signed in.

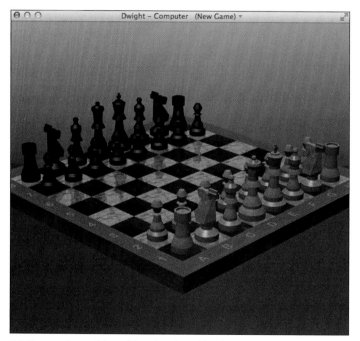

5.3 Change the position of the chessboard by dragging a corner of it.

Dictionary

Dictionary, like all the other cool applications in Mavericks, does more than just the obvious.

You can use it as a standard dictionary (the New Oxford American Dictionary, to be exact) or as a thesaurus (the Oxford American Writer's Thesaurus). You can also use it to find terms in the Apple dictionary or to discover articles on Wikipedia. To begin a search, simply type a word or topic in the search field in the upper-right corner of the window (next to the magnifying glass icon), as shown in Figure 5.4. Dictionary displays what it finds in all four sources or only the one you select from the toolbar.

5.4 Dictionary is a great tool for students, writers, business professionals, and anyone else who needs the definition of, or articles on, a word.

DVD Player

DVD Player performs as advertised: It plays DVDs. It can also perform all the basic functions of a regular DVD player. The upside to using this application instead is that you don't have to leave your Mac to catch a flick.

You control the playback of movies with an on-screen remote, shown in Figure 5.5, as opposed to one that is handheld.

You can also control playback of your DVDs with the Mac keyboard, using the keyboard shortcuts listed in Table 5.2.

5.5 The DVD Player on-screen remote control.

Table 5.2 DVD Player Keyboard Shortcuts

Function	Keys
Play/Pause	Space bar
Stop	⌘+.
Scan Forward	⌘+Shift+→
Scan Backward	⌘+Shift+←
Volume Up	⌘+↑
Volume Down	⌘+↓
Mute	⌘+Option+↓
Close Control Drawer	⌘+]
Eject DVD	⌘+E

Font Book

Fonts are very important for creating the look and feel of your Mac, as well as any documents you may create with its applications. Font Book is a fantastic utility that allows you to manage the fonts you have installed on your Mac.

Font Book, shown in Figure 5.6, can install and delete fonts without you having to reboot your Mac. Use it to organize your fonts into collections, enable the fonts you want to use, or disable the fonts you don't want to use rather than completely deleting them from the system.

5.6 Font Book helps to organize and manage your font collections.

Refer to the Font Book Help section (choose Help ➪ Font Book Help) to find out more about this exceptional utility.

Stickies

Stickies is a nifty little application for keeping lists, creating reminders, and quickly entering any information you want. It uses the metaphor of the tiny yellow notes that we all have dangling off our computer monitors (except these stickies don't fall off and drift under your desk when you're not looking). Stickies automatically saves your notes, as shown in Figure 5.7.

Make a note of it!

Stickies lets you keep notes (like these) on your desktop. Use a Stickies note to jot down reminders, lists, or other information. You can also use notes to store frequently used text or graphics.

• To close this note, click the close button.

• To collapse this note, double click the title bar.

Your current notes appear when you open Stickies.

5.7 An example of a sticky note.

Note The Stickies app and the Stickies Dashboard widget (see more in Chapter 2 regarding widgets) do not share notes. Thanks to the technical editor of this tome, Paul Sihvonen-Binder, for this excellent reminder.

Additional applications

Table 5.3 lists a brief description of other applications that come with Mavericks. They are covered in greater detail in other chapters.

Table 5.3 More Mavericks Applications

Application	Function
App Store	Provides a one-stop shop for thousands of Mac apps. Information about using this feature can be found later in this chapter.
Automator	Automates the tasks you find repetitive and mundane. Chapter 14 covers Automator in depth.
Calendar	Lets you create calendars to keep up with your hourly, daily, weekly, monthly, and annual tasks and appointments. Chapter 8 goes into much more detail about Calendar.
Contacts	Keeps contact information in one handy location. See Chapter 8 for more information.
Dashboard	Organizes tiny applications called widgets. Much more on Dashboard and widgets is found in Chapter 2.

continued

Table 5.3 continued

Application	Function
FaceTime	Allows you to make video calls to other Mac users, as well as iPhone 4 (and newer), iPad 2 (and newer), and iPod touch owners. See Chapter 12 for more information on FaceTime.
Game Center	Allows you to play games by yourself or against opponents online. With Game Center, you can play games against others who are using a Mac, iPad, iPhone, or iPod touch.
Image Capture	Captures images from your scanner and/or digital camera. Learn much more in Chapter 12.
iTunes	Provides your Mac entertainment hub. Chapter 11 gives you the inside scoop.
Mail	Houses the Mavericks e-mail application. Discover how to use Mail in Chapter 10.
Maps	Helps you find destinations and plot courses to them, as well as sync said destinations with other devices. You'll find more on Maps later in this chapter.
Messages	Sends messages instantly to friends, family, and colleagues. Messages is covered later in this chapter.
Mission Control	Helps organize your desktop clutter. Chapter 1 covers much more about Mission Control.
Photo Booth	Takes pictures and videos using the built-in Mac camera. Read more about it in Chapter 12.
Preview	Opens multiple file types, such as JPEGs, TIFFs, and PDFs. See Chapters 7 and 12 for more about Preview.
QuickTime Player	Plays video and sound files in a multitude of formats. See Chapter 12 for more info.
Reminders	Helps you keep track with items on your to-do list(s).
Safari	Houses the OS X web browser. Chapter 9 prepares you to cruise the Internet jungle in style.
System Preferences	Allows you to make Mavericks behave the way you want it to. I cover how to tweak settings for your network, change the appearance of your Mac, and much more in Chapter 3.
TextEdit	Houses the Mavericks word processor. Begin creating documents by perusing the information about TextEdit later in this chapter.
Time Machine	Backs up your files and folders to keep them safe and allows you to restore them if necessary. Chapter 14 has the lowdown on this very popular Mavericks feature.

Navigating Mavericks Applications

Many of the basic functions and menus of Mavericks applications and utilities are accessed in the same way. For example, opening a file from within almost any application is done by choosing File ⇨ Open. Some keyboard shortcuts also are used universally in Mavericks applications.

Opening and closing applications

This one is basic, but necessary, so I'll keep it short and to the point. Use one of these methods to open an application:

- **Choose Go ⇨ Applications or Go ⇨ Utilities from within the Finder, and double-click the application or utility you need.**
- **Click the application icon in the Dock.**
- **Click the Launchpad icon in the Dock, and then click the application's icon.**
- **Choose Apple menu ⇨ Recent Items, and select a recently used application from the list.**

You can use one of these techniques to close an open application:

- Choose the application title menu (immediately to the right of the Apple menu), and select Quit.
- Press ⌘+Q.
- Click and hold the application icon in the Dock, and then select Quit from the resulting pop-up menu, as shown in Figure 5.8.

5.8 Easily quit an application from the Dock.

Using commands and keyboard shortcuts

Table 5.4 lists some common commands for Mavericks applications, as well as the keyboard shortcuts that make issuing those commands even easier.

Table 5.4 Commands and Keyboard Shortcuts

Command	Function	Keyboard Shortcut
Open	Opens a file or document.	⌘+O
Save	Saves the contents of a document.	⌘+S
New	Creates a new blank document.	⌘+N
Close	Closes the active window.	⌘+W
Page Setup	Opens a dialog for selecting the correct paper size and orientation for printing.	⌘+Shift+P
Print	Opens a dialog for printing the current document.	⌘+P
Copy	Copies highlighted text.	⌘+C
Cut	Cuts highlighted text from a document.	⌘+X
Paste	Pastes copied or cut text into a document.	⌘+V
Select All	Highlights all text in a document.	⌘+A
Find	Finds words in the document or window.	⌘+F
Find Next	Finds the next instance of a word in a document or window.	⌘+G
Find Previous	Finds the previous instance of a word in a document or window.	⌘+Shift+G
Force Quit	Opens a window to force an application or utility to quit.	⌘+Option+Esc
Minimize	Minimizes the active window to the Dock.	⌘+M
Preferences	Opens the application preferences.	⌘+,
Hide	Hides the active application.	⌘+H
Quit	Quits the active application.	⌘+Q

Genius

If you are a Windows user who is switching to a Mac, many of the keyboard shortcuts with which you are familiar have Mac equivalents. For example, to print a job in Windows, you would press Ctrl+P and on a Mac you would press ⌘+P. Pressing Ctrl+C copies an item on Windows, while ⌘+C does the same trick on a Mac.

Accessing applications with a Stack

If Launchpad isn't your thing, Mavericks has a neat feature called Stacks that allows you to place folder aliases on the right side of the Dock. You can add a Stack for your Applications folder to the Dock for quick, easy access to all the applications and utilities on your Mac. Follow these steps:

1. **Open the hard drive by doing one of the following:**

   - **Double-click the hard drive icon.**

   - **Press ⌘+N from within the Finder, and select the hard drive icon from the Devices section**.

2. **Drag the Applications folder to the right side of the Dock, and drop it.**

3. **Click the Applications folder icon to open the Stack.**

The Stack can display in a fan pattern, as shown in Figure 5.9; in a grid, as shown in Figure 5.10; or as a list. As you can see, Fan mode doesn't show all the items in the folder if it contains lots of items. Notice at the top of the fan in Figure 5.9 that it says 23 More in Finder next to the arrow. This means that there are 23 more application icons that can't be shown in the fan due to its configuration; this is where the Grid mode shines.

Viewing applications in full-screen mode

Many apps running in Mavericks can do so in full-screen mode, including Mail, Safari, Terminal, and iCal. This mode allows the app to be the center of your attention, totally hiding anything else on your desktop and changing your workspace to accommodate only the functions of the app.

5.9 A Stack of applications in Fan mode.

5.10 A Stack of applications in Grid mode (use the scroll bar to find applications that don't fit in the window, if necessary).

If the application you are currently running supports full-screen mode, you see a small icon in the upper-right corner of the application's window that looks like two arrows pointing diagonally in different directions, as shown in Figure 5.11. Click this icon to take the app into full-screen mode.

5.11 Click the full-screen mode icon in the upper-right corner to dedicate your screen to one app at a time.

You can move between open windows in full-screen mode by swiping a laptop trackpad or the Apple Magic Mouse or Magic Trackpad. Exit full-screen mode by clicking the blue box containing two arrows pointing toward one another (this appears when you hold your mouse pointer in the upper-right corner of the screen) or by pressing the Escape (ESC) key.

Working with Documents in TextEdit

TextEdit is the built-in word-processing application for Mavericks, and it can handle a good deal of your basic document-writing needs. TextEdit is one of those names that advertise just what the application does: It edits text. The TextEdit interface is simplicity itself, as are the functions it provides. Although you don't get all the frills of a full-fledged word processor, like Microsoft Word, Apple's Pages, or OpenOffice, TextEdit is surprisingly more capable than it appears at first glance (it can even open documents created by the aforementioned big boys).

Setting TextEdit Preferences

I am a big fan of making things work the way you want them to on your computer, rather than the way Apple (or anyone else) says you should. The way I work may do wonders for my production but cause you to groan with frustration or yawn in tedium. Most applications allow you to change the default behaviors to match your style of working (or playing, as the case may be), and TextEdit is no exception.

To alter the TextEdit default behaviors, choose TextEdit⇨Preferences from the menu or press ⌘+,. The Preferences window opens and permits access to two tabs: New Document and Open and Save. The New Document preferences are shown in Figure 5.12.

5.12 The TextEdit New Document preferences options.

Table 5.5 offers a breakdown of each option in the New Document preferences.

Table 5.5 TextEdit New Document Preferences

Preferences	Function
Format	Lets you select Rich text (RTF) or Plain text (TXT) as your default format for new documents. The Wrap to page option causes text to wrap to document margins instead of window margins.
Window Size	Sets the default window size for new documents by width (measured in characters) and height (measured by line).
Font	Lets you choose the default font for new plain or rich text documents. Click Change to make a different selection.
Properties (RTF only)	Allows you to type information you want included with each document you create, such as your name, your company, or any necessary copyright information.
Check spelling as you type/ Check grammar with spelling	Activates the spelling and grammar checkers.
Correct spelling automatically	Corrects spelling mistakes on the fly. Use this option with caution because TextEdit may change something that it mistakenly thinks is misspelled.
Show ruler	Displays a ruler at the top of each window.
Data detectors	Automatically recognizes dates, locations, contacts, and times, and creates items such as iCal events and Address Book contacts for them.
Smart copy/paste	Automatically adds any necessary spaces when text is added or deleted.
Smart quotes	Uses curly quote marks instead of straight ones.
Smart dashes	Automatically substitutes an em dash (—) when you type double hyphens (--).
Smart links	Automatically turns Internet addresses into links that open the appropriate website when clicked.
Text replacement	Attempts to replace typos with common words it thinks you intended. For example, if you type "arw," TextEdit substitutes "are" instead.
Restore All Defaults	Reverts to the TextEdit default preferences.

Figure 5.13 shows the Open and Save Preferences. To see how these options can customize your TextEdit experience, see Table 5.6.

5.13 The Open and Save preferences options for TextEdit.

Table 5.6 TextEdit Open and Save Preferences

Preferences	Function
Display HTML/RTF files as HTML/RTF code instead of formatted text	Opens HTML and RTF files automatically as native HTML or RTF code, retaining no formatting at all. This is beneficial to web developers who need to edit their code.
Add ".txt" extension to plain text files	Automatically tags plain text files with the .txt file extension.

continued

115

Table 5.6 continued

Preferences	Function
Plain Text File Encoding	Lets you decide which text encoding to use by default when opening and saving plain text files. I suggest sticking with Automatic unless you really know what you are doing with these settings.
HTML Saving Options	Lets you choose the default document type, styling, and encoding to use when saving documents as HTML files.
Preserve white space	Preserves blank areas that are already in your document so they aren't lost during formatting.
Restore All Defaults	Reverts to the TextEdit New Document and Open and Save default settings.

Creating and saving documents

Open TextEdit by choosing Go from within the Finder, selecting Applications, and double-clicking the TextEdit icon. TextEdit automatically opens a window so you can browse your Mac for a document or open a new one by clicking the New Document button in the lower-left corner. Click New Document to open a blank document, as shown in Figure 5.14.

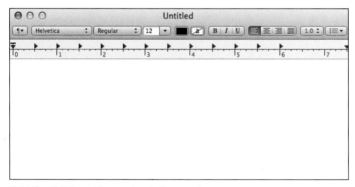

5.14 TextEdit is waiting patiently for your input.

Creating a new document doesn't get much easier, but what if TextEdit is already open? Simply do one of the following:

- Choose File ➪ New.
- Press ⌘+N.

A shiny new document opens. To get started with your document, just begin typing. After you create a document, you typically want to save it so you can refer to it again later.

To save a document, do the following:

1. **Choose File ⇨ Save, or press ⌘+S, to open the Save dialog.**

2. **Type a name for your document in the Save As field.**

3. **Navigate to the location on your Mac where you want to save the document.**

4. **Click Save.**

Formatting TextEdit documents

Sometimes, simply typing text into your documents may be good enough for the task at hand, but other situations may call for something nicer, neater, and more polished. The look and feel of a document can be very important—even more so to the reader than the writer—and something as simple as font choice can affect how the reader responds to the text. Because TextEdit uses RTF, tasks like manipulating fonts and adding pictures are almost too easy.

Using fonts

OS X Mavericks comes with a wide variety of built-in fonts to spice up your word processing world. To manipulate fonts in a document, do the following:

1. **Open an existing file or create a new one in TextEdit by doing one of the following:**

   - **Choose File ⇨ Open or File ⇨ New.**

   - **Press ⌘+O or ⌘+N.**

2. **Highlight the text you want to change by clicking and dragging the mouse over it.** You can highlight all the text in the document by pressing ⌘+A or choosing Edit ⇨ Select All.

3. **Choose Format ⇨ Font to change the fonts used in your document.** You can change the font size, make the letters bold, underline words, change the color of the text, and more, but I cover that a bit later in this chapter.

4. **Choose Format ⇨ Text to manipulate text on the page.** Move the alignment of the text to the left, right, or center. You can also change the spacing between lines, change the direction of your writing from right to left (necessary for text in some languages, such as Hebrew), create tables from existing text, and more.

The Fonts window, shown in Figure 5.15, is the central location in TextEdit for choosing and styl-izing fonts. Open the Fonts window by choosing Format ⇨ Font ⇨ Show Fonts.

5.15 The Fonts window in TextEdit makes it easy to change the look of your text.

The toolbar at the top of the window allows you to make changes to the appearance of the text, such as:

● **Text Underline and Text Strikethrough.** Decide whether to use a single or double line for the underline or strikethrough, as well as what color the line should be.

● **Change the color of the text.**

● **Change the background color of your document.**

Select the font to use in your document by browsing the Collection and Family lists. You can change the size of the font, as well as its typeface characteristics (such as making it bold or italic).

Checking spelling and grammar

No matter who you are or how well educated you may be, at some point, someone catches you in a spelling or grammatical error. Thankfully, writers have brilliant editors who come behind us and clean up our frequent messes, but most folks aren't so blessed. It is to those unlucky enough not to have editors that I dedicate this section of the chapter.

TextEdit may be a simple program, but it's quite a smart one, too. Do you have a problem spelling words like "millennium" or "weird"? Does "I am doing well" come out as "I is doing well"? If so, TextEdit has your back.

To check spelling and grammar in your documents, do the following:

1. **Choose Edit ⇨ Spelling and Grammar ⇨ Show Spelling and Grammar to open the Spelling and Grammar dialog, shown in Figure 5.16.**

2. **Click Find Next, and TextEdit goes through each spelling or grammar violation.** It even makes suggestions for rectifying the problems.

5.16 You have no more excuses for poor spelling or bad grammar if you use TextEdit.

3. **Click Change if you agree to the suggested changes, click Ignore to skip and move to the next violation, or click Learn to teach TextEdit the spelling of a word that may not be in its vocabulary.**

4. **Close the Spelling and Grammar dialog by clicking the red dot in the upper-left corner when finished.**

Genius

TextEdit can check your spelling and grammar on the fly, too. Choose Edit ⇨ Spelling and Grammar, and click Check Spelling While Typing to have TextEdit check each word as you type. Choose Edit ⇨ Spelling and Grammar, and click Check Grammar With Spelling so TextEdit checks your grammar along with the spelling of your words. To have TextEdit look over your document at any time, press ⌘+;.

Opening an existing document

To open a document from within TextEdit, do the following:

1. **Choose File ⇨ Open to display the Open dialog.**

2. **Select the On My Mac button in the upper-left side of the Open dialog to open a document that is stored on your computer, or click the iCloud button to open a document you're storing in iCloud. If you're not signed in to iCloud in System Preferences, you can see only the contents of your computer and won't have to choose between it and iCloud.**

3. **Navigate the Mac hard drive or iCloud account until you find the file you want to open.**

4. **Select the name of the file, and click Open to display the document in TextEdit.**

You can now view, print, or edit your document as needed.

Saving a document in a different format

You may notice a File Format menu at the bottom of the TextEdit Save As dialog, shown in Figure 5.17. The default TextEdit file format is RTF, which stands for Rich Text Format. Most word processors on any computing platform (including Mac, Windows, and Linux) can open RTF documents, so you don't have to worry whether other computer users can view or edit your TextEdit documents.

5.17 Save your TextEdit documents in any of these formats.

RTF allows you to make formatting changes to your document, such as adding some punch to your fonts by changing their size and color.

If you click the File Format pop-up menu, you see the other formats in which TextEdit can save your document (refer to Figure 5.17). What is the coolest thing about the availability of these formats? Not only can TextEdit save your document in the selected format, but it can also open any document that uses it. This gives you extreme flexibility when it comes to opening and saving files that originate with users of other operating systems and word processors.

Genius

There is another file format called plain text (.txt). Plain text doesn't allow you to format your documents with fancy fonts or pictures. However, programming is done in this format. It is also a format that all word processors (even those that run in command-line operating systems, like DOS and UNIX) can open, read, and edit. To create a plain text file, choose Format ➪ Make Plain Text from the menu.

Table 5.7 describes the available file formats so you can decide whether something other than RTF is right for you.

Table 5.7 TextEdit File Formats

Format	Uses
Rich Text	Rich Text Format (RTF) is the default file format. This format allows you to make formatting changes to your document, such as changing font size and color.
Rich Text with Attachments (RTFD)	This is essentially RTF with graphics included, such as pictures.
Web Page (.html)	HTML stands for HyperText Markup Language, which is a programming language used to create web pages. It allows you to edit web pages or quickly create new ones.
Web Archive	This is used primarily as the format in which Safari saves web pages. TextEdit can open, edit, and save these files.
OpenDocument Text (.odt)	OpenDocument is a relatively new standard for word processing files that is native to the OpenOffice.org office suite.
Word 2007 Format (.docx)	Microsoft made a break from the traditional Word file format (.doc) with Office 2007.
Word 2003 Format (.xml)	Open, edit, and save files that were created from Word 2003 using XML (Extensible Markup Language), another programming language used extensively on the web.
Word 97 Format (.doc)	This format should be very familiar to anyone who's used Microsoft Word in the past. It is one of the most widely used formats on the planet.

Getting Started with Messages

Instant messaging is one of the most popular forms of communication today. On the Internet, you can have instant conversations with anyone, anywhere in the world. Messages is a great instant messaging client that can do much more than just send text clips back and forth. You can also exchange files, such as pictures, documents, and music. Because Messages is also on the iPad, iPod touch, and iPhone, you can converse with users of those devices from your Mac; it's the same app, just on different platforms. To start using Messages, you need to set up an account and add some contacts to your Buddy List.

Setting up a Messages account

Messages can use several types of instant messaging accounts, which are laid out for you in Table 5.8.

Table 5.8 Messages Account Types

Account Type	Description
Apple ID	Using your Apple ID you can send and receive unlimited messages to any Mac or iOS device (iPhone, iPad, or iPod touch).
AIM	AIM stands for AOL Instant Messenger. You can use your existing AIM account or sign up for a new one by clicking Get a Messages Account in the second pane of the Welcome to Messages dialog. You can also sign up at www.aim.com by clicking Get a username.
Jabber	Jabber is an open-source implementation of instant messaging. Get a login name by going to www.jabber.org.
Google Talk	If you have a Google account, you can log in to chat with Google Talk users with Messages. Learn more about Google Talk at www.google.com/talk/.
Yahoo!	If you prefer Yahoo! as your chat provider, simply type your Yahoo! Messenger account information. If you need an account, simply go to http://messenger.yahoo.com and click the Register link.

After you get your account affiliations in order, it's time to start up Messages. From within the Finder, press ⌘+Shift+A to open the Applications folder and double-click the Messages icon, or simply click the Messages icon in the Dock. When you open Messages for the first time, you are greeted with a welcome screen. If you have an Apple ID and want to use it for Messages, enter your Apple ID information and click Sign In to begin. If you don't have an Apple ID yet, or want to use one of the other account types, simply click Not Now and then click the Skip button in the warning dialog to move forward and set up an account. When the Choose a Messages account to add dialog pops up, select the type of account you want to use and then enter the appropriate information to get started. If you've somehow gotten past this dialog or if this isn't your first time opening Messages, please follow these instructions to add an account:

1. **Select Messages, and choose Preferences from the menu.**

2. **Click the Accounts tab, and then click the plus sign (+) in the lower-left corner of the window.**

3. **In the Account Setup window, shown in Figure 5.18, choose the account type you want to use, type the information for the account, and click Done. (If you have a Jabber account, select Other Messages account..., click Continue, and then choose Jabber from the Account Type pop-up menu.)** Your new account is now added to the list.

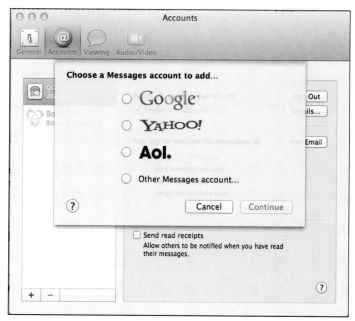

5.18 Type your account information so you can start messaging.

Note

With some account types, you can chat only with people who are using the same account type. For example, if you have an Apple ID account but your friend is using Jabber, you can't send that person an instant message unless one of you signs up for an account with the service the other is using.

Adding buddies to your Buddy List

You can use the people in your Contacts or you can use your Buddy List to chat with friends, family, and colleagues.

After you add an account, you are logged in to it automatically and the Messages window appears, as shown in Figure 5.19.

To chat with folks in Contacts, you first must add them to Contacts, which you can discover how to do by perusing Chapter 8.

To add buddies to your Buddy List, choose Window ⇨ Buddies, select the correct account if you have multiple accounts enabled, click the plus sign (+) in the lower-left corner of your Buddy List, and choose Add Buddy. Type your buddy's account information in the window, similar to the one shown in Figure 5.20, and click Add.

5.19 The Messages window is where your chats take place.

5.20 Adding a buddy to your Buddy List couldn't be much easier.

Your newly added buddy should show up in your Buddy List, ready and waiting to chat with you. You may have the ability to do everything with Messages: text, audio, and video. However, if your buddy has a slower Internet connection or computer, or uses a different chat client altogether, he may not be able to join you in one form of chat or another. You can check his Messages abilities quite easily with the following steps:

1. **Select your buddy's name in the Buddy List.**

2. **Choose Buddies ⇨ Show Profile from the menu.**

3. **Your buddy's iChat capabilities are listed in the Profile tab of the Info window, as shown in Figure 5.21.**

5.21 A typical Info window for someone in your Buddy List showing his Messages capabilities.

Different ways to chat

You have your Messages account, and you've added some buddies to your Buddy List. The only thing left to do is start chatting. As I mentioned earlier, Messages has three ways to converse with someone: text, audio, and video. I show you how to get started with each method in this section.

Text chats

Text chats are the most common method of instant messaging, but as more and more people get broadband Internet connections (such as cable and DSL), the trend will most likely be toward video.

To start a Text chat:

1. **Open the Messages window by pressing ⌘+N, if it's not already open, that is.**

2. **Select the person with whom you want to chat.** If they are in your Buddy List, type their name in the To field. If the person is in your Contacts, click the + button on the right side of the To field, click the Contacts tab, and find and select them. You can add several people to one chat if you like.

3. **Start typing away in the text field at the bottom of the Messages window.** Soon you'll be chatting like there's no tomorrow.

4. **After you finish typing a response, press Return to send it.**

Audio chats

You may wonder why you would want to use audio chat when you have a phone. In some cases (when traveling internationally, for example), phone conversations may not be free, but audio chats are always free.

To begin an audio chat:

1. **Select the buddy you want to chat with from your Buddy List.**

2. **Click the phone in the bottom of the Buddy List window to initiate the audio chat session.** Your buddy receives an invitation to the audio chat. He can choose to send a text reply instead of speaking with you, decline the invitation altogether and bruise your ego, or accept and begin conversing with you.

Video chats

Video chats are where it's at! The ability to see and speak to one another across the miles (for free, no less) is the dream of every displaced parent and grandparent. It was a godsend when I had to be away from my wife and kids for two weeks on business.

Note

To video chat via the Internet, you must have a broadband connection—no ifs, ands, or buts about it. Dial-up simply doesn't have the ability to stream video.

To initiate a video chat:

1. **Select the buddy you want to chat with from your Buddy List.**

2. **Click the small video camera at the bottom of the Buddy List window to initiate a video chat.** Your buddy receives an invitation like the one sent for an audio chat. She can choose to send a text reply, or decline or accept the invitation. It may take a few seconds to connect to one another, depending on the speed of your Internet connections.

After you establish a connection, you can see one another and talk, just as if you were in the same room. You see your buddy in the large window and yourself in a smaller preview window (so you can see how goofy you look to your friend).

126

Use Special Effects with Video Chats

Spice up your video chats with special effects exactly like those used in Photo Booth (see Chapter 12 for more information). To add special effects (and some pizzazz) to your snapshots, click Effects in the lower-left corner of the video chat window. Choose from any of the effects on the list to make you appear in the video chat window using those effects. There are filter effects (such as Glow) and distortion effects (such as Dent), or you can use video backdrops.

Managing and Reading Your Library with iBooks

Although I'm certainly not in the camp of folks who say that print is dead, it is obvious that many people prefer their books in a digital format as opposed to the good ol' analogue standard. I, for one, prefer the feel of a hardback or paperback book, but I do have quite a digital collection. It's one thing to take a bag full of your favorite books to the beach, but it's another thing entirely to haul that same bag on board an airplane! And although I do prefer a paper book in hand, I'm limited to carrying only a couple at a time, but I can take umpteen of them on my iPhone or iPad.

Having said all that, I'd like to introduce you to iBooks for OS X. iBooks is the same app that you've probably used on your iPhone or iPad, but it's now tailored to OS X's interface. If you utilize iCloud you can read a book on the subway ride home, and when you get home you can pick up right where you left off on your iMac. Technology's pretty cool, huh? iBooks allows you to synchronize book purchases, bookmarks, notes, and more across devices, so your reading experience is wonderfully, and almost transparently, consistent.

Open iBooks by clicking its icon in the Dock, from within Launchpad, or press ⌘+Shift+A from within a Finder window and find its icon there. Follow along to begin using iBooks:

1. **Click the Get Started button in the iBooks window.**

2. **If you have an Apple ID click the Sign In button to sign in, which allows you to download items from the iBooks Store and sync items via iCloud.**

3. **Click the Store button in the upper-left corner of the iBooks window.** Agree to the Terms and Conditions, review your billing information for making iBooks Store purchases, and start shopping or reading. If you've made purchases in the iBooks Store before on other devices, those purchases are now available in iBooks for OS X.

Now that you're in the iBooks Store, feel free to browse to your heart's content (and make a few purchases if the fancy strikes). It's easy to find books that suit your tastes, and quite a few free books are available as well. Use these tips for getting around in the iBooks Store:

- **Use the search field in the upper-right of the iBooks Store window, or use the items in the Quick Links section to help you peruse the vast offerings.** You can also use the Featured, Top Charts, NY Times, and Top Authors buttons at the top of the iBooks Store window to help you see what goodies are available.

- **Click the icon of a book to see more about it (some books even allow you to pre-view them).**

- **Click the price of the book to purchase it and begin downloading.** Click the Downloads button in the upper-right corner of the window to view the progress of your downloads, as shown in Figure 5.22.

- **Click the arrow to the right of the price to add the book to your wish list, to share it via Messages, Mail, and so on, or copy its link.**

5.22 Click the Downloads button to view the progress of books you're downloading.

When you're ready to actually begin reading your books, iBooks is a very friendly interface in which to do so. You can use the search field to quickly find titles, or you can browse your collection using the All Books, Collections, Authors, Categories, or List buttons at the top of the iBooks window.

After you've found the title you want, double-click to open it. iBooks opens your book in a new window and you can now begin reading. Move from page to page using the arrow keys on your keyboard, or swipe your trackpad or Magic Mouse from side to side using two fingers.

Use the tools in the upper-left corner of the window to go back to your iBooks library, view the books table of contents, or view your notes. The tools in the upper-right corner of the window allow you to change the appearance of the books' text and pages as shown in Figure 5.23, search the text, create or view bookmarks, and view the book in full screen.

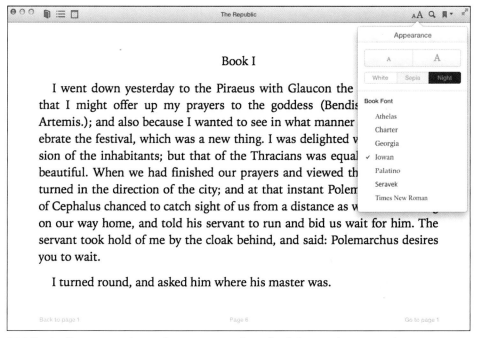

5.23 iBooks allows you to change the appearance of your books' text and pages to suit your tastes.

Discovering Our World with Maps

Maps has been around since the beginning of Apple's iOS, the operating system that powers their iPhones and iPads, but it is making its OS X debut in Mavericks. Maps isn't just for looking at dots on a globe (although it's quite good for that): It's for seeing places you've never been, getting a birds-eye view of places you have been, and finding out how to get there from here. What's more, you can map out directions for your destination using the large display of your Mac and then transfer them to your iPhone for maximum portability. Maps utilizes your Mac's graphics power to display 3D maps quickly and smoothly, allows you to bookmark favorite places, and even helps you discover a location's most popular attractions, restaurants, and more. Open Maps from within your Applications folder, and we can get started.

The Maps interface is simple and intuitive, as you can see in Figure 5.24.

Table 5.9 provides a brief description of the tools found in the Maps interface.

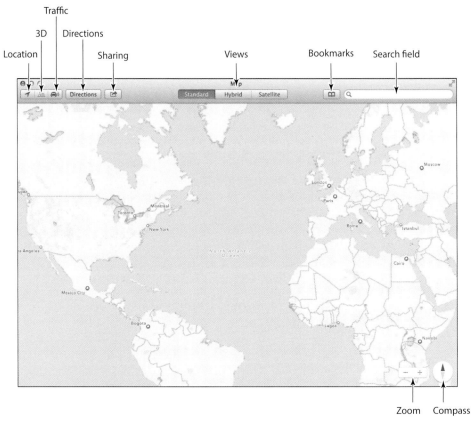

5.24 Maps makes it simple to discover locations around the globe.

Table 5.9 Tools in the Maps Interface

Tool	Function
Location	Click to see your current location.
3D	Click to see a 3D landscape of your map. You will have to zoom in a bit before items display in 3D.
Traffic	Click to see local traffic patterns on a map.

Tool	Function
Directions	Click to open the Directions sidebar, where you can enter information necessary to get you from point A to point B.
Sharing	Click to share your map or directions in myriad ways, including e-mail, Twitter, and Messages, create a Bookmark, or add the location to a contact.
Views	Choose among Standard, Satellite, and Hybrid views (combination of Standard and Satellite). Satellite and Hybrid views combined with 3D provide Flyover views.
Bookmarks	Click to show the Bookmarks banner. From here, you can click a bookmark to go right to its location, search for bookmarks using the Search field, and edit the list of bookmarks.
Search field	Enter a location name to find it in Maps. Be as specific as you can to help Maps find the correct location.
Compass	Click and drag to change the directional view of the map. The red arrow points to due North.
Zoom	Click the minus sign (–) to zoom out or the plus sign (+) to zoom in.

Getting directions

It's kind of a shame that most of the young people today won't get the pleasure of learning how to fold a huge paper map as I and my ancestors before were so (un)fortunate to do. Well, maybe the resultant saved time and avoided aggravation is a good thing for mankind's future.

If you are like me and remember the days of searching for directions on crinkly paper maps, you'll certainly and quickly learn to appreciate the simple utility of the Maps app when it comes to this task. Here's the way we get directions in the 21st century:

1. **Open the Maps app.**

2. **Click the Directions button in the toolbar to open the Directions sidebar.**

3. **Enter a Start location and End location (click the button with the squiggly line to reverse the two), and click the Directions button.** Your directions appear in the sidebar, as shown in Figure 5.25.

Now that you have directions, here are some of the things you can do with them:

- To save your directions, choose View ➪ Add Bookmark to create a Bookmark for them.
- Click the Share button to share your directions.
- Export your directions as a PDF or print them via the File menu.

5.25 Getting directions in Maps is as simple as a few clicks.

Viewing locations

Maps provides a variety of ways to view your locations; some are bare-bones basic, and others are pretty cool:

- **Standard.** Standard view affords the typical topographical map that we're used to seeing with the paper variety. These maps are clean and uncluttered, and many prefer them for just those reasons.

- **Satellite.** Satellite provides a true view of your locations from space! It's extremely helpful when checking out landmarks with which you're unfamiliar.

- **Hybrid.** Hybrid is a combination of Standard and Satellite views, which is especially helpful when navigating a location that is populated by numerous trees or tall buildings.

- **Flyover.** This is the coolest view of all, and it's also extremely helpful in places that you're not very familiar with. The three-dimensional view of the landmarks confirms you're in the place you need to be, and it's a great way to take virtual tours, as shown in

Figure 5.26. You can achieve Flyover view by clicking the 3D button while in Satellite or Hybrid viewing mode; you may need to zoom in a bit, too.

5.26 Flyover view is one of the best features in Maps.

Acquiring New Applications in the App Store

The App Store is Apple's way of saying "boxed software is so 1980s." In the App Store, you can download literally thousands of applications and utilities for your Mac (some are free, some are not). The great thing about the App Store is that you can browse for the application you want, download it instantly, and fire it right up. There are no order forms to fill out, no waiting for the software to be delivered by a courier, and no boxes or discs to store. The App Store, shown in Figure 5.27, even keeps a running record of the software you download and alerts you when updates are available. It's truly the one-stop shop for Mac applications.

Note This may seem rather obvious to some, but you must have an Internet connection to use the App Store. No Internet, no App Store.

Signing in and viewing your account

If you have an iTunes Store or iCloud account, or any type of account that requires an Apple ID, you are ready to sign in and begin using the App Store. If you don't have an Apple ID, you need to get one before you can purchase and download items.

5.27 Thousands of apps are ready for download in the App Store.

To create an Apple ID:

1. **Open the App Store by clicking its icon in the Dock.**

2. **Choose Store ⇨ Create Account from the menu.**

3. **Follow the instructions in the Welcome to the App Store window to create your Apple ID.**

Now that you have an Apple ID, you can sign in to the App Store and start browsing the virtual shelves. To sign in to your Apple ID, choose Store ⇨ Sign In from the menu, or click Sign In under the Quick Links section on the right side of the window. Type your Apple ID and Password in the appropriate fields, and click Sign In.

You can also view and edit your Apple ID account:

1. **Choose Store ⇨ View My Account from the menu, or click Account in the Quick Links section on the right side of the window.**

2. **Type your Apple ID and Password in the appropriate fields, and click View Account.**

3. **Inspect and edit your information if necessary, and click Done to return to the App Store.**

Browsing for applications

The App Store makes it simple to find the application you've been looking for. You can search for apps in three ways:

- **Click the Featured tab at the top of the window to see the latest and greatest apps to come to the App Store.** Apple gives some of the more well-known apps the Mavericks's share of the headlines at the top of the Featured page.

- **You can see lists of the best-selling and most popular apps by clicking Top Charts at the top of the window.** The apps are divided into three categories: Top Paid, Top Free, and Top Grossing.

- **Click Categories to see a wide array of app categories, as illustrated in Figure 5.28.** If you know what kind of app you want but aren't sure which particular one to get, this is the place to start.

Viewing apps you've purchased

Pretty soon you may begin to lose track of everything you've purchased from the App Store. Thankfully, unlike the clerk behind the counter at your local software haunt, the App Store remembers everything you purchase; it even shows you the status of the app on your Mac.

Simply click Purchased at the top of the App Store window to see a list of the apps you've bought. The button to the right of the app name alerts you to its status. For example, if you previously installed an app, the button says Installed. If not, simply click Install to do so.

Categories

Business iFax – Send & Receive … 2X Client RDP / Remot… Templates for MS Office		**Developer Tools** Xcode TextWrangler LiveReload		**Education** Typist Eigenmath Smartr	
Entertainment Tuba for YouTube Free MPlayerX Screensaver + free		**Finance** Mint QuickView Stock + MoneyControl – Incom…		**Games** Full Deck Solitaire Zombies Ate My Friends Green Jelly	
Graphics & Design SketchBook Express Picture Collage Maker … Softmatic ScreenLayers		**Health & Fitness** Sleep Pillow iMuscle 2 Relax Melodies		**Lifestyle** Wallpapers HD Lite Desktop Aquarium free Day One	
Medical Essential Skeleton 2 Grays Anatomy Studen… Essential Anatomy 2		**Music** VirtualDJ Home Logic Pro X Mixxx		**News** Pocket Instant RSS Notifier ReadKit	
Photography Fotor Photo Editor – Ph… iPhoto My Splash Effects		**Productivity** OS X Mountain Lion Pages Evernote		**Reference** Kindle Bible+ Bible Glo	
Social Networking Twitter TweetDeck by Twitter FaceTime		**Sports** TennisBoard3Dx Marathon Pace Calcula… DiverLog Lite		**Travel** Universal Translator Garmin WebUpdater Garmin BaseCamp	

5.28 Search categories of apps when you only have an idea of what you seek.

Keeping your apps up to date

From time to time, developers release updates to their software to iron out bugs or add some cool new features, and you want to know when this happens. The App Store makes it simple: Just click Updates at the top of the window to see a list of available updates. To update your apps:

1. **Click Update next to the name of the app you want to update.**

2. **Type your Apple ID and password, and click Sign In to download the latest and greatest version of your app.**

3. **The App Store provides you with a progress bar to keep track of how much longer it will take to retrieve the update.** You can pause if you have to take a break and click Resume when you're ready to continue the download.

4. **After the download is complete, the update automatically installs.**

What Can I Do
with Utilities?

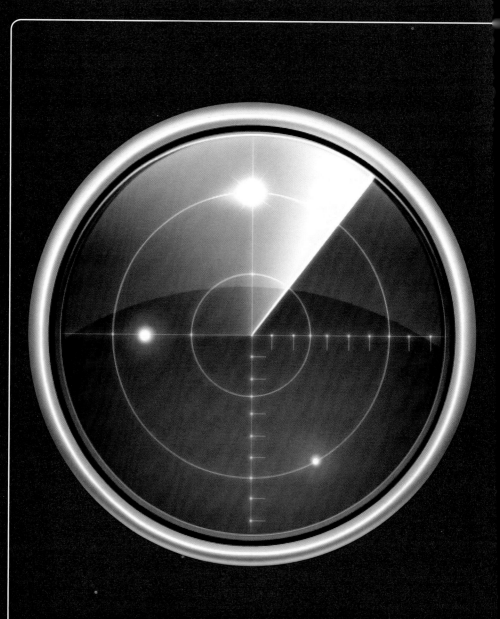

Utilities do lots of the dirty work for your Mac. They diagnose problems with your network, help you partition or format drives, take screenshots, manage passwords, and much more. Some utilities are more specialized than others, but there's a little something for everyone in Mavericks's utilities. In this chapter, I explore the Mavericks utility offerings and the basics on how they can be used to enhance your Mac experience. I also delve a bit into Terminal as homage to the Mavericks UNIX underpinnings. These utilities (for the most part) can be found in the Applications Utilities directory on your Mac.

Working with Software Utilities

Software utilities help you with matters related to software functions, such as monitoring color profiles and taking screenshots. Even though some of these utilities may touch hardware from time to time, typically their work is software-centric.

Note   All the utilities in this chapter have Help systems that can teach you much more about those that interest you the most. To access the Help system for any application, simply click Help in the menu bar.

Using AppleScript Editor

AppleScript Editor is a tool that helps you write and edit AppleScripts. "Great," I can hear you say, "but what are AppleScripts?" AppleScript is a scripting language built in to OS X. The scripts you can produce with it are called AppleScripts. You probably have already used an AppleScript without being aware of it. They generally are used by applications (and other utilities) to perform tasks and commands behind the scenes. AppleScript Editor is typically used by application developers, but some savvy Mavericks users may find it useful to write their own AppleScripts to automate repetitive tasks. For much more about AppleScript and AppleScript Editor, go to the AppleScript Help by clicking the Help menu and making a selection, or visit some (or all) of the following websites:

- www.macosxautomation.com/applescript/
- http://mac.tutsplus.com/tutorials/automation/the-ultimate-beginners-guide-to-applescript-2/
- http://macscripter.net/

Managing color profiles with ColorSync Utility

This utility manages the Mac color profiles for devices such as monitors and printers. If you have to ask what a color profile is, you probably don't want to mess with this one. However, if you do know what a color profile is, you can open ColorSync by choosing Applications ⇨ Utilities and double-clicking its icon.

Repairing color profiles

Sometimes, your color profiles may catch a bug or need other repairs, and ColorSync Utility is up to the task of color profile doctor. To find problem profiles and repair them, follow these steps:

1. **Click the Profile First Aid tab at the top of the ColorSync Utility window.**

2. **Click Verify in the lower-right corner, and ColorSync Utility finds any profiles with health issues, as shown in Figure 6.1.**

3. **Click Repair to have ColorSync Utility provide proper care to the sickly profiles.**

6.1 ColorSync Utility finds profiles with problems and resolves their issues.

Viewing installed color profiles

It's simple to view all the color profiles installed on your Mac. Follow these steps:

1. **Click the Profiles tab at the top of the ColorSync Utility window.**

2. **Decide which profile category you need: System, Computer, User, or Other.** Click the arrow to the left of the category to see its profiles.

   - **Profiles in the System category are those installed and used by Mavericks itself, and they are located in the System ⇨ Library ⇨ ColorSync ⇨ Profiles directory.**

   - **Profiles in the Computer category are those installed by you or another adminis- trator for use by all account holders on the Mac, and they are located in the Library ⇨ ColorSync ⇨ Profiles directory.**

141

- **User profiles are those installed by you or another administrator for use by an individual account holder on the Mac, and they are located in the account's Home folder ⇨ Library ⇨ ColorSync ⇨ Profiles directory.**

- **Profiles in the Other category are those installed by third parties in directories other than those mentioned previously.**

3. **Select a profile to see all its attributes, as shown in Figure 6.2.** Click Open, located on the upper right of the Profiles window, to see even more detailed information about the profile.

6.2 View color profile information in the Profiles tab.

 Genius You can see a really neat 3D rendering of the profile color gamut in the graph that appears in the lower right of the window. Click and drag your mouse anywhere in the graph, and the color gamut rotates for you.

Assigning profiles to devices

A nice feature, especially when it comes to high-end printing and color matching, is the ability to assign a profile to a device, such as a printer or display. To assign a profile to a device, follow these steps:

1. **Click the Devices tab at the top of the ColorSync Utility window.**

2. **Browse the list of devices to find the one to which you want to assign the profile, and then select it, as shown in Figure 6.3.**

6.3 You can assign profiles to a device for more precise color management.

3. **Click the arrow next to Current Profile, and choose Other from the pop-up menu.**

4. **Browse your Mac for the profile to which you want to assign the device, and click Open.**

Editing Quartz filters

Quartz filters can be used when printing to customize the color of a file, among many other things. ColorSync Utility affords the ability to edit these Quartz filters and even create new ones.

To edit existing Quartz filters or create new ones, follow these steps:

1. **Click the Filters tab in the toolbar.**

2. **Click the disclosure triangle next to the filter that you want to edit, or click the plus sign (+) at the bottom left of the filter list to create a new one.**

3. **Adjust the settings for each part of the filter by clicking the disclosure triangles next to each part and using the pop-up menus to change the settings as required.**

Calculating colors on your screen

If you really like one of the colors you see on your display, you can use the ColorSync Utility Calculator to calculate its color percentages. Follow these steps:

1. **Click the Calculator tab in the toolbar.**

2. **Click the magnifying glass at the bottom of the window.**

3. **Drag your mouse pointer (which now looks like a circle with a cross hair in the center) over the pixel on your screen with the color values you want to see.**

4. **Click the pixel to see the color values represented, as shown in Figure 6.4.**

6.4 Calculate the color values of any pixel on your screen.

Measuring color values with DigitalColor Meter

DigitalColor Meter measures the color values on your display so you can enter them into other programs, such as graphics applications.

To see the values associated with a particular pixel on your screen, simply hold your mouse pointer over the pixel. DigitalColor Meter shows you the color and the values represented.

Using Grab

This utility takes screenshots of items on your Mac. In fact, Grab was used extensively in the creation of art files for this book. For more in-depth information about Grab, see Chapter 12.

Working with Grapher

Grapher is an algebra geek's dream come true, and it's also a neat utility that graphs equations, visualizing them in two or three dimensions. You can even animate your graphs with this baby and share them as QuickTime movies. For more information about Grapher, go to its help center by clicking the Help menu.

Storing passwords with Keychain Access

Keychain Access manages your plethora of passwords in one convenient location. Keychain Access can store passwords of any type (including those used for accessing servers and websites), as well as other sensitive information, such as bank accounts and credit card numbers. The purpose of Keychain Access (along with securely storing private information) is to remember your passwords for you, which is very helpful given the crazy number of passwords the typical Internet user is required to have these days.

When you first log in to Mavericks, a default login keychain is created. This keychain uses the same password as your user account. I strongly suggest perusing the Help feature of Keychain Access if you want to get more familiar with its functionality.

Setting up VoiceOver

VoiceOver allows your Mac to describe the contents on your screen verbally. Your Mac literally speaks to you and reads the contents of your open documents and windows. This is obviously a fantastic utility for anyone who has difficulty seeing what's on the screen.

You can configure VoiceOver to your specific needs by customizing its many options, as shown in Figure 6.5, including:

- **Have your Mac speak a greeting to you upon login.** Among other uses, this feature is helpful if some instructions need to be provided for a user before he can get started working with the computer.

- **Configure Mavericks to tell you when the Caps Lock key is pressed, which can wreak havoc if you're trying to enter a case-sensitive password.**

- **Adjust the rate, pitch, volume, and intonation of your Mac's voice, which is helpful for various hearing difficulties.**

- **Configure the layout of a connected braille display.**

145

6.5 Configure VoiceOver to suit your needs and better utilize your Mac.

Working with Terminal

Terminal is your gateway to entering the command-line world of UNIX. In my opinion, in order to even think of yourself as an OS X aficionado, you must have at least attempted some basic UNIX commands using the old-fashioned way. To take a step back in computing time, open Terminal by choosing Go menu ⇨ Utilities (or press ⌘+Shift+U). Next, double-click the Terminal icon to open a new window, as shown in Figure 6.6.

6.6 This is what computing looked like before the advent of the graphical user interface.

Terminal, like other applications, can be modified to work the way you want it to. Click the Terminal menu and select Preferences (or press ⌘+,) to open the Preferences window.

Startup

When you first open Terminal, it automatically opens a new Terminal window. The Startup options in the preferences window, shown in Figure 6.7, enable you to define the state in which Terminal starts up.

Choose one of the following:

- **On startup, open.** Decide which settings to use for the new window, or open a series of windows called a window group (more on window groups later in this chapter).

- **Shells open with.** Determine whether to open Terminal in its default shell, which is called *bash*, or in a different shell. A shell is software that allows a user to interact with the UNIX services and provides the commands that can be executed by the user. You can download and install other UNIX shells from the Internet. To use a shell other than bash, select the Command (complete path) radio button and type the path to the directory in which the shell is located.

- **New windows open with and New tabs open with.** Determine which settings to use when opening new windows or new tabs.

6.7 Decide how Terminal reacts when you first start it up.

147

Genius   If you use Terminal often (and rest assured, you're an official card-carrying geek if you do), it's a good idea to keep a shortcut to it in your Dock. That way, the comfort of the command line is within easy reach. I've used OS X for years, and I like to keep the Terminal feature close by my side. You never know when the uncontrollable urge to chmod, mkdir, or ping might strike you!

Settings

The Settings section, shown in Figure 6.8, lets you adjust the look and behavior of your Terminal windows.

6.8 Even geeks like to customize their work environment!

The list on the left side of the Settings window contains preformatted window settings that you can choose. Set one as your default by highlighting the desired setting and clicking Default. Add or delete saved settings by clicking the plus (+) or minus (−) sign.

Table 6.1 gives a brief description of what each tab in the Settings section allows you to modify.

Table 6.1 Options Available in the Settings Tabs

Tab	Options
Text	Change the appearance of text, including the font and the colors designated for certain types of text. Also, control how the cursor is displayed.
Window	Set the default title of windows, as well as what other information appears in the title bar, such as the dimensions of the window or the name of the currently active process. Choose the default background color of windows, the default size of new windows, and how far back a user can scroll.
Shell	Have the shell issue a command by default as soon as a new window is opened; tell Terminal how to behave when a user exits a shell and whether it should prompt the user before closing the window.
Keyboard	Assign commands to shortcut keys to make entering commands even faster.
Advanced	Settings allow you to change the Terminal emulation, alarms, and character encodings.

Window Groups

In the Window Groups window, you can delete, import, and export your window groups. Window groups are useful for users who utilize several windows, allowing them to run multiple tasks during their Terminal sessions.

Creating window groups causes Terminal to keep each window's individual settings intact, so they are in the same state when you reopen them as they were when you closed them. To create a window group, follow these steps:

1. **Open the windows you will be working with, and make sure they are set up in the format you need.**

2. **Choose the Window menu, and select Save Windows as Group.**

3. **Give the window group a descriptive name, such as "Network diagnostics," and click the Save button.** Select the check box in the Save window to have this window group open automatically when you first open Terminal.

Encodings

The options in the Encodings window allow you to enable and disable international character encodings so Terminal can display international characters.

Tabbed windows

Some users may prefer to have several Terminal windows open at once, but I like the simplicity of having one window running multiple tabs, as shown in Figure 6.9.

6.9 Tabbed Terminal windows are the way to go for me.

To create a new tab, choose Shell ⇨ New Tab and select the setting for the new tab. For example, choose Basic to select a default shell interface. Close tabs by clicking the X in the upper-left corner of the tab. You can also save tabbed windows as a window group by choosing Window ⇨ Save Windows as Group and giving the group a descriptive name.

Entering UNIX commands

To effectively navigate in a CLI (command-line interface), you need to understand how UNIX views the structure of your files and folders on the hard drive. UNIX calls each folder on your Mac a directory, and it recognizes the drives as volumes. The beginning—or top—level of your startup drive is known as the root directory, which is represented by a slash (/).

Let's begin learning how to get around in UNIX by opening a new window. To do so, choose Shell ⇨ New Window and select the setting for the new window.

When you first bring up a Terminal window, it opens in your home directory, which is represented by a tilde (~). To move to another directory, type its path on the command line. For example, to move to the root directory of your hard drive, simply type **cd /** and press Return (cd stands for change directory). To move back from the root directory to your home directory, simply type **cd ~** and press Return.

Moving to a subdirectory can be a little trickier; however, knowing where directories are located on your drive helps immensely. Directories are separated by slashes when typing their path. For example, type the following to move to the Utilities folder on your hard drive and press Return:

```
cd /Applications/Utilities
```

Common commands

You can bend Mavericks to your will using Terminal just as you can with the mouse. Typing commands in the CLI executes functions that range from listing items in a directory to performing diagnostics on your network. As I covered in the previous section, entering and executing a command is as simple as typing it and pressing Return; that's it!

Table 6.2 lists some of the most commonly used UNIX commands and gives a brief explanation of the functions they perform.

Table 6.2 Common UNIX Commands

Command	Function
ls	Lists files in the current directory.
ls –a	Lists all files (including hidden files) in the current directory.
cd	Changes directories. Type this command, followed by the path of the directory to which you want to change.
man	Displays the manual page for a command.
su	Stands for superuser. Temporarily enables the root user account, discussed in Chapter 4. Type **su** followed by the command you want to invoke as the superuser, and then press Return. Type the password for the root account when prompted.
mv	Moves or renames a file. Type **mv** followed by the name of the file (and in some cases, the path to the file) you want to move, and then type the path and name of the file to which you want to move it. This action creates a new file in the new location and deletes the original.
rm	Deletes a file. Type the command followed by the path and name of the file you want to delete.
rm –r	Deletes a directory and all its contents. To use this command, type **rm –r** *directory name* (where *directory name* is the name of the directory you want to delete) and press Return.
pwd	Displays the path to the directory in which you are currently working.
cp	Copies a file. Type **cp** followed by the path and name of the file you want to copy, and then type the path and name of the file to which you want to copy it. This creates a new file in the new location, but also retains the original.
mkdir	Creates a new directory. Type **mkdir**, and then type the path and name of the new directory.

X11

Also known as the X Window System, X11 allows you to run UNIX applications alongside those in OS X. Because the Mavericks version of UNIX, Darwin, is a fully compliant and certified UNIX variant, it can compile and run the full gamut of your UNIX applications. Thousands of applications are available, many of which use graphical user interfaces. Although Apple no longer includes X11 by default as part of OS X, they continue to support its development. Apple directs users to the XQuartz project to download the X11 app. For more information visit http://xquartz. macosforge.org.

Finding additional UNIX information

UNIX adds a whole other dimension to Mavericks that many regular users may never discover. However, you can find hidden treasures in UNIX that are well worth learning about. Here are some additional resources on UNIX:

- www.apple.com/opensource/
- http://developer.apple.com/opensource/
- www.unix.org

These links are accurate at the time of this writing. The Internet is chock-full of more UNIX goodness, so feel free to scour it for all the command-line enlightenment you can stand.

What's Up, Man?

Literally hundreds of UNIX commands are at your disposal in Mavericks, and each might have several options that further expand its abilities. Needless to say, I simply cannot explain the functions of all those commands. But fear not: A UNIX command can tell you everything you need to know—the man command. In a Terminal window, type **man** followed by the name of the command about which you need more information and press Return. The man (or manual) page for that command appears. The man page describes what that command can do and what options are available for it.

When you first open the man page for a command, you see only a few lines of it. To navigate through the man page, follow these steps:

1. **Press the up and down arrows on your keyboard to scroll up or down one line at a time.**
2. **Press the space bar to move to the next page.**
3. **Press Q to exit the man page.**

Administering System Utilities

System Utilities help you manage, monitor, and configure items related to the internal system functions of OS X. These include things like the load on your processor and general information about the computer.

Tracking your Mac with Activity Monitor

Activity Monitor keeps track of all the goings-on in Mavericks, such as what applications are running and how much processor capacity is being used, as shown in Figure 6.10.

Select an activity or process from the list to quit, inspect, or sample using the buttons in the toolbar. You can also monitor the CPU and hard drive using the tabs at the bottom of the Activity Monitor window: CPU, System Memory, Disk Activity, Disk Usage, and Network.

Discovering errors with Console

Console displays messages generated by your Mac or its applications when an error occurs. This utility is great for tracking down problems with OS X. For example, if you are having an issue with a certain app crashing, the log for that application (found in Console) could be useful to the technical support representative when you call the developer of the app for help.

6.10 Keep up with the CPU and hard drive activity of your Mac.

Moving information with Migration Assistant

Migration Assistant moves all the user account information from one Mac to another using a FireWire cable. You can bring over your network information, passwords, the contents of your user account folders, and so on in one fell swoop. Migration Assistant also helps you restore information from a Time Machine backup.

Using Remote Install OS X

Remote Install OS X helps install OS X on a Mac that doesn't have an optical drive. For example, the MacBook Air doesn't have an internal optical drive of its own, so it relies on optical drives in other computers or an external optical drive.

Using System Information

System Information gives you all the information you could ever want about your Mac hardware, software, and network functionality. Select an option from the list on the left, as shown in Figure 6.11, and System Information gives you more information than you bargained for.

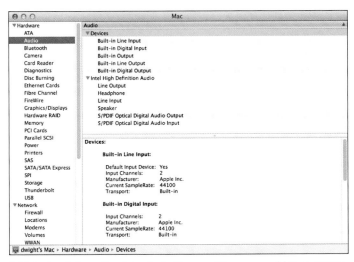

6.11 System Information is loaded with everything you could ever want to know about your Mac.

Using Hardware Utilities

Utilities of the hardware variety concentrate on helping you configure and use the various types of hardware you may want to connect to your Mac.

Configuring devices with Audio MIDI Setup

Audio MIDI (Musical Instrument Digital Interface) Setup helps set up audio and MIDI devices that you connect to your Mac, including those that are built in, such as the speakers shown in Figure 6.12.

Configure multiple drives with RAID Utility

RAID (Redundant Array of Inexpensive Disks) Utility allows you to configure multiple hard drives to act as one contiguous drive. This is good if you have a massive amount of information to store. For example, if you have a server utilized by many users who create very large files (an advertising agency is a good example), this utility comes in handy. You must have a RAID card installed on your Mac to use RAID Utility, which means that (at the time of this writing) only a Mac Pro can use it because it's the only Mac that can accept a RAID card.

6.12 Audio MIDI Setup helps you set up audio devices, such as speakers, on your Mac.

Managing Network Utilities

Two network utilities in Mavericks allow you to manage, configure, and diagnose issues with your network.

AirPort Utility

AirPort Utility helps you manage your AirPort Base Station or Time Capsule. You can use it to do all the following (and more):

- **Discover and install new firmware updates for your AirPort Base Station or Time Capsule**
- **Share your Internet connection**
- **Control who can access your wireless network**
- **Monitor and diagnose any problems with your AirPort Base Station or Time Capsule**
- **Restore your AirPort Base Station or Time Capsule to its factory defaults**
- **Set up a password to protect your AirPort Base Station or Time Capsule settings**

Consult the AirPort Utility help for more information about how to utilize this great tool.

Network Utility

Network Utility monitors network traffic and diagnoses any issues that may creep up. This utility is great, but you almost have to be a network administrator to understand and utilize some of its diagnostic tools. And you almost need to be a programmer to access the thing; Apple has seen fit in this version of OS X to bury Network Utility in the CoreServices directory. To open Network Utility:

1. **From the Finder, press ⌘+Shift+C to open the Computer directory.**
2. **Double-click the icon for your Mac's hard drive and browse to System ⇨ Library ⇨ CoreServices.**
3. **Double-click the Network Utility icon.**

The Info tab, shown in Figure 6.13, can provide invaluable information about your connection to the network, which can come in handy when troubleshooting networking issues.

6.13 Network Utility provides you with vital information about your Mac's network connections.

Note If you're trying to see if a certain device responds to you using its IP address, the Ping section of Network Utility is for you. Just type the IP address of the device with which you are trying to communicate and click Ping to see if it responds over the network.

Additional Utilities

If you're looking at your Utilities folder right now, you might notice that I don't touch on Boot Camp or Bluetooth File Exchange. That's because they are discussed elsewhere in this book; Boot Camp is covered in Chapter 15, and Bluetooth File Exchange is discussed in Chapter 13.

How Do I Work with PDFs in Preview?

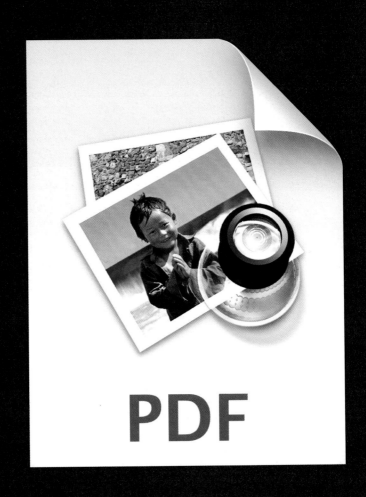

Portable Document Format files (PDFs) are the de facto standard for disseminating documents over the Internet and throughout many corporations. This is due largely to their portability across multiple operating systems, their relatively small file sizes, and the availability of security options for sensitive information. Mavericks includes an application called Preview that can open, edit, and save PDFs (most of the graphics on your screen are created with PDF technology). In this chapter, I show you how to work with PDF files using Preview.

Opening and Saving PDFs in Preview

PDF files have become a standard document format that almost anyone who uses a computer has seen at some point. Most documents on the Internet are PDF files. Anyone on any computer can open PDFs, whether the computer runs OS X, Windows, or Linux, as long as a PDF reader application, such as Preview or Adobe Reader, is installed.

Preview can open many types of files; see Chapter 12 for a comprehensive list. This chapter maintains a laser-like focus on PDFs. To open a PDF file in Preview, do the following:

1. **From within Finder, choose Go ⇨ Applications and then double-click the Preview icon to open the application.** You could also launch Preview from Launchpad.

2. **The Preview window appears if you've enabled your iCloud account.** You have the option of choosing to browse for files that are stored locally or in iCloud. Click either the iCloud or On My Mac button in the upper left of the window. If you have iCloud enabled on your Mac, you may add documents to your iCloud account by dragging and dropping them into the Preview window. If the Preview window doesn't appear when launching Preview, choose File ⇨ Open or press ⌘+O to display the Open dialog.

3. **Browse to the file you want to open, click its icon to highlight it, and then click Open, as shown in Figure 7.1.**

7.1 Choose the file you want to open in Preview.

Genius

If the Preview icon is in your Dock (either because it's already open or because you keep an alias for it there), you can simply drag and drop a PDF file onto the Preview icon to open it.

If you make changes to an open PDF, Preview automatically saves them as versions of the document. This allows you to view the file as it has appeared throughout the time you worked with it. It also eliminates the need to repeatedly save your documents as you make changes.

Preview automatically saves versions of a document you are editing once an hour, but it does so more often if you make frequent changes. Preview also saves versions of documents when you open, save, duplicate, lock, or rename them, or when you revert to previous versions. Preview trims the number of saved versions to make them easier to browse and also deletes all saved versions when you delete a document.

Although this process is automatic, you can also save versions of PDFs on your own. If you make changes to a PDF in Preview and want to save those changes, press ⌘+S. You can also choose File ⇨ Duplicate.

If you make changes to a file but you want to save the changed version under a different name and/or in a different location, follow these steps:

1. **Choose File ⇨ Duplicate from the menu to create an exact copy of your original document.**

2. **Press ⌘+S or click the red Close button in the upper-left corner of the document window to open the Save As dialog, shown in Figure 7.2.** The Save As dialog looks a little different, depending on which method you choose to open it, but the next step is the same.

3. **Type a new name for the file, choose a location in which to save it, and click Save.**

7.2 You can duplicate files and save them under a new name or in a new location.

Preview has a really cool way of browsing through the versions of a document. It is very reminiscent of the way Time Machine lets you browse through backed-up files; see Chapter 14 for more info.

To browse through the many different versions of a document and possibly revert to one of them:

1. **Open the document of which you want to browse versions.**

2. **Choose File ⇨ Revert to ⇨ Browse All Versions from the menu, and your screen is transformed into something resembling the latest sci-fi blockbuster, as shown in Figure 7.3.**

7.3 Soar through space and time to find the version of the document you need.

3. **Click the gray tick marks on the right side of the window or drag the slider to find the version you want to see.**

4. **Perform one of these tasks:**

    - To restore the document to a previous state, select the version and click Restore.

    - To create a new document from a version of a previous one, select the version, hold down the Option key, and click Restore a Copy.

    - To return to your document without reverting to any previous versions, click Done.

If you've ever double-clicked a file to open it, only to have it open in an application you didn't expect, you'll love this little nugget. To make a certain file type open only in an application you designate, do the following:

1. **Click the file once to highlight it, and then press ⌘+I to open its Info window, as shown in Figure 7.4.** You can also Control+click (or right-click) the file and select Get Info from the pop-up menu to open the Info window.

2. **If the gray triangle to the left of the Open with section is pointing to the right, click it to expand that section.**

3. **Click the pop-up menu to choose the application you want to set as the default for opening this file.**

4. **To make the selected application the system-wide default for opening all files of this type, click Change All.**

5. **Close the Info window by clicking the red button in the upper-left corner.**

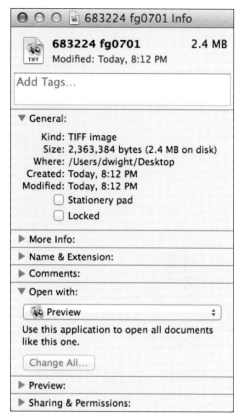

7.4 Get Info on any file by highlighting it and pressing ⌘+I.

Setting the Preview Preferences for PDFs

The way you set the preferences for Preview affects how you use the application. I'm a big advocate for making Mavericks and all its applications work the way you want them to. It's very important that your application preferences fit your work style.

The Preview preferences are divided into four categories: General, Images, PDF, and Signatures. However, the only two covered in this chapter are PDF and Signatures. (The other two are discussed in Chapter 12.) Open Preview and press ⌘+ to open the Preferences window.

PDF

The options under the PDF tab in the Preview preferences are shown in Figure 7.5.

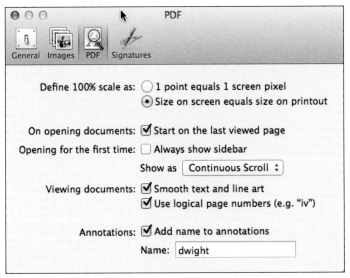

7.5 The PDF preferences for Preview.

Table 7.1 covers the functions of the different options under the PDF tab.

Table 7.1 PDF Preferences

Preference	Function
Define 100% scale as	Determine whether 100 percent scale of a PDF is based on screen pixels or the actual printout.
On opening documents	Select the check box to begin viewing a PDF from the last page you viewed the previous time it was open.
Opening for the first time	Determine whether to always show the sidebar when opening a PDF for the first time, as well as choose scrolling options (Continuous Scroll, Single Page, Two Pages).
Viewing documents	Select these check boxes to smooth lines in text and line art or to use logical page numbers when viewing PDFs.
Annotations	Select this check box to assign a name to annotations you make in a PDF, and then type that name in the Name field.

Signatures

How cool would it be if you could add your own John Hancock to your PDF files? You're about to find out, because that is exactly what Preview lets you do with one of its latest options.

To add a signature to your arsenal of PDF tricks, follow these steps:

1. **Open the Signatures pane of the Preview preferences window, and click Create Signature.**
2. **Sign your name (in black ink) on a white piece of paper.**
3. **Hold the paper up to your Mac's camera.** Be sure that the signature on the paper is resting on the blue line in the preview window, as shown in Figure 7.6.

7.6 You can add your signature to Preview using your Mac's built-in camera.

4. **Click Accept, and your signature is added to the list in the Signatures preferences pane.**

You can add or remove signatures from the list by using the plus (+) and minus (–) signs in the lower-left corner of the Signatures preferences pane. Read on to find out how to insert signatures into your PDFs.

Viewing and Editing PDFs

Mavericks is a whiz at opening, viewing, editing, and creating PDF files. I covered opening files earlier in this chapter; I concentrate on viewing and editing them in this section. The creation of PDFs is covered later in this chapter.

To get started, you need to open a PDF, as described earlier.

Annotating PDFs

To annotate a PDF is to highlight, strike through, or underline text that needs to be edited or removed. Annotation also means to add notes or links to a document or to spotlight an area of the page with an oval, arrow, line, or rectangle. Figure 7.7 shows an example of annotations in a PDF.

To annotate a PDF, do the following:

1. **Click and drag the mouse cursor over the text you want to mark up to highlight it.**
2. **Choose Tools ⇨ Annotate.**
3. **Select which type of annotation to use:**

   - Highlight Text (⌘+Control+H)
   - Strike Through Text (⌘+Control+S)
   - Underline Text (⌘+Control+U)
   - Add Oval (⌘+Control+O)
   - Add Rectangle (⌘+Control+R)
   - Add Line (⌘+Control+I)
   - Add Text (⌘+Control+T)
   - Add Outlined Text
   - Add Speech Bubble
   - Add Thought Bubble
   - Add Note (⌘+Control+N)
   - Add Signature

Genius If annotating PDFs is something you do often, memorize the keyboard shortcuts for them. Keyboard shortcuts can save you much more time than you realize. It's worth taking the time to learn them if you work in a fast-paced environment.

Note The annotations and other editing tools can be accessed quickly by opening the Edit toolbar. Simply click the Edit button to the left of the search field in the toolbar, and the Edit toolbar appears beneath it.

7.7 Mark up and annotate PDFs in Preview.

Adding your signature to a PDF

Some PDFs may require your signature, so Mavericks has added this really cool tool to Preview. As covered earlier in this chapter, you can create a signature in Preview via the Preferences pane. To add a created signature to your PDF, do the following:

1. **Open the PDF to which you want to add the signature.**

2. **In the Edit toolbar, click the Signature button and select the signature you want to place in your PDF, as shown in Figure 7.8.** If you don't see the Edit toolbar, choose View ⇨ Show Edit Toolbar or click the Edit button in the toolbar.

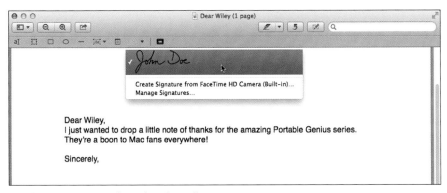

7.8 Choose a signature from the Edit toolbar.

167

3. **Click and drag the signature to the location in the document you prefer.**

4. **Resize the signature if necessary by dragging the handles (gray dots) found on each side and in each corner of the signature window, as shown in Figure 7.9.**

Dear Wiley,
I just wanted to drop a little note of thanks for
They're a boon to Mac fans everywhere!

Sincerely,

John Doe

Deleting pages from a PDF

7.9 Signatures can be resized by dragging the size handles.

Just a few years ago, the only way to delete or rearrange PDF pages was to pay through the nose for a third-party program. Thanks to Apple, Preview now has these capabilities, which means you can provide a professional level of service without having to shell out a professional level of money.

To delete a page from a multipage document, do the following:

1. **If you can't see all the pages of the PDF in the sidebar, choose View ⇨ Thumbnails and then choose View ⇨ Sidebar ⇨ Expand All.**

2. **Find the page you want to delete in the sidebar, and click to select it.** You can select multiple pages by holding down the ⌘ key while clicking the individual pages. The sidebar must be displaying thumbnails, not Table of Contents. To set the sidebar to display thumbnails, click the Thumbnails button in the View section of the toolbar at the top of the PDF's window.

3. **Choose Edit ⇨ Delete or simply press the Delete key to remove the page from your PDF.**

4. **Save your PDF (⌘+S) to keep the changes, or press ⌘+Z to undo a change.**

Rearranging pages in a PDF

As mentioned in the previous section, rearranging pages in a PDF is a treat for anyone who doesn't have an expensive third-party application. To shuffle your PDF pages, do the following:

1. **If you can't see all the pages of the PDF in the sidebar, choose View ⇨ Thumbnails and then choose View ⇨ Sidebar ⇨ Expand All, or simply click the triangle next to the file name in the sidebar.**

2. **Search the sidebar for the page you want to move.** The sidebar must be displaying thumbnails, not Table of Contents. To set the sidebar to display thumbnails, click the Thumbnails button in the View section of the toolbar at the top of the PDF window.

3. **Click and drag the page to the location in the sidebar you prefer, and drop it in place, as shown in Figure 7.10.**

4. **Save the changes by pressing ⌘+S, or undo them by pressing ⌘+Z.**

Note

If you try to make changes to a locked PDF, Preview gives you two options to continue working with the document. To create a new document that retains the changes you made, click Duplicate. If this doesn't sound appealing, click Undo Change to just forget the whole affair. A second option is to unlock the file by clicking the word Locked in the title bar and selecting Unlock from the pop-up menu. Using this option allows you to save changes directly to the original document.

7.10 Drag pages from their old location to a new one to rearrange the contents of your PDF.

Magnifying the contents of a PDF

Sometimes, the fonts in a PDF may be too small to view, or you may simply want to read a section of the document without having to zoom in on the entire page. Preview has a nifty tool called the Magnifier (catchy name) that can accommodate you. Here's how to zoom in on a specific section of a page:

1. **Open a PDF, and go to the page you want to view.**

2. **Choose Tools ⇨ Show Magnifier from the menu, and the Magnifier window appears in your PDF window, as illustrated in Figure 7.11.**

3. **Click and drag the Magnifier to the location of the PDF on which you want to zoom in.**

4. **When finished, choose Tools ⇨ Hide Magnifier or press the ESC key to go back to normal viewing.**

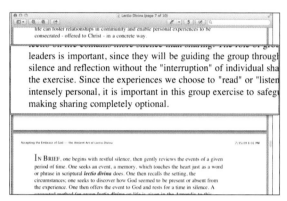

7.11 Magnifier zooms in on specific sections of a PDF.

Changing the page view

If your PDF contains multiple pages, consider viewing the contents of the document in its entirety so you can jump from one page to another rather quickly. The View button can be found all the way to the left in the toolbar. (If the toolbar isn't visible at the top of the PDF window, press ⌘+B.) It is a pop-up menu that contains five options for selecting a specific type of view:

- **Content Only view shows only the currently selected page in your PDF.**

- **Thumbnails view opens the sidebar on the left side of the PDF window and displays thumbnail images of each page in your PDF.**

- **Table of Contents view displays the PDF table of contents (assuming it contains one) in the sidebar.**

- **Highlights and Notes view displays every page that contains a highlight or a note in the sidebar.**

● **Bookmarks view shows a list of pages you've bookmarked in the sidebar.**

● **Contact Sheet view displays every page of the PDF in a single window, as shown in Figure 7.12.**

7.12 Choose Contact Sheet view to see all pages of a PDF simultaneously in one window.

Rotating pages in a PDF

Sometimes, when a PDF is created, some pages may appear in portrait orientation but should be in landscape (or vice versa) for readability. Preview can save your neck some strain by helping you easily rotate pages. Here's how:

1. **Open a PDF, and go to the page you want to rotate.**

2. **Choose Tools ⇨ Rotate Left or Tools ⇨ Rotate Right from the menu to rotate the page 90 degrees in one direction or the other, as illustrated in Figure 7.13. You can also click the Rotate button in the toolbar, but you are limited to rotating 90 degrees counterclockwise per click.**

3. **Save the changes by pressing ⌘+S, or undo them by pressing ⌘+Z.**

Compressing PDFs

PDF files are sometimes larger in terms of file data size than they need to be, and this is just a waste of valuable hard drive space (even in this age of terabyte-plus storage). Preview has a nice way of allowing you to reduce the file size of a PDF:

1. **Open a PDF that you want to compress (reduce), and press ⌘+Shift+S to make a duplicate.**

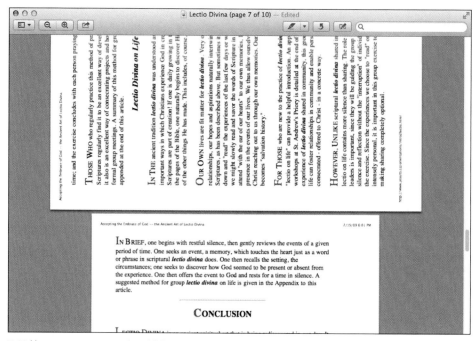

7.13 You can rotate pages in a PDF so you can read them without having to look at them sidewise.

2. **Press ⌘+S to open the Save As dialog sheet.**

3. **Choose Reduce File Size from the Quartz Filter pop-up menu, as shown in Figure 7.14.**

4. **Click the Save button to compress the PDF to a smaller file size.**

7.14 Reduce the file size of a PDF easily with a Quartz filter.

Creating Your Own PDFs

Once upon a time, PDFs could be generated only by expensive software. OS X has changed that due to its extensive use of the PDF file format throughout the operating system. Mavericks affords you the ability to create PDFs from any document you please, for free!

To create a PDF using Mavericks, do the following:

1. **Open a document in an application.** If you want to follow along, I'm using TextEdit.

2. **Choose File ➪ Print.**

3. **Click PDF in the lower-left corner of the window to see the options you have at your beck and call, as shown in Figure 7.15.**

4. **Select Save as PDF from the menu to open the Save dialog, shown in Figure 7.16.**

5. **Give the PDF an appropriate name, decide where on your Mac to save it, and click Save.**

The ability to create PDFs with any document on your Mac without expensive third-party software is a huge boon, no doubt about it. However, that third-party software (specifically Adobe Acrobat) has always had the ability to make PDF files secure from prying eyes.

This is a great feature and is required by some corporations when disseminating sensitive information. Previous versions of OS X were lacking in this department, but Mavericks comes to the rescue of the security-obsessed among us. To secure your PDFs, refer to Step 5 in this section. Prior to clicking Save, click Security Options to see the PDF Security Options window, as shown in Figure 7.17. Table 7.2 spells out the available security options. Click OK to assign those you have chosen for a file.

7.15 Mavericks gives you several options for creating PDF files from any document you want.

7.16 The options in the PDF Save dialog.

7.17 Secure your PDFs from anyone not authorized to view them.

Table 7.2 PDF Security Options

Option	Function
Require password to open document	Select this check box to enable the password feature. Type a secure password in the Password field, and then retype it in the Verify field.
Require password to copy text, images, and other content	Check this box to prevent someone from copying elements of the PDF and pasting them into an unsecured document without knowing the password to do so. Type a secure password in the Password field, and then retype it in the Verify field.
Require password to print document	If this check box is selected, a user must know the password in order to print this document. Type a secure password in the Password field, and then retype it in the Verify field.

How Do I Organize My Life with Calendar, Contacts, Notes, and Reminders?

If your life is anything like mine, you need as much organization as you can get. Enter Calendar, Contacts, Notes, and Reminders. With Calendar, you can create calendars for family or work events, while Contacts keeps all your contacts in one location. You can create events in Calendar with reminders for important dates (no more excuses if you forget your anniversary, guys). Contacts allows access to your contacts through any application programmed to use it, including Mail or Messages. Notes is a nifty tool for jotting down your thoughts, and Reminders keeps you abreast of all the tasks in your life.

Creating Calendars

Open Calendar to get started; choose Go ⇨ Applications in the menu and double-click the Calendar icon, or use Launchpad to find and start Calendar.

You can create calendars that reflect the different areas of your everyday life, such as your work schedule, bill due dates, or school events. Having a separate calendar for each makes it easier to organize your time.

You can create a new calendar in two ways:

- **Choose File ⇨ New Calendar.** If you are signed in to iCloud, choose File ⇨ New Calendar ⇨ iCloud.

- **Press ⌘+Option+N.** This action won't work, though, if you are trying to create a new iCloud or other network-based calendar.

Performing either of these opens the Calendars list (in the upper-left corner of the window) and displays an untitled calendar. Next, simply type a name for the calendar. Create as many as you need before proceeding.

Your calendars are now ready to be put to work. There are a number of ways in which you can manage them:

- **Arrange calendars in the list by clicking and dragging them into the order you prefer, as shown in Figure 8.1.**

- **Rename a calendar by right-clicking (or Control-clicking) it in the Calendars list and selecting Get Info from the pop-up menu.** Type a new name for the calendar in the Name field.

- **The events you enter (more on that a bit later in this chapter) are represented by the color of their respective calendars.** You can change the color of a calendar by right-clicking (or Control-clicking) it in the Calendars list and then selecting Get Info. Click the color button in the upper-right corner of the window, and select a color from the list.

8.1 Click and drag calendars into the order you prefer.

- **Notice the check box to the left of each calendar you create.** It indicates whether events are displayed for the calendar in question. Deselecting some of these check boxes can help make sense out of a particularly busy schedule.

- **Create groups to arrange similar calendars together in the calendar list.** Choose File ⇨ New Calendar Group or press ⌘+Shift+N, and give the new group a descriptive name. Arrange calendars into groups by dragging and dropping them below the desired group. Groups are available only if you aren't logged into iCloud; however, you may log out of iCloud, create groups, and then log back into iCloud. Any groups you create when logged out of iCloud remain intact and functional.

Genius

You can change the way your calendars are displayed in the Calendar window by clicking the Day, Week, Month, and Year tabs at the top. Click the arrows in the upper-left area of the Calendar window to scroll to the previous or next day, week, or month. The Full Screen button is the one with two opposite-pointing arrows in the upper-right corner of the Calendar window. To exit Full Screen, press ESC.

Adding events to calendars

A calendar without an event is about as useful as a car without tires, and it probably won't even get you as far. Events are the items that you add to your calendars to make them come alive; they are your life, but organized.

To create a new event:

1. **Select the day the event begins.**

2. **Press ⌘+N or choose File ⇨ New Event to open the Quick Event dialog and create a new event for that day.**

3. **Type a descriptive name for the event.** The event information window opens automatically.

You now have your first event, but you most likely want to edit the contents of it before considering it a done deal.

Editing calendar events

After you create an event, some tweaking may be in order. To edit your event, follow these steps:

1. **Open the event information window, shown in Figure 8.2, by double-clicking the event or by clicking the event to highlight it and pressing ⌘+E.**

2. **Click each item in the event information window to edit it.** Table 8.1 lists the available items and their functions.

3. **Click Done.**

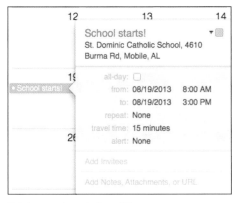

8.2 An event ready for editing.

Table 8.1 Event Information

Item	Function
event name	Enter a name or brief description of the event.
location	This is where the event is to be held.
all-day	Select this check box if the event lasts an entire day, as opposed to an hour or two. All-day events are highlighted in the calendar.
from and to	Select begin and end dates and times for your event.
repeat	Click the options menu next to this item if you want the event to be repeated (for a recurring event like a birthday or weekly meeting).
travel time	Enter the time it takes to travel to and from the event.
calendar selector	Choose the calendar to which this event belongs. The selector is found in the upper-right corner of the event information window.
alert	Select from several alert types, such as e-mail, on-screen messages, and sound. You can set multiple alerts for each event.
invitees	Invite others to add this event to their calendars.
attachments	You can attach documents and other files to your events. For example, you could attach a grocery list to a scheduled shopping trip.
url	Include a relevant website or shared calendar address.
notes	Type any additional information you may need for the event.

Setting Calendar Preferences

You can change the Calendar preferences to customize how it works. Choose Calendar ➪ Preferences to see what options are available, as shown in Figure 8.3.

8.3 The Calendar preferences window.

The General tab allows you to make the most basic of setting adjustments. The settings are listed in Table 8.2.

The Accounts tab allows you to subscribe to CalDAV and Exchange servers, which some companies and organizations use to share calendars among several users. To subscribe to your company's or organization's CalDAV server, click the plus sign (+) in the lower-left corner and type the server information. (If you don't have this information, contact your IT department.) You may also subscribe to other accounts that you have, such as iCloud, Google, Facebook, and Yahoo!.

Table 8.2 The Calendar General Preferences Tab

Setting	Function
Days per week	Set the number of days for your normal week. For example, you might change this to 5 to reflect a five-day workweek.
Start week on	Choose on which day to start your week.
Scroll in week view by	Select to view either weeks or days when in week view.
Day starts at	Decide at what time your typical day begins.
Day ends at	Set the time your typical day ends.
Show X hours at a time	Choose how many hours to display when in Day and Week viewing modes.

continued

Table 8.2 continued

Web site	Description
Default Calendar	Select the calendar to which new events are automatically added.
Show Holidays calendar	This calendar displays national holidays for your part of the world.
Show Birthdays calendar	Select this option to display a calendar that lists birthdays from your Contacts.

The Advanced tab, shown in Figure 8.4, helps you set preferences for time zone support, to-do's, events, alarms, and invitations.

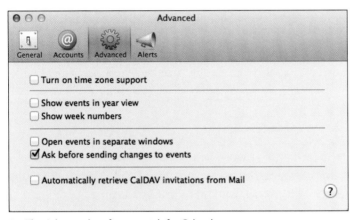

8.4 The Advanced preferences tab for Calendar.

Table 8.3 lists the Advanced preferences available for Calendar.

Table 8.3 The Calendar Advanced Preferences Tab

Setting	Function
Turn on time zone support	This allows you to view your schedule as it would be in a time zone other than your default. When you check this box, select the appropriate time zone from the pop-up menu that appears. This option is great for those who travel or work with others in different time zones.
Show events in year view	When using this option, days in which you are busiest appear darker than those when you are less busy.
Show week numbers	Select this option to see week numbers. This option works only in Week, Month, and Year views.
Open events in separate windows	This option causes events to open in a separate window when double-clicked. This is a good trick for comparing two or more events.

Setting	Function
Ask before sending changes to events	Check this box to have Calendar alert you and make certain you want to send changes you've made to events.
Automatically retrieve CalDAV invitations from Mail	Select this check box to have event invitations shown in Calendar instead of just Mail.

The Alerts tab allows you to set default times for alerts of appointments, all-day events, and birthdays. From this tab, you can also turn on or off shared calendar messages and invitation messages in Notification Center.

Sharing Calendars

Life is much easier when everyone is on the same page—be it your company or your family. Calendar offers two ways to share your calendars with others: publishing and exporting.

Publishing and sharing a calendar

When you publish a calendar (or share it, if you are using iCloud), you place a copy of it on the Internet or a local WebDAV server. Other users can access it through Calendar, another third-party calendar application, or a standard web browser using any computing platform.

Follow these steps to publish a calendar that's not part of your iCloud account:

1. **Open the calendar list, and find the calendar or calendar group to which you want to publish in the calendar list.**

2. **Right-click (or Control-click) the calendar, and select Publish from the menu.** The Publish calendar window appears, as shown in Figure 8.5. The Publish option appears only for local calendars, not iCloud or other network-based calendars.

3. **When the window opens, type a name for your calendar if you don't want to use the default.**

4. **Type the information for the server you will use to share the calendar into the Base URL field.** Type the server login name and password to gain access to it.

5. **When the options are set to your liking, click Publish.**

Publish calendar

Publish calendar as: Birthdays

Base URL: https://www.example.com/folder/

Login:

Password:

☐ Publish changes automatically ☐ Publish alerts
☑ Publish titles and notes ☐ Publish attachments
☐ Publish to do items

Cancel   Publish

8.5 Publish calendars to share them over a network or through the Internet.

Follow these steps to share a calendar to iCloud:

1. **Open the calendar list, and find the calendar to which you want to publish in the calendar list.**

2. **Click the broadcast icon (looks like radio waves) to the right of the calendar name; hold your mouse pointer over the calendar name to see the broadcast icon.** The Share "calendar name" with window appears.

3. **Type the name or e-mail addresses of those you want to share the calendar with. Press Return after each entry. Click the triangle next to each entry to set the access privileges (View & Edit or View Only).**

4. **Check the Public box if you want to allow people to subscribe to a read-only version of the calendar.**

5. **Click Done to share the calendar via iCloud.**

Exporting a calendar

Exporting a calendar is a good way to move calendars from one computer to another. You can also edit calendars that you've exported, although you cannot edit calendars that you've published from another computer.

To export a calendar, follow these steps:

1. **Open the calendar list, and click to select the calendar or calendar group from which you want to export the calendar list.**

2. **Choose File ➪ Export ➪ Export to open the Save As window, as shown in Figure 8.6.**

3. **Give a descriptive name to the file, choose a location to save it, and click Export.**

4. **Share the exported calendar by e-mailing it, placing it on a shared server, or using any other way you can think of.**

Genius

The default format of exported calendars in Calendar is ICS. ICS files can be imported into almost any third-party calendar application, so you don't have to worry about your Windows or Linux pals not being able to view your calendar. Likewise, you can use your friends' calendars in Calendar if they export them from their applications using the ICS format.

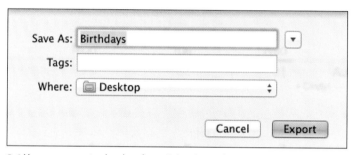

8.6 You can export calendars from Calendar and import them onto other computers.

Backing up a calendar

It's always a good idea to back up your calendars in case you need to restore them sometime in the future. The Calendar Archive feature is just the tool for such a task; all your calendars are backed up in this single file.

Here's how to create an archive:

1. **Choose File ⇨ Export ⇨ Calendar Archive to open the Save As window.**

2. **Give a descriptive name to the file.**

3. **Choose the location to which you want to save the file, and click Save.**

Note

There's no real need to perform this procedure if your calendars are stored on an external server, such as iCloud or Google. Those calendars are automatically backed up. However, if you're a stickler for being on the safe side, it can't hurt to back up your calendars yourself.

Subscribing to calendars

It stands to reason that if some people are publishing their calendars, there must be others subscribing to them. There are two ways to subscribe to calendars. This is the easy way:

1. **Choose File ⇨ New Calendar Subscription from the menu.**

2. **Type the URL of the calendar to which you want to subscribe in the Calendar URL field, as shown in Figure 8.7.**

3. **Click the Subscribe button to see the information window for the calendar.**

Enter the URL of the calendar you want to subscribe to.

Calendar URL: https://example.com/calendar.ics

Cancel   Subscribe

8.7 Subscribing to calendars is a snap with Calendar.

4. **Decide whether to remove Alerts and/or Attachments (which I recommend if you don't know the person who created the calendar).** You can also choose how often the calendar should automatically refresh in case changes are made by its creator, as well as a location for the calendar. (If you are using iCloud, you can choose between iCloud or your Mac.)

5. **Click OK to complete the subscription process.**

This is the even easier way:

1. **If someone sends you the link to his or her calendar in an e-mail, or if you click the link to a calendar from a web page, Calendar automatically begins the subscription process.**

2. **Click the Subscribe button to see the information window for the calendar.**

3. **Decide whether to remove Alerts and/or Attachments (which I recommend if you don't know the person who created the calendar).** You can also choose how often the calendar should automatically refresh in case changes are made by its creator.

4. **Click OK to complete the subscription process.**

Printing calendars

If you're like me, you understand that, although the concept of a paperless office sounded pretty cool in the 1980s, it most certainly—and to some degree, thankfully—hasn't come to fruition. Sometimes I just like to have a printed page in hand as opposed to being tied to my desk or lugging around a laptop. I love my Mac, but we're not permanently attached at the hip. Calendar can provide you with great printed calendars to use for yourself or to give to others. This is a great tool for offices and schools, or any other organization or team, for that matter. Another plus: Printed calendars are much easier to hang on your fridge than your computer screen is.

To print your calendars, follow these steps:

1. **Choose File ➪ Print.**

2. **Select from among the myriad options shown in Figure 8.8, and click Continue.**
   Table 8.4 lists the printing options and gives brief explanations of them.

3. **Click Print in the Print window.**

8.8 The Calendar printing options.

Table 8.4 The Calendar Printing Options

Option	Function
View	Choose what view to use for your printed calendar from the pop-up menu.
Paper	Select a paper size on which to print your calendar.
Time range	Decide when the printed calendar (or calendars) should begin and end using the Starts and Ends pop-up menus.
Calendars	Select the check boxes next to the calendars with events you want to include.
Options	Determine whether to print all-day events, timed events, mini-calendars, and calendar keys, and whether to print only in black and white.
Text size	Choose what size font to use when printing your calendars.
Zoom	Drag the slider to enlarge the preview image.

Working with Contacts

Have you ever needed to find an elusive phone number or address for a prospective client and had to thumb through ten devices and books to find it? Apple created Contacts just for you. Creating contacts in Contacts can make rounding up all those Christmas card addresses much easier.

Contacts are files that contain information for people in your life, such as street addresses, e-mail addresses, birthdays, and even their pictures. To get started, open Contacts by clicking Go ⇨ Applications and then double-clicking the Contacts icon. You can also enter Launchpad and click the Contacts icon.

Contacts is fairly useless without data, so let's start adding some.

Creating a contact card

A contact card contains all of a person's information, so you need to create one. You can create a new card in several ways:

● **Choose File ⇨ New Card from the menu.**

● **Press ⌘+N.**

● **Click the + button at the bottom of the All Contacts page in the Contacts window.**

These actions create a new blank card awaiting your input, as shown in Figure 8.9.

Genius You can add new contact cards quite easily when you receive a vCard in an e-mail. A vCard is a digital business card that some people attach to e-mails so others can easily save their contact information. In Mail, simply double-click a vCard in an e-mail to create a new card in Contacts.

After you finish typing the necessary info, press Tab on your keyboard to move to the next available field. If you don't need to use a particular field, leave it blank and it won't appear on the card after you save it. If the contact is a company, check the Company check box. This enables the company to be found in your contacts list alphabetically by the first letter of its first name. For example, Alabama Power appears in the A section, rather than under the P's (for Power). To add a new field, choose Card ⇨ Add Field and select one from the list.

8.9 Creating a new contact card is really easy.

After you finish typing the information, press ⌘+S or click Done at the bottom of the card window to save it. You can always edit the information in the card by clicking to highlight it in the Name column of the Contacts window and then clicking Edit beneath the card window. The Edit button turns blue and changes to say Done when in editing mode.

Creating a contact group

A great feature that I use quite a bit in Contacts is groups. Using groups, you can create different categories of contacts, such as Family, Work, and Church. As with contact cards, you can use a couple of techniques to create new groups:

- **Press ⌘+Shift+N.**
- **Choose File ⇨ New Group from the menu.**

Genius

There's an even faster way to create a group. Select multiple cards from the Name column by holding down the ⌘ key while you click the names and then choosing File ⇨ New Group from Selection.

After the group column opens on the left side of the window, be sure to give your group a descriptive name of the items it will contain. To add cards to the groups, drag and drop them from the name column onto the preferred group in the Group column, as shown in Figure 8.10. This action doesn't remove the card from the name column; it just associates it with the selected group.

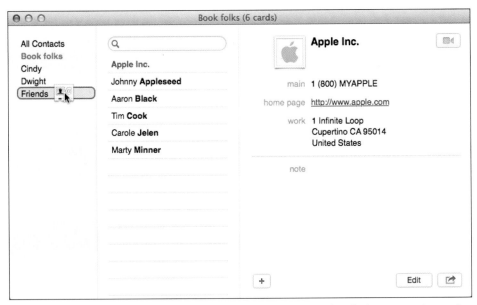

8.10 Drag and drop the names of the contact cards onto the group under which you want them to be listed.

Creating a Smart Group

Smart Groups are groups to which contact cards are automatically added if they meet certain specified criteria. For example, if you create a Smart Group to look for contact cards with certain last names, a new card created using that last name is automatically added to the Smart Group. To create a Smart Group, follow these steps:

1. **Press ⌘+Option+N, or choose File ➪ New Smart Group from the menu.** The Smart Group window appears, as shown in Figure 8.11.

2. **Give the Smart Group a descriptive name.**

3. **Decide whether the Smart Group will contain cards that match any or all of the conditions you are about to set.**

4. **Add or remove conditions by clicking the + or – buttons on the right.**

5. **Click OK to save the new Smart Group, or click Cancel to delete it.**

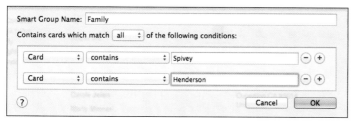

8.11 Add some intelligence to your Smart Group.

You can change a Smart Group's criteria at any time by Control-clicking its name in the Group column and selecting Edit Smart Group.

Genius

If your contact list is a mile long, you can quickly find a contact with just a smidgen of information. Simply type something about the contact (such as her name, e-mail address, or the city in which she lives) in the search field, which is denoted by the magnifying glass at the top of the Contacts page. As you type, the closest matches appear in the contacts list.

191

Importing contacts

Contacts can import files from other applications when created in the following formats:

- **vCard**
- **LDIF (LDAP Interchange Format)**
- **Tab-delimited**
- **Comma-separated (CSV), which is usually the most compatible with other applications**

Caution

When you import a Contacts Archive, your existing Contacts database is replaced. This causes you to lose all existing contact cards in Contacts. You are prompted by Contacts to be sure that you want to continue this action. Make sure that you have a backup archive before continuing (see the export instructions in the next section).

Consult each application to find out how to export contacts from it in one of these formats. To import contacts to Contacts, follow these steps:

1. **Choose File ➪ Import.**

2. **Browse to the file you want to import, and click it to highlight it.**

3. **Click Open in the bottom-right corner. If you import a vCard with a contact already in Contacts, you must choose how to handle the conflict by clicking the Review Duplicates button.** As shown in Figure 8.12, you can choose to update the old card with the new information, keep the old card, keep only the new card, or keep both cards.

8.12 Decide the ultimate fate of a vCard.

Exporting contacts

The file format preferred by Contacts for exporting contacts is vCard. vCard is a standard format common to most applications that have functionality similar to Contacts.

To export vCards from Contacts, follow these steps:

1. **Select the contacts you want to export.**

2. **Choose File ⇨ Export, and select Export vCard.**

3. **Give the exported vCard a name.**

4. **Browse to the destination on the Mac hard drive to which you want to save the exported file, and click Save.**

Genius Notice in the File ⇨ Export menu that there is another selection called Contacts Archive. Choose this format if you want to make a complete backup file of your Contacts database. I highly recommend doing this after importing a large number of files to make sure you don't lose all the work you've just done. At the very least, I suggest performing one of these backups once a month.

Eliminating duplicate contacts

While populating your Contacts, you may inadvertently enter the same contact multiple times or you may find that you have duplicate contacts, with slightly different information. Contacts is quite adept at handling these situations.

Follow these steps to search for and resolve duplicate contacts:

1. **Open Contacts.**

2. **Choose Card from the menu, and select Look for Duplicates.**

3. **Contacts searches for duplicates.** If it finds any, it lets you decide if you want to merge the information, as shown in Figure 8.13. If so, click Merge; otherwise, click Cancel.

8.13 You can easily merge duplicate contacts in Contacts.

Setting Contacts Preferences

As with most other applications, Contacts has many preferences to help you customize your experience. Open the preferences by choosing Contacts ➪ Preferences from the menu or pressing ⌘ +,.

General

The General preferences allow you to make several basic appearance and behavior modifications, as shown in Figure 8.14.

8.14 The Contacts General preferences, at your service.

While these options are fairly self-explanatory, Table 8.5 gives a brief description of each.

Table 8.5 Contacts General Preferences

Option	Function
Show first name	Display a contact's first name before or after the last name.
Sort By	Decide to sort contacts by first or last name.
Address Format	Select the country that uses the address format you want to use.
Default Account	Choose which account should be the default by using the pop-up menu. This option appears only if you have multiple accounts to select from.

Accounts

The Accounts preferences, shown in Figure 8.15, allow you to synchronize contacts with other accounts (such as iCloud) or share your Contacts with others.

194

8.15 Sync your contacts with other accounts.

Click the + button in the lower-left corner to add Contacts servers to your accounts list, and config-ure them as needed for proper access and synchronization.

Template

Use the Template preferences shown in Figure 8.16 to modify the fields automatically displayed when creating new contact cards. Remove fields by clicking the minus sign (–) to the left. To add fields, click the plus sign (+) or choose a field type from the Add Field pop-up menu.

vCard

The vCard options, shown in Figure 8.17, allow you to change the default vCard format version in Contacts and to specify how much information you want to share when sending others your vCard.

Table 8.6 explains the vCard options.

8.16 I love the Template preferences because they allow customization of the fields on contact cards.

8.17 The vCard options in the Contacts preferences

Table 8.6 vCard Options for Contacts

Option	Function
vCard Format	Choose between versions 3.0 and 2.1. Version 3.0 is the default; choose 2.1 if others have problems importing your vCards.
vCard 2.1 Encoding	Select the appropriate encoding for your language. English speakers generally want to stick with Western (Mac OS Roman). This option is available only if you select 2.1 for the vCard format.

Option	Function
Enable private me card	When this check box is selected, you can deselect the items you don't want exported with your contact card. For example, you may want to share everything except your personal e-mail or home address.
Export notes in vCards	Select this check box to include notes you have typed in your contacts' vCards.
Export photos in vCards	Select this check box to include any photos that you associate with the contact card (or cards) being exported.

Getting Maps for Addresses

A great feature included in Contacts is the ability to see maps of the addresses in your contact cards. This functionality really shines when you need to get to a client's location but aren't sure where it is. Here's how to use this cool feature:

1. **Click the card you need so you can see the contact information.**

2. **Hold your mouse pointer over the address so the Show Map option appears to the right of it, as shown in Figure 8.18.**

3. **Click Show Map. Maps automatically opens and displays a map of the location.**
   From here, you can get directions from your current location to the address.

Contacts and Maps work well together to give you accurate information; this feature is a pleasure to use.

8.18 Choose Show Map to see a detailed map of a location.

Syncing Contacts and Calendars with Devices

Mavericks can connect to and synchronize contacts and calendar information with the iPad, iPhone, and iPod touch using iTunes, which makes keeping contact information and calendar data consistent across multiple devices very easy.

To synchronize, follow these steps:

1. **Connect your iPad, iPhone, or iPod touch to your Mac.**

2. **Open iTunes.**

3. **Click your device's name in the source list under Devices to highlight it.**

4. **Click the Info tab to see the sync settings for Contacts and Calendars, as shown in Figure 8.19.**

8.19 iTunes keeps your iPhone and iPod touch in sync with your contacts and calendars.

5. **Select the check boxes next to Sync Contacts and Sync Calendars.**

6. **Click Apply in the lower-right corner (you may need to scroll down to see it), and click Sync.**

iTunes informs you when the synchronization process is complete.

Making Notes

Notes is a nifty little app for putting your thoughts to "paper" (the digital kind, that is). Do you need to put a grocery list together? Notes is your tool. Maybe you just thought of the title and synopsis of the next great bestselling novel? Notes has your back. Notes has been around on the iPhone since its inception, so if you are an iPhone or iPad aficionado, you will feel instantly comfortable with Notes for Mac.

Notes is all about jotting stuff down, so let's see how to get started in doing just that.

From the Finder, press ⌘+Shift+A to open the Applications folder, and double-click the Notes icon to launch the Notes app, or simply click the Notes icon in the Dock (if it's there). After the Notes window, shown in Figure 8.20, is open, beginning a new note couldn't be any simpler: Just start typing.

8.20 Notes is ready for plenty of note-taking action!

Creating additional new notes is as simple as beginning the first one: Click the + button in the lower-left corner of the Notes window, and start typing. Your first note can still be hanging out in the sidebar on the left side of the window. If you want to get back to it, or any other note, simply select it in the sidebar. The search field at the top of the sidebar is a great help when your list of notes gets too long to quickly browse. You can also add pictures to your notes by dragging and dropping them right into the note.

If you want to change the fonts, align the text, or add bullets to a list, use the selections found in the Format menu.

You can organize your notes into folders:

1. **Choose View ⇨ Show Folders List to expand the sidebar.**

2. **Choose File ⇨ New Folder to create a new folder in the sidebar.** Give the folder a descriptive name.

3. **Drag notes from the Notes list into the folder in which you want it to reside.**

Note If you are logged into iCloud (check System Preferences ⇨ iCloud if you aren't certain), Notes automatically syncs your notes with it. Contacts, Calendars, and Reminders are auto-synced as well.

After a note has outlived its purpose, it's time to delete it. Again, simple enough: Open the doomed note, click the Trash icon (looks like a little trash can) at the bottom of the page, and click the Delete Note button.

Like other apps in Mavericks, Notes is nice about sharing with others. To share your thoughts, click the Sharing button at the bottom of the page and select Email or Message.

Reminders

Reminders is something of a newcomer to the world of OS X (as of 10.8), helping us to remember important dates and tasks. You can keep as many to-do lists as you can type.

Create and edit reminders

The Reminders window is split into two parts: The left side is a listing of Lists and Reminders, and the right side (notepad) is where you enter items into the list selected on the left.

To add a new list, just click the + button at the bottom of the Reminders window, shown in Figure 8.21, or press ⌘+l, and give it a descriptive name.

Add items to your list just by typing them on the first available line on the notepad. Notice the check box to the left of each item. Click that box when you have finished a task, and it moves to the Completed list. If you accidentally move something to the Completed list, it's simple to retrieve:

1. **Select the Completed list on the left side of the Reminders window.**

2. **Find the item you accidentally marked as completed.**

3. **Click the box to deselect the item and move it back to its parent list.**

8.21 Reminders provides a list of items you need to tend to.

In addition to making lists for things like groceries and goals, you can create reminders based on calendar dates:

1. **Click the Calendar icon at the bottom left of the Reminders window.**

2. **Select the date for your reminder.**

3. **Type the reminder's title in the first available space on notepad.** If you need to edit the reminder information, hold your mouse or trackpad pointer over the reminder and note the Inspector button (looks like a small circle containing a lowercase "i") that appears to the right of it.

4. **Click the Inspector button to see the reminder's information.** When the Inspector window opens, as shown in Figure 8.22, type the required data. You can choose from the following:

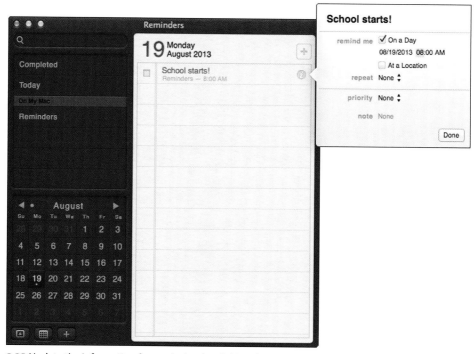

8.22 Update the information for reminders by clicking the Inspector button.

- **On a Day.** Check this option to be reminded of the item on a certain day and time.

- **At a Location.** Choose this option to be reminded of the item after you've arrived at or left a particular location. For this notification to work, you must have Location Services turned on for Reminders in the Privacy pane of the Security & Privacy preferences (System Preferences ➪ Security & Privacy ➪ Privacy ➪ Location Services ➪ Enable Location Services ➪ Reminders).

- **Repeat.** If this is a reminder that will occur regularly, click the Repeat pop-up and select the appropriate interval.

- **Priority.** Use the Priority pop-up to designate the importance of a reminder.

- **Note.** Add any notes you feel are necessary for the item.

5. **Click Done, and the new reminder appears in the Reminders list.**

Reminders can be easily deleted by selecting the reminder (click below its name or to its right) and pressing the Delete key on your keyboard.

Reminders accounts

Reminders is intelligent enough to allow the use of several different accounts for your reminders, so you can have separate accounts for work and personal items. It's simple enough to set Reminders to use a particular account:

1. **Choose Reminders ➪ Accounts from the menu to open the Mail, Contacts & Calendars preferences pane.**

2. **If you don't have an account set up, or the account that you need isn't set up, click the account type from the list and follow the instructions to add it.**

3. **Select the account from the list on the left side of the preferences pane.**

4. **Select the check box next to Calendars & Reminders to begin syncing with the account, as shown in Figure 8.23.**

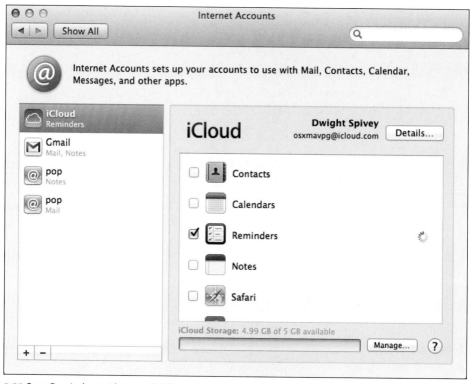

8.23 Sync Reminders with several different account types.

How Do I Master the Web with Safari?

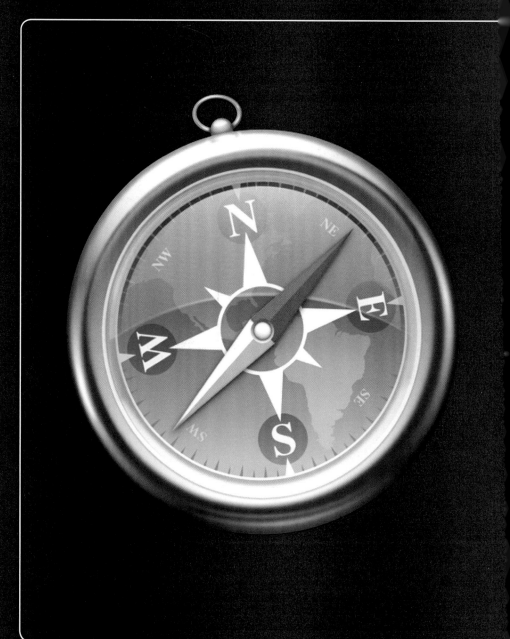

Since the advent of television, nothing has affected our daily activities quite like the Internet. Checking e-mail and surfing the web have become as routine as waking up in the morning. Mavericks comes loaded with the seventh version of one of the web's best surfboards: Safari. Safari is a lightning-fast and standards-compliant browser that has even the most demanding of browser critics smiling. Most computer users are quite familiar with the bare basics of web browsing, so in this chapter, I jump right into the meat and potatoes of using and customizing Safari.

Setting Safari Preferences

The heart of Safari is its preferences. They tell Safari how you want it to behave in both everyday browsing and special circumstances. In this section, I discuss preferences in some detail so that you can use them to streamline and customize your surfing experience. To open Safari's preferences, hold down the ⌘ key and press the , (comma) key, or select Safari ➪ Preferences from the menu.

General

The General pane of the Safari preferences is shown in Figure 9.1.

9.1 The options in the Safari General preferences pane.

Table 9.1 gives the scoop on all the available options.

Table 9.1 Safari General Preferences

Option	Description
Default web browser	If you've installed web browsers other than Safari, such as Firefox or Opera, choose one to be the default for your Mac.
Default search engine	Set Google, Yahoo!, or Bing as your default search engine for Safari.
Safari opens with	Choose whether Safari should launch a new window when you first open it or whether it should open any windows that were previously open the last time you used it.

Option	Description
New windows open with	Select whether new windows should open with your homepage, a blank page, your bookmarks, or the same page as the previous window.
New tabs open with	Choose to open new tabs in Top Sites (more on Top Sites later in this chapter), your homepage, an empty page, or the same page as the current tab, or to display your bookmarks.
Homepage	Type (or paste) the URL of the Internet site you want to be your homepage. Click Set to Current Page to make the website you are currently viewing your homepage.
Remove history items	Delete items from your browsing history after the prescribed length of time you choose from the pop-up menu.
Top Sites shows	Set the number of sites you want to view in the Top Sites window (6, 12, or 24).
Save downloaded files to	Select in which folder your downloaded files are to be saved.
Remove download list items	Safari keeps a history of files you've downloaded. This option lets you choose from the pop-up menu how often items on that list should be purged.
Open "safe" files after downloading	Select this option to have Safari automatically open certain types of files, such as disk images and zipped archives, when they finish downloading.

Tabs

Tabs allow you to have multiple sites open at once, but within one window, as opposed to having a window open for each site you're visiting. The Tabs pane, shown in Figure 9.2, lets you tell Safari when to open pages in tabs instead of new windows, whether to allow a ⌘+Click to open a link in a new tab, and whether to make a new tab or window the active one. Keyboard shortcuts are listed to help you easily open and navigate to new tabs and windows.

9.2 Tell Safari how to utilize tabs in the Tabs preferences pane.

AutoFill

Safari uses AutoFill to remember the information you type into forms on websites. This way, it can automatically enter that information for you in the future. The following options, shown in Figure 9.3, are available:

● **Using info from my Contacts card.** This option lets Safari use the information you've entered about yourself in the Contacts application. Click Edit to open Contacts and change your information.

9.3 AutoFill helps you quickly enter information on web pages with fields.

● **User names and passwords.** Select this option to have Safari save the usernames and passwords that you use to log on to secure websites. I do not recommend this option if security is of any importance to you. Click Edit to see a list of websites and their corresponding usernames.

● **Credit cards.** Safari can securely remember credit card information that you enter when making purchases via the Internet. You can add or remove cards by clicking the Edit button.

● **Other forms.** Safari remembers the information you type into fields of websites, such as online application forms or addresses for driving directions. Click Edit to see all the sites in which you've entered information in the past.

Passwords

The Passwords pane, shown in Figure 9.4, helps you keep track of passwords you've stored in Safari for websites that require secure access.

Caution

Be wary of your surroundings if you decide to check the Show passwords box (which I heartily do not recommend). You never know who might be peeking over your shoulder.

9.4 Manage your stored passwords using the Passwords preferences pane.

The Passwords pane allows you to:

- **View all your stored passwords by the website name**

- **Search for a particular site by entering the website name in the search field**

- **Remove all the stored passwords by clicking the Remove All button at the bottom of the pane, or remove passwords individually by selecting the website you want to get rid of and clicking the Remove button**

- **Make the passwords visible by checking the Show passwords check box**

Security

The Security settings for Safari are shown in Figure 9.5.

Note

One of my few gripes with Safari is the inability to allow some websites to open pop-up windows while blocking others. With Safari, it's all or nothing: Either you enable pop-up blocking or you don't. Some sites have legitimate uses for pop-ups, and when visiting them, you have to temporarily turn off pop-up blocking and remember to turn it back on after leaving.

9.5 Choose how best to secure your browsing expeditions.

Table 9.2 covers the options available in the Security pane.

Table 9.2 Safari Security Options

Option	Description
Fraudulent sites	Select the check box to have Safari warn you when you visit a site that may be fraudulent.
Web content	Java and JavaScript are used for interactive elements on many web pages. Select the check box next to the JavaScript option to enable it in Safari. Select the Block pop-up windows option to avoid those pesky ads that infest some websites.
Internet plug-ins	Plug-ins help Safari view or play certain types of content on websites, such as movies and sound files. Check the Allow Plug-ins box to let Safari utilize these extended capabilities. Click the Manage Website Settings button to customize access that websites have to individual plug-ins. (This is probably not necessary for most users.)

Privacy

The Privacy preferences pane, shown in Figure 9.6, affords options to keep your browsing habits from being known all over the free world. Some websites can be a bit too intrusive, and others can be downright sly in how they share your personal information.

The Privacy pane can protect you in five areas:

- **Cookies and other website data.** This section allows you a bird's-eye view of the cookies and other information websites have stored on your system. Click Remove All Website Data to remove all cookies and stored information. Click Details to see a list of all the websites that have stored tracking info and cookies on your Mac.

9.6 Protect your personal information while browsing the Web.

- **Block cookies and other website data.** These options allow you to determine which sites (if any) can store cookies and other website data on your Mac. Be careful choosing the Always option; some sites require cookies to function properly.

- **Limit website access to location services.** Some sites use your current location to help you find services and places of interest in your local surroundings. The Location services section lets you decide whether and how these sites gather your location information.

- **Website tracking.** Select the Ask websites not to track me check box to politely request that websites not track your browsing activities.

- **Smart Search Field.** In most browsers today, when you perform an Internet search, the default search engine automatically begins suggesting possible matches for your search, based on the letters you have typed. Check the Prevent search engine from providing suggestions box to prevent this from occurring. Check the box for Do not preload Top Hit in the background to prevent just such an action from occurring. Both options are personal preference items, so you be the judge regarding whether to enable them.

Notifications

Websites can send notifications to Notification Center, but whether you allow them to is entirely up to you, much like storing a website password is your decision to make. Whenever you allow a website to send notifications (you are prompted if one attempts to do so), the website is listed in the Notifications preferences pane, shown in Figure 9.7.

9.7 Manage the websites that can send notifications to your Mac using the Notifications pane.

Click Remove All to clear the list of websites, or selectively dismiss websites using the Remove button.

Extensions

Finally! It only took the Apple folks five versions to do so, but they eventually included the use of third-party extensions in their browser (which other browsers have done for quite some time). Third-party extensions provide even more functionality to Safari, allowing you to do anything from get the latest weather report to get notified of new e-mail right in your browser. The Extensions pane of the Safari preferences, shown in Figure 9.8, allows you to find and manage extensions.

Toggle the Off/On button to enable or disable the use of extensions, and click Get Extensions in the lower-right corner of the window to be whisked away to the official Apple Safari Extensions Gallery website (or go to https://extensions.apple.com).

After extensions are installed, they display on the left side of the Extensions pane. Select each extension to view its information, adjust its settings, or uninstall it if you're not particularly impressed with it.

9.8 Expand Safari's capabilities using Extensions.

Advanced

The Accessibility options in the Advanced pane, as shown in Figure 9.9, allows you to make small text display with a larger font for easier reading. You can also press the Tab key to highlight and navigate items on a web page without using a mouse.

Some computers and other network devices (such as printers and routers) have web pages that you can view via a browser, and if these devices are running the Bonjour protocol, Safari can see them quite easily without having to enter IP addresses and such. Check one or both options in the Bonjour section to make Bonjour sites available quickly in the Bookmarks menu and/or the Favorites bar.

Internet plug-ins can cause a drain on battery power if you're using a laptop. The Stop plug-ins to save power option can prevent this from happening when battery power is running low.

The Style sheet drop-down menu lets you choose a Cascading Style Sheet of your own to use when browsing the web.

9.9 The Advanced preferences pane in Safari.

The Default encoding menu lets you select a different encoding if text appears garbled on the websites you visit. If you need to change encoding for only a single page, go to View⇨Text Encoding and select a language to use.

This Website Won't Open in Safari!

Sometimes, web developers put (usually) superficial limitations on which browsers can access their websites; for example, the developer may harbor a personal preference for Internet Explorer. Thankfully, this practice is declining with the increased use of browsers such as Safari and Firefox. However, you can bypass these contrived limitations with the following steps:

1. **Select the Show Develop menu option in the Advanced Preferences pane of Safari.**

2. **Choose Develop⇨User Agent.**

3. **Select the browser version you want Safari to emulate from the list.** Safari can even pretend it's a browser on a Microsoft Windows PC.

4. **Refresh the offending web page. This (usually) bypasses the bogus limitation.**

Click Change Settings next to the Proxies option to allow your Mac to access the Internet when using a firewall. You may want to ask your IT department what proxy settings to use if you are on a corporate network.

Selecting the Show Develop menu in menu bar option displays the Develop menu, which is used mainly by programmers for testing their web pages. You may need to use this menu to access websites designed for other browsers, as described in the sidebar.

Using Bookmarks

Bookmarks are links that you create for your favorite websites so you can easily and quickly visit them. To bookmark a website, follow these steps:

1. **Choose Bookmarks⇨Add Bookmark, or press ⌘+D.**

2. **Select a location for the bookmark to reside by using the pop-up menu.**

3. **Give the bookmark an appropriate name.**

4. **Click Add, as shown in Figure 9.10, to create the bookmark.**

9.10 Create bookmarks so you can quickly access your favorite locations on the web.

Genius Safari has an even easier way to create a bookmark. Simply click and drag the address of the page in the Address field to the Bookmarks bar, give it a name, and click OK.

Organizing bookmarks

Like toys in a child's room, bookmarks can quickly get out of hand if they aren't organized. To open the Bookmarks window, as shown in Figure 9.11, choose Bookmarks⇨Show Bookmarks, or press ⌘+Option+B.

The bookmarks list is on the left side of the window (under the Bookmarks column), and it houses your bookmark collections (or folders). Each collection can contain subfolders as well as bookmarks.

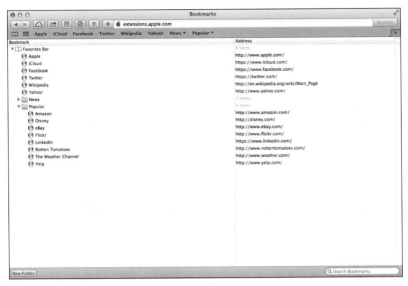

9.11 Bookmarks waiting to be whipped into shape.

You can organize bookmarks in the Bookmarks window by doing the following:

- **Arrange bookmarks in a collection.** Select the collection you want to organize, and drag and drop the bookmarks in the order you want them to appear.

- **Arrange bookmark folders in the order you want them to be listed.** Click and drag the bookmark folder you want to move to its new position in the bookmarks list.

- **Create new collections.** Click the New Folder button under the left column to create a new bookmark collection, and give the collection a descriptive name.

- **Create subfolders in collections.** Select the collection to which you want to add a sub-folder. Click the New Folder button under the left column, and give the subfolder a descriptive name.

- **Change the name or address of a bookmark.** Select the collection that contains the bookmark you want to change. Right-click (or Control-click) the bookmark, and select either Rename Bookmark or Edit Address to make your changes.

- **Delete a bookmark or collection.** Right-click (or Control-click) the item you want to remove, and select Delete from the list.

Genius

You can keep bookmark folders in the Bookmarks bar to provide fast access to mul-tiple sites. Apple provides a News folder and a Popular folder in the Bookmarks bar; experiment with them to see how beneficial they are.

Note You can view your browsing history by choosing History ⇨ Show History from the menu or by pressing ⌘+Option+2.

Importing and exporting bookmarks

Most browsers can export a list of their bookmarks so you can easily back them up or use them in another browser. To import bookmarks into Safari, follow these steps:

1. **Choose File ⇨ Import Bookmarks.**

2. **Browse your Mac by using the Import Bookmarks window, and find the bookmarks file you want to import.**

3. **Highlight the file, and click Import.** The Bookmarks window automatically opens and reveals the list of imported bookmarks so you can organize them.

To export bookmarks from Safari, follow these steps:

1. **Choose File ⇨ Export Bookmarks.**

2. **Name your bookmarks file in the Export Bookmarks window.**

3. **Browse your Mac for a location to save the bookmarks, and click Save.**

Customizing the Main Safari Window

You can personalize your browsing experience by making some custom changes to the main window in Safari. Several options can make Safari more efficient for you:

● **Hide or show the status bar at the bottom of the Safari window.** As shown in Figure 9.12, this area displays the address for links, how many elements of a page have been loaded, and more. Choose View ⇨ Hide Status Bar or View ⇨ Show Status Bar (depending on its current state).

9.12 Viewing the URL for a link using the status bar at the bottom of Safari's window.

● **Choose whether to display the Bookmarks sidebar.** Choose View ⇨ Hide Bookmarks
Sidebar or View ⇨ Show Bookmarks Sidebar.

● **Decide whether to display the Tab bar.** Choose View ⇨ Show Tab Bar or View ⇨
Hide Tab Bar.

● **Choose whether the Reading List sidebar is visible by choosing View ⇨ Show
Reading List Sidebar or View ⇨ Hide Reading List Sidebar.**

● **Hide the URL field so it doesn't clutter your browser window.** Choose View ⇨ Hide
Toolbar or resurrect it by choosing View ⇨ Show Toolbar.

● **Add or remove items from the toolbar.** Choose View ⇨ Customize Toolbar. In the
resulting dialog, shown in Figure 9.13, click and drag items you want to add from the
window to the toolbar and drop them in place. To remove items from the toolbar, drag
them out and drop them outside of the Safari window where they disappear in a puff
of smoke.

9.13 Customize the toolbar to add your favorite items or remove those that are simply in your way.

Genius

You can rearrange the items in your toolbar with typical OS X ease. Hold down the ⌘
key, and then click and drag an item in the toolbar to move it to a better location.
Other items in the toolbar shift automatically to accommodate the item being
moved.

Viewing Your Favorite Pages with Top Sites

Top Sites shows you a preview of the websites you frequent, and it works in typical Apple fashion: really cool and really easy. To view your Top Sites, as shown in Figure 9.14, click the Top Sites button (looks like three rows of four squares) on the left side of the Bookmarks bar, or press ⌘+Option+1. Next, simply click a site's page in the Top Sites window to visit it.

Note

One of the major features of Safari in Mavericks is the combination of the Search and URL fields in the main window. If you want to search for a particular subject, type the subject in the URL field and your default search engine looks it up as you type and after you press Return.

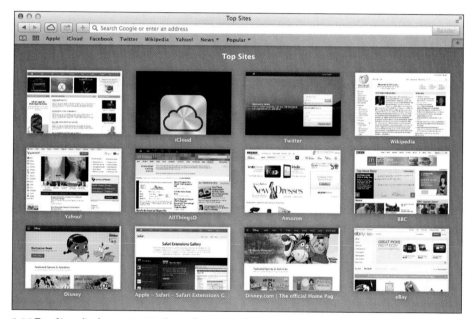

9.14 Top Sites displays up to 24 of your favorite websites as thumbnails.

You can remove websites from or pin sites to your Top Sites page quite easily:

- To remove a website, hold your mouse pointer over the image of the website until the edit button appears in the upper-left corner of the image; click the X to remove the site.

- To pin a website, hold your mouse pointer over the image of the website until the edit button appears in the upper-left corner of the image; click the pushpin icon to pin the site.

Private Browsing

Are you the type who doesn't like the world knowing your business? Do you value your privacy when surfing the web? Are you a super spy who doesn't want your evil arch nemesis to know what websites you've been visiting? You're in luck if you use Safari as your browser of choice.

Private Browsing prevents anyone else using your Mac from ever knowing what pages you've viewed during your browsing session. To enable Private Browsing, choose Safari ➪ Private Browsing and click OK to enable Private Browsing, as shown in Figure 9.15.

Do you want to turn on Private Browsing?

Safari can keep your browsing history private. When you turn on private browsing, Safari doesn't remember the pages you visit, your search history, or your AutoFill information.

Cancel   OK

9.15 Enable Private Browsing for added privacy.

Genius

To quit Private Browsing, choose it from the Safari menu again and close any windows you had open (not tabs, but the actual window). If you don't close the window, someone else could use the Forward and Back buttons to view the sites you were visiting.

Viewing Windows Media Files

Watching videos on the web is becoming more common, and two of the most popular formats for doing so are QuickTime and Windows Media. Mavericks has QuickTime built in, but it has no way for you to view Windows Media files out of the box. Don't worry: Windows Media Components for QuickTime by Flip4Mac makes this a non-issue. To get the WMV (Windows Media) components, follow these steps:

1. **Go to** http://windows.microsoft.com/en-us/windows/windows-media-components-quicktime**, and click the appropriate links to download the WMV Components disk image.** Safari automatically opens the disk image, as shown in Figure 9.16.

2. **Control-click Flip4Mac.pkg, and select Open from the menu to open the installer file.** Click Open if your Mac warns you that Flip4Mac WMV.mpkg comes from an unidentified developer.

3. **Click Continue when prompted, and accept the license agreements.**

4. **Click Install, and type the username and password of an Administrator account to begin the installation.** When you see the Install Succeeded prompt, you are finished and can now view Windows Media files on your Mac.

9.16 You are just a few steps away from viewing Windows Media files in Mavericks.

Note The WMV components work with any browser on your Mac, not just Safari. Nothing further needs to be done in your other browsers to view Windows Media files.

Using the Reading List

The Reading List is a new feature in Safari 5 that allows you to save links to pages you want to come back to and read later. Accompanying the Reading List is the Reader, which enables you to read the articles in your Reading List (as well as many that aren't) without the annoyance of ads and other distractions typical to most web pages.

To add a site to your Reading List, follow these steps:

1. **Open the website you want to add to your Reading List.**

2. **Press ⌘+Control+2 to open the Reading List sidebar.**

3. **Click the + button immediately to the left of the URL/Search field to add the site to the Reading List.** Safari saves the page for offline reading.

Genius You can quickly add a site to your reading list by clicking its link while holding down the Shift key.

When you're ready to read your article using Reader, follow these steps:

1. **Press ⌘+Control+2 to open the Reading List sidebar.**

2. **Select the article you want to view.** After the site loads, a Reader icon displays on the right side of the address field (if the article is text based).

3. **Click the Reader icon to view the article free of distractions, as shown in Figure 9.17**

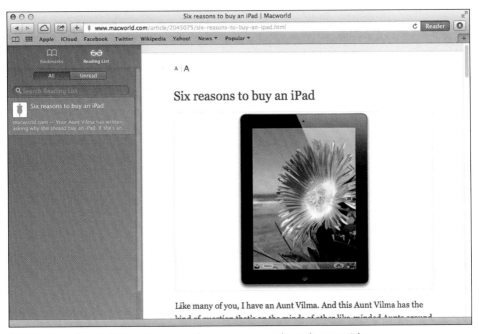

9.17 Reader cuts out all the extraneous info so you can simply read your article.

Finding Text on a Website

Sometimes, you may be looking for a specific word or phrase on a web page, but it's so packed with information that it could take you half the day to find it. Safari provides a great mechanism for finding text on a web page that can quickly point you to what you need. To search for text on a web page, follow these steps:

1. **Press ⌘+F to open the Find field near the upper-right corner of the window.**

2. **Type the search term or phrase in the Find field (in this example, iPad), and Safari immediately begins searching as you type, as shown in Figure 9.18.**

3. **Safari displays the number of matches it finds for your search term to the left of the Find field.** The page is grayed out, and the instances of the search term are highlighted.

4. **Click the left and right arrows to cycle through the matches.**

5. **Click Done next to the Find field when you are finished.**

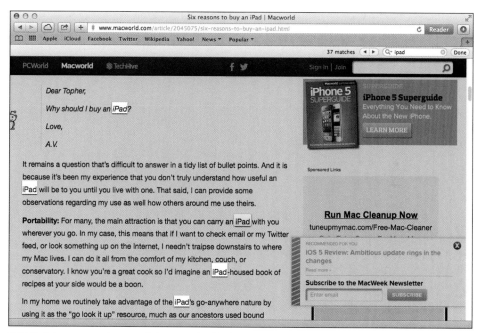

9.18 Safari grays out the rest of the page, highlighting only the instances of your search term—in this case, the word *iPad*.

Troubleshooting

Safari can make web surfing a joy, but nothing is perfect. Just like anything else, Safari sometimes doesn't behave. This section provides a quick look at some of the most common problems experienced when surfing the web with Safari, what causes them, and suggestions for fixing the situation.

A web page won't open

A web page may not open for many reasons, including these:

● **The page may be temporarily down.** If so, try accessing it later.

● **You may not have an Internet connection.** Even if you were cruising the web seconds before, something may have caused you to lose connectivity.

- **The cached site is corrupt.** If this is the case, your browser keeps trying to open the corrupt cache site instead of refreshing it. To fix this, try emptying the cache and reloading the website. Choose Safari ⇨ Empty Cache from the menu, and select Empty.

- **Be sure that you are typing the correct website address.** This mistake has bitten me more than once!

A file won't download

Sometimes, when you click a link on a site, the file may appear not to download (for example, you can't find it on your Mac) or it may, indeed, not be downloading. You can view the files being downloaded or files that have previously been downloaded by clicking the Downloads button, which is found in the upper-right corner of the Safari window and looks like a square containing a downward-pointing arrow. The Downloads window displays a list of downloaded files, as shown in Figure 9.19.

9.19 A list of my recently downloaded files.

Here are a few things to check when this problem occurs:

- **From the Downloads window, see if the file download is in the list to find out if Safari tried to download it, but failed.**

- **If you see the file in the Downloads window but can't find it on your Mac, click the magnifying glass to the right of the filename.**

- **If a link simply doesn't download the promised file, contact the proprietors of the site.** Perhaps there is a missing or broken link to the file.

A downloaded file won't open

Sometimes, that file you're downloading just won't cooperate and open. What to do? Here are some suggestions:

- **Is the file completely downloaded?** If not, resume the download or start over.
- **Try downloading the file again.** It may have been corrupted during the download process.
- **Some files may not be supported by OS X.** Find out what type of file it is (the extension on the end of the file is a dead giveaway), and search Google for software that opens that type of file on a Mac.

AutoFill isn't working

I think AutoFill is pretty convenient. When it's not working, I'm not a happy camper. If it's not working on your Mac:

- **Be sure that AutoFill is turned on.** Choose Safari ➪ Preferences, and click the AutoFill tab. Select the check box next to each of the options you want to use.
- **The information needed may not have been entered before.** If that's the case, type the info again.

Images aren't displaying correctly

One day, you might be surfing along when suddenly a page that should be chock-full of images has none. In some cases, this may not be a big deal, but in others, it may be huge. (How can you properly shop for a new Mac if you can't see what it looks like?) Here are a couple of ideas:

- **Try reloading (refreshing) the page by pressing ⌘+R on the keyboard.**
- **Contact the webmaster of the site.** The links to the images on the site may be missing or broken.

How Do I Stay Connected with Mail?

Mail is the easy-to-use Mavericks e-mail application, and it is head and shoulders above most e-mail programs that I've used. Mail was already a great e-mail client in its previous incarnation, but it takes another leap forward with Mavericks. The ease with which you can set up several popular e-mail accounts, including iCloud, Gmail, and Microsoft Exchange Server, is unparalleled. This version of Mail's collaboration with Maps, Notification Center, and the widescreen, two-column view makes it an instant hit.

Getting Around in Mail

Mail is a very straightforward application: Most of its tools are in plain view for easy clicking capability. Figure 10.1 shows the Mail main window so you can get familiar with its features.

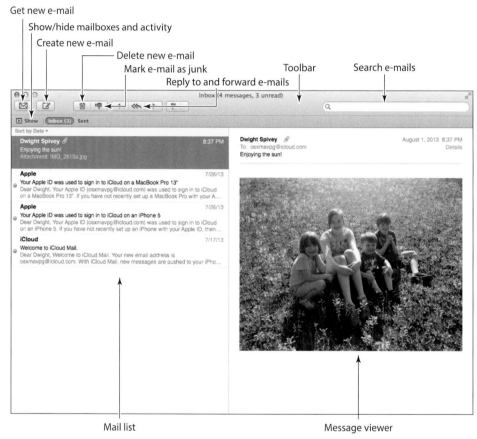

Get new e-mail

Show/hide mailboxes and activity

Create new e-mail

Delete new e-mail

Mark e-mail as junk   Toolbar   Search e-mails

Reply to and forward e-mails

Mail list   Message viewer

10.1 The Mail main window in the default layout.

Table 10.1 explains a few of the features available in the main window. Others are discussed in further detail throughout this chapter.

Table 10.1 The Mail Main Window Features

Feature	Description
Junk	Junk e-mail is anything you don't want, whether it's unsolicited advertising or messages from your long-lost cousin who just found out you won the lottery. Highlight the offending message in the Mail list, and click the Junk button to permanently mark an e-mail as junk. This filters future e-mails like it automatically into the Junk folder.
Search	Type a search term into the Search field, and Mail finds all e-mails that contain the term.
Show or Hide	Click to show or hide the Mailbox pane (which shows you all the Mailboxes you have configured) and Mail activity window (which displays a progress mail activity bar when sending or receiving mail).

Customizing the Toolbar

The toolbar is where the main Mail controls reside, but you aren't limited to the default set of controls. You can quite easily modify them to your liking by following these steps:

1. **Choose View ⇨ Customize Toolbar.**

2. **From the huge list of available controls, shown in Figure 10.2, select those you want to add to the toolbar.**

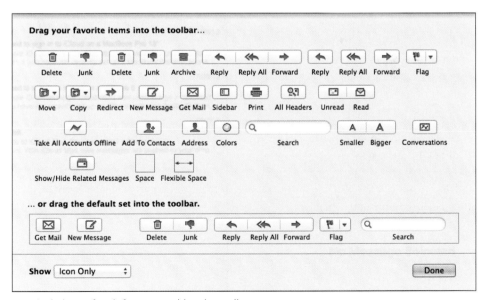

10.2 A plethora of tools for you to add to the toolbar.

3. **Click and drag the controls you want to add to the toolbar, and drop them where you want them.** You may also want to rearrange the controls by using the same drag-and-drop technique. The neat thing is how the other controls move out of the way of the one you are moving.

4. **Delete controls from the toolbar by clicking and dragging them out of the window, and then dropping them.** They disappear from the toolbar in a puff of smoke!

5. **Click Done when you're finished.**

Managing E-mail Accounts

Mail won't do much more than take up space on your hard drive if you don't have an e-mail account. When you sign on with an Internet service provider (ISP), it should provide you with all the information you need to add an e-mail account to Mail. If you're using one of the more well-known e-mail services, Mail most likely configures your account by itself using only your e-mail address and password. However, just to be on the safe side, be sure to get all the e-mail information from your ISP before you begin to use Mail.

Setting up an account

The first time you start Mail, you are asked to set up an account, as shown in Figure 10.3. If you've already enabled iCloud for your e-mail, you won't see this screen; you're whisked immediately to your iCloud inbox, so you can just skip this section altogether.

To set up an account, follow these steps:

1. **Select the type of account you have from the list provided, and click Continue.** Don't worry if you don't see your account type; simply choose Add Other Mail Account.

10.3 Select an e-mail account type to get started with Mail.

2. **Type a name for the account.** Recipients of your messages see the name for this account. Make sure it's the way you want it displayed!

3. **Type the e-mail address to use for the account.**

4. **Type the password for your e-mail account, and click the Set Up button (or Create, depending on the account type).**

5. **Decide whether to set up Notes, Calendars, Contacts, and Messages with the same account, and click Done.** Mail does the rest for you! Some account types may not support these options, so if you don't see them, don't panic.

You can set up additional accounts just as easily. Follow these steps:

1. **Choose Mail⇨Preferences, or press ⌘+,.**

2. **Click Accounts in the Preferences window to open the Accounts pane, and click the plus sign (+) in the lower-left corner to add an account.**

3. **Select the type of account you want to add, and click Continue, as shown in Figure 10.4.**

4. **Type the required information in the Add Account window, and click Set Up or Create (depending on the account type).**

10.4 Automatically adding accounts within Mail preferences.

Manual setup

Mail supports POP, IMAP, and Exchange e-mail accounts, and you can add any of these types manually if you prefer this to an automatic setup. Ask your ISP or network administrator what type of account you have and what settings you need to create your account.

To manually create a new account, follow these steps:

1. **Choose Mail ➪ Preferences, or press ⌘+,.**

2. **Click Accounts in the Preferences window to open the Accounts pane.**

3. **Click the plus sign (+) in the lower-left corner to add an account, select Add Other Mail Account, and click Continue.**

4. **Type the correct information in the Full Name and Email Address fields of the Add Account window but enter an incorrect password in the Password field; click Create.**

5. **You'll receive an error message stating that the account must be manually configured because you didn't enter a correct password; simply click Next to set up the account manually.**

6. **In the Incoming Mail Server Info window, shown in Figure 10.5, choose your Account Type (in my case, IMAP), and type the required information as provided by your ISP or network administrator; click Next.**

7. **Consult your ISP or network admin regarding the security options in the next Incoming Mail Server Info window, set them as needed, and click Next.**

8. **In the Outgoing Mail Server Info window, shown in Figure 10.6, enter your SMTP server information, along with your username and password if they are required by your e-mail provider or ISP.** This is necessary for you to send e-mail to other people.

10.5 This information is required to receive e-mail.

10.6 Type this information, and you're almost finished configuring your Mail account.

9. **Click Create to add the new account to Mail.**

Setting Preferences in Mail

Just like any other app, Mail works best when it works best for you. Because only you know what works best for you, Mail provides the ability to change its default behavior to suit your needs using Preferences. Press ⌘+, to open the Mail preferences window.

General

The options in the General pane are shown in Figure 10.7.

10.7 The Mail General options.

Table 10.2 gives the scoop on each of these options.

Table 10.2 Mail General Preferences

Option	Description
Default email reader	Choose an e-mail app to be the default for your Mac if you've installed others in addition to Mail, such as Thunderbird or Outlook.

continued

Table 10.2 continued

Option	Description
Check for new messages	Determine how often Mail automatically taps your e-mail provider on the shoulder to see if any new messages have arrived in your inbox.
New messages sound	Select an alert sound for Mail to use to notify you when new messages arrive. Select the Play sounds for other mail actions check box to sound alerts when you send messages or when Mail wants you to be aware of other activities, such as when new messages are sent or when an error occurs.
Dock unread count	The Mail icon in the Dock shows you how many unread messages you have. It also tells Mail where to look to find those unread messages.
New message notifications	This allows Notification Center to alert you when receiving new messages in your Inbox Only, from VIPs or Contacts, or from All Mailboxes.
Add invitations to Calendar	You can set Mail to automatically add any invitations you may receive in an e-mail to Calendar.
Downloads folder	Choose where Mail saves attachments by default.
Remove unedited downloads	Mail temporarily saves attachments in the Mail Downloads folder unless you specify that it save them elsewhere. These are deleted after you delete the e-mail to which they were attached unless you change that behavior here.
If outgoing server is unavailable	If you send an e-mail and Mail tells you it is unable to reach the outgoing mail server for your account, you can use the pop-up menu here to have Mail either show you a list of alternative outgoing servers to use or hold the message until your original outgoing server is available.
When searching all mailboxes, include results from	Select any or all three (Trash, Junk, and Encrypted Messages) of the available options for Mail to include when searching other mailboxes.

Accounts

The Accounts pane lets you see and edit your account information and decide how Mail handles certain behaviors for your accounts. Earlier in this chapter, I discussed adding and removing accounts from this pane. Now, let's look at the other options available for your accounts. The Accounts pane is separated into three tabs: Account Information, Mailbox Behaviors, and Advanced.

Account Information

The Account Information tab, shown in Figure 10.8, allows you to set up the information necessary to receive e-mail from any one account, as well as to enable or disable (without deleting it) the account. This information is available from your e-mail provider or your company's IT administrator.

The Outgoing Mail Server pop-up menu lets you specify an SMTP server to send mail from this particular account. If you haven't set up an outgoing server, click the pop-up and select Edit SMTP Server list to enter the information as provided by your e-mail provider or IT admin.

Select the Use only this server check box to prevent Mail from using a different SMTP server if the one assigned to this account is unavailable for any reason.

10.8 Account Information is where you tell Mail the settings for your e-mail account.

Mailbox Behaviors

The options in the Mailbox Behaviors tab, shown in Figure 10.9, differ depending on whether the account type is IMAP or POP. It includes these options:

- **Drafts.** Decide whether to keep copies of drafts on your e-mail provider's servers or not. I advise you to select this check box so that if something happens to your Mac, your draft messages can still be accessed from another computer. This option is available only for some IMAP accounts.

- **Sent and Junk.** Choose whether Mail should erase Sent or Junk mail from their respective mailboxes, and choose how to handle deleted sent and junk messages.

● **Trash.** Tell Mail how to handle messages that you delete. Moving deleted messages to the Trash mailbox gives you the opportunity to find them again if you need them. Storing deleted messages on the e-mail server is a good idea so you can get to these messages if you need to, but they won't take up extra space on your Mac (if you deselect the first option, that is).

10.9 Tell Mail how to handle items in your mailboxes with the Mailbox Behaviors tab.

Advanced

The Advanced tab allows you to tell Mail to automatically check for new messages, automatically erase deleted messages from an IMAP account in which you don't move deleted messages to the Trash, and keep copies of e-mails on your e-mail provider's server. You can also specify the IMAP Path Prefix, port number, and the authentication type necessary to communicate with your e-mail provider's SMTP server.

Caution The Remove copy from server after retrieving a message option should be dese-lected if your e-mail account uses POP. Selecting this check box prevents you from retrieving e-mails from your e-mail provider if you have problems with your Mac. Deselecting this check box keeps copies of e-mails on your e-mail provider's server as a backup.

Junk Mail

Everyone gets junk e-mail from time to time, and the Junk Mail pane, shown in Figure 10.10, helps you kick those unwanted messages to the curb. It also tells Mail which e-mails are not junk.

10.10 Configure how Mail detects and handles junk e-mail messages.

These options are available:

- **Enable junk mail filtering.** Select this check box to turn on the junk mail filters.

- **When junk mail arrives.** Tell Mail how to handle junk e-mails that arrive. You can mark them as junk but still keep them in your Inbox so you can inspect them, move them automatically to a Junk mailbox so you can peruse them at your leisure, or customize how they are handled.

- **The following types of messages are exempt from junk mail filtering.** This option is invaluable because it lets Mail know which messages it should never mark as junk. If your messages are from senders in your Address Book, from senders of previous e-mails, or addressed to your full name, you can instruct Mail not to filter them as junk.

- **Trust junk mail headers in messages.** Some e-mails already contain indicators that they are junk. Selecting this option lets Mail rely on those indicators to filter the messages out as junk.

- **Filter junk mail before applying my rules.** Later in this chapter, I cover how to set rules for Mail. Selecting this option lets the junk mail filter run on all e-mails before your rules are carried out.

- **Reset.** Click Reset to return Mail to its default junk filtering options. Use this one with caution; after you reset the junk filter, it forgets any settings and rules you applied to it.

- **Advanced.** Click Advanced to set your own custom rules for what Mail should do with junk e-mails. Select the Perform custom actions radio button in the When junk mail arrives section to access the Advanced button.

Fonts & Colors

This one doesn't get much simpler. Use the Fonts & Colors pane to set the default font for your Message List, messages, notes, and fixed-width fonts. If you are sending a plain text message (as opposed to the default HTML), you can choose to use a fixed-width font. You can also set the default colors for quoted text, which is the text that is included when you reply to or forward an e-mail.

Viewing

The Viewing pane, as shown in Figure 10.11, is where you tell Mail how to display your e-mails.

The available options include the following:

- **Use classic layout.** Select this option to have your messages appear in a list on top of the preview pane, as in earlier versions of Mail.

- **Show header detail.** The pop-up menu and check boxes below it let Mail know how you want the header information to appear in your e-mails. To clarify, headers are items that are commonly seen at the top of e-mails, such as From and To. The three boxes under the pop-up menu perform the following tasks:

  - **Display unread messages with bold font.**

- **Display remote images in HTML messages.** Select this option to have pictures and graphics appear in e-mails.

- **Use Smart Addresses.** You can decide to have Mail display the name of the recipient in the address field, as opposed to their actual e-mail address by selecting this option.

- **View conversations.** Mail allows you to view related e-mails as a group, which is called a conversation. The self-explanatory options in this section let you determine how these messages are displayed in conversation view.

10.11 You can customize how your messages are displayed in Mail with these options.

Composing

The Composing pane includes many options, as shown in Figure 10.12, and they are divided into three sections: Composing, Addressing, and Responding.

Composing

The following options (refer to Figure 10.12) help you when creating a new e-mail or when replying to one:

● **Message Format.** Determine the default format to use when creating new e-mail. If you choose plain text, you can't use the advanced graphics features of Mail, such as Stationery.

● **Check spelling.** You can check spelling as you type, after you hit Send, or never.

● **Automatically Cc myself.** Select this check box to send a copy of e-mails you send to others to yourself. This may not be necessary because Mail puts a copy of your sent messages in the Sent folder anyway.

Addressing

The Addressing section (refer to Figure 10.12) helps configure how Mail works with e-mail addresses in new e-mails and notes:

● **When sending to a group, show all member addresses.** If you send e-mail to groups, selecting this option displays the e-mail address for each individual in the group.

10.12 The options in the Composing pane configure how Mail puts together an e-mail.

- **Mark addresses not ending with.** This option helps you prevent sending unintentional e-mails to folks by marking e-mail addresses that don't end with a particular domain name.

- **Send new messages from.** Choose which e-mail address to show in the From field when sending messages to others.

Responding

The Responding options in the Composing pane (refer to Figure 10.12) let Mail know how it should reply to those who have been courteous enough to send you messages:

- **Use the same message format as the original message.** It's a good idea to reply to someone using the same format as his or her original e-mail. For example, if you reply to a plain text e-mail with rich text, the recipient may not be able to read it.

- **Quote the text of the original message.** Select this option to display the original message and subsequent exchanges under your reply.

- **Increase quote level.** Select this option to distinguish individual quotes using colors and indentions.

- **When quoting text in replies or forwards.** To include all text from the original e-mail in a reply or forward, select the first radio button. To include only text you've selected in the original e-mail, select the second radio button.

Signatures

The Signatures pane, shown in Figure 10.13, allows you to create and edit personal e-mail signatures. A signature can contain any information you like, such as your address, phone number, fax number, and so on. You can create as many signatures as needed, which comes in handy if you have multiple accounts because you can assign specific signatures to each one.

Follow these steps to create a signature:

1. **Select the account to which you want to assign the signature, or choose All Signatures to allow all accounts to use the new signature.**

2. **Click the plus sign (+) to add a new signature.**

3. **Give the signature a descriptive name (middle window), and type the signature information in the large text field on the right.**

4. **To edit the fonts and colors in the signature, highlight the text you want to change, right-click (or Control-click) the highlighted text, choose Font⇨Show Fonts or Font⇨Show Colors, and make the changes you desire.**

5. **If you want to keep uniformity throughout the message and signature, select the Always match my default message font check box.**

6. **Select the Place signature above quoted text check box to situate your signature after your message but before the quoted text.**

7. **If you want to use one signature with multiple accounts (not all, though), drag the signature from the middle window and drop it onto the account names to which you want it applied.**

10.13 Signatures give your e-mails a personal touch, much like signing a handwritten letter.

Rules

Under the Rules tab, Mail allows you to create your own rules and dictate how it distributes and marks certain messages. These rules can be based on criteria that you set, allowing a high level of customization.

Using the four plus (+) and minus (−) buttons on the right side of the pane, as shown in Figure 10.14, you can add, edit, duplicate, and delete rules.

10.14 Create your own rules to customize how Mail distributes your messages.

To add a new rule to the Rules list, follow these steps:

1. **Click the Add Rule button.**

2. **Type a descriptive name for your new rule.** A rule tells Mail that if a certain condition exists, it should perform a certain task or action.

3. **Create a rule:**

   a. **Determine if any or all conditions must be met using the pop-up menu.**

   b. **Select the conditions using the appropriate pop-up menus.** To add more conditions, click the plus sign (+). To remove conditions click the minus sign (–).

   c. **Select the task to be performed using the pop-up menus in the Perform the following actions section.** Click the plus sign (+) to add more actions or the minus sign (–) to remove actions.

4. **Click OK to create the new rule.**

Composing E-mail

Composing and sending e-mail is a snap with Mail. To begin sending that world-changing memorandum, do the following:

1. **Click the New Message button in the toolbar, which looks like a piece of paper with a pencil writing on it.**

245

2. **In the New Message window, type the e-mail address of the person you want to receive your message in the To field, as shown in Figure 10.15.** To send a copy of the e-mail to other folks, type their addresses in the Cc field.

10.15 Putting together the perfect e-mail.

3. **Type the topic of your e-mail in the Subject field.**

4. **Select the account from which you are sending the e-mail, as well as a signature if you like, by using the pop-up menus in the From menu.**

5. **You can click the Customize button on the left (it looks like a small rectangle containing three lines stacked next to a tiny downward-pointing arrow), and choose whether any other fields, such as Priority, should appear in the New Message window.**

6. **Type the content of your e-mail, and click the Send button (the one that looks like a paper airplane) in the upper-left corner.**

7. **Congratulate yourself for being a full-blown member of Internet society.**

Genius

Just like the toolbar in the main Mail window, the toolbar in the New Message window can be modified to suit your style. With a New Message window open, choose View ⇨ Customize Toolbar to arrange, remove, or add items to enhance your productivity.

Using Stationery

One of the coolest features in Mail for Mavericks is the ability to customize e-mails with Stationery. Stationery is preformatted e-mails that Apple provides with Mail. This feature can transform any ordinary e-mail into a stunning creation. To use Stationery, follow these steps:

1. **Open a New Message window.**

2. **Click the Show Stationery button (it looks like a small rectangle containing a piece of paper) in the upper-right corner of the toolbar.**

3. **Browse the topics listed on the left of the Stationery field (below the Subject field and immediately above the e-mail content window), as illustrated in Figure 10.16, and select the Stationery that is appropriate for your message.**

4. **Customize the content of your e-mail by dragging and dropping your own images into the image placeholders (if any), and type your own text in the preformatted text fields.**

10.16 Create beautifully formatted e-mails with Stationery.

Adding attachments

Sometimes, you want to e-mail a picture or send along an accompanying document with your message; these additions are called attachments. To add an attachment to your e-mail, follow these steps:

1. **Open a New Message window, and type the addresses of your recipients.**

2. **Click the Attachment button (the one with the paper clip) in the toolbar.**

3. **Browse your trusty Mac for the file you want to attach, select it, and click Choose File.** If you are sending a picture from your iPhoto or Photo Booth libraries, click the Photo Browser button (the icon looks like a mountain with the moon next to it) in the toolbar, click and drag a picture from the Photo Browser window, and drop it into the body of the e-mail. You can also simply drag and drop items, such as pictures, as shown in Figure 10.17, into the body of your e-mail to attach them.

10.17 Drag and drop your picture into an e-mail.

Keep Your Recipients Anonymous

Sometimes, when sending an e-mail to multiple recipients, you need to hide their names and e-mail addresses. This technique is called Blind Carbon Copy (Bcc for short), and Mail makes it a snap to do:

1. **Open a new message window.**

2. **Click the Customize button located to the left of the From field, and select Bcc Address Field.**

3. **Type the addresses of the recipients to remain anonymous in the Bcc field. This conceals their identities from the other recipients.**

Formatting content

Add a little pizzazz to your message by customizing its fonts and colors. To format an e-mail, follow these steps:

1. Open a New Message window.

2. Type the text of your e-mail.

3. Highlight the text you want to format.

4. **Click the Show formats bar button (the icon looks like the letter A) in the toolbar, and select the font you want to use.** You can alter the font typeface and size, underline the text, change the font color, and add a shadow to the text and modify it.

Receiving, Replying to, and Forwarding E-mail

Your Inbox typically attempts to receive e-mails automatically every few minutes, but you can also have Mail check the server for new e-mails manually in one of the following ways:

- Click the Get new messages in all accounts button on the left side of the toolbar. The icon looks like an envelope.

- Press ⌘+Shift+N.

- Choose Mailbox ⇨ Get New Mail, and select the account you want to check.

You don't have to be working in Mail to see when new e-mail arrives, but Mail must be running, of course. The Mail icon in the Dock displays a red circle containing the number of unread e-mails in your Inbox so you can easily tell when you have new mail. Also, if you've set up Mail to allow notifications, you see them pop up in Notification Center.

When someone sends you an e-mail, it shows up in your Inbox for the account the e-mail was sent to. It appears in the Mail list in bold letters and has a blue dot to the left of the From field. The Inbox button in the toolbar also displays the number of unread e-mails it contains in parentheses. Simply click the e-mail in the Mail list to read it in the Message Viewer.

To reply to or forward an e-mail you've received, follow these steps:

1. **Highlight the e-mail to which you want to respond in the Mail list.**

2. **Click the Reply button to respond to the person who sent you the e-mail, the Reply All button to send a message to all recipients of the e-mail, or the Forward button to send the e-mail to other parties.**

3. **Type text or add attachments to your message.**

4. **Click the Send button in the toolbar.**

Organizing with Mailboxes

In this section, I show you how to use mailboxes to keep your e-mail organized. You learn the basic functions of standard mailboxes, how to back up a mailbox, how to utilize Smart Mailboxes, and more.

Using standard mailboxes

Standard mailboxes keep your e-mail organized, and each account can have several. Table 10.3 lists some of the types of standard mailboxes that accounts can have.

Table 10.3 Functions of Standard Mailboxes

Mailbox	Description
Inbox	Incoming messages to your e-mail account are stored here.
Drafts	Sometimes, you may want to save an e-mail you've typed so you can send it at a later time. The Drafts folder is where those saved e-mails reside until you are ready to send them.

Mailbox	Description
Sent	Copies of messages you have sent to people are kept here.
Trash	This is where your deleted messages reside until you are ready to completely erase them from your Mac.
Junk	Messages that are flagged as junk mail are deposited into this mailbox. This way, they don't intrude with your normal activities but can be sifted through later at your convenience.

Creating custom and Smart Mailboxes

Mail lets you create your own mailboxes to suit your individual needs. You can make custom mail-boxes that are named for different items or topics (such as Bills), or you can use Smart Mailboxes. A Smart Mailbox allows you to create rules that the Smart Mailbox follows. For example, you can set up a Smart Mailbox that automatically grabs and stores any e-mail that comes from a particular person.

To create a new custom mailbox, follow these steps:

1. **Choose Mailbox from the menu, and select New Mailbox.**

2. **In the New Mailbox dialog, as shown in Figure 10.18, select a location where the new mailbox can be saved.**

3. **Give the new mailbox a descriptive name, and click OK.** The new mailbox appears in the Mailbox pane on the left side of the Mail window.

10.18 Creating a new mailbox.

To set up a Smart Mailbox (I love these things), follow these steps:

1. **Choose Mailbox from the menu, and select New Smart Mailbox.**

2. **In the sheet that appears, as shown in Figure 10.19, give the mailbox a descriptive name.**

10.19 Make a Smart Mailbox to help you organize and save time finding e-mails.

Back Up Those Mailboxes!

It is always a great idea to keep a backup of your e-mails in case something happens to Mail, Mavericks, or worse, your Mac. You can restore your lost e-mails to their proper places if you've been making consistent backups of your mailboxes.

To back up a mailbox, follow these steps:

1. **Select the mailbox you want to archive.**
2. **Choose Mailbox ⇨ Export Mailbox.**
3. **Select the folder in which you want to save the mailbox archive, and click Choose. An archive of the mailbox is created in the appropriate folder using the MBOX format.**

To restore a mailbox, follow these steps:

1. **Choose File ⇨ Import Mailboxes.**
2. **Select the Apple Mail radio button, and click Continue.**
3. **Browse your Mac to find the archived mailbox you want to restore, select it, and click Choose.**

3. **Select what the mailbox should contain and how the items in it should match the criteria you are about to define.**
4. **Define the criteria for items that the mailbox should or should not contain.** Click the plus sign (+) to the right to add a new criterion or the minus sign (–) to remove it.
5. **Decide whether to include messages that are in the Trash or Sent mailboxes, and select or deselect the check boxes as appropriate.**
6. **Click OK to create the new Smart Mailbox.**

Troubleshooting

Occasionally, you may have trouble with Mail. The most common problem is the inability to send or to receive e-mails. The final two topics in this chapter attempt to help resolve these problems.

Unable to send messages

Sometimes, you may find that you can't send messages. The reason may be that the Send button is grayed out, or you might receive an error message stating that you cannot connect to the SMTP server for your ISP. Try these things when facing this daunting situation:

- **If you have an Internet connection, open Safari and see if you can load a web page.** If not, choose Apple menu ⇨ System Preferences ⇨ Network, and make sure you have a connection.

- **Check the SMTP settings for your account.**

  a. **Choose Mail ⇨ Preferences.**

  b. **Click the Accounts button, and click the account with which you are having trouble.**

  c. **Be sure the Outgoing Mail Server (SMTP) option is set correctly.**

  d. **If your SMTP server isn't set up at all, check with your ISP for the proper settings.**

- **Make sure you have the latest software updates for Mavericks.** Choose Apple menu ⇨ Software Update, and install any available updates.

Unable to receive messages

Starting to feel lonely? Maybe it's because you haven't received an e-mail from your friends and family lately. Well, don't feel too unloved yet; check the following to see if Mail is receiving e-mail:

- **Is your account offline?** If so, that prevents you from being notified of any new messages. You can tell that an account is offline because it has a small lightning bolt icon to the right of it in the sidebar, as shown in Figure 10.20. To put it back online, click the lightning bolt and select the Take All Accounts Online option.

10.20 An account is offline if you see the lightning bolt next to it.

- **Are you currently connected to the Internet?** If not, be sure to connect.

- **Send a message to yourself to test your connection settings.** Check with your e-mail provider to make sure you are using the correct settings for your account.

- **Is the name of your mailbox grayed out?** If so, choose Window ⇨ Connection Doctor and follow any instructions that may be given for any accounts that are having difficulty connecting to your ISP.

253

How Can I Use iTunes with Multimedia?

Gotta have that music! And those movies. Don't forget about the television shows and podcasts, too! In today's world, we want our entertainment now. We want it affordable and portable, and we prefer it digital. Mavericks meets all those needs with a nifty tool called iTunes. Since its introduction in 2001, iTunes has become an integral part of our entertainment arsenal. When you throw an iPod, iPad, or iPhone into the mix, iTunes becomes an absolute necessity. Thankfully, it's just as intuitive and easy to use as everything else Mac; you'll be addicted to its charms before you know it!

Getting Around in iTunes

iTunes can handle most of your digital entertainment needs, but you need to know how to use its menus, buttons, and features before you can get much use out of it. The first two sections of this chapter cover where to find everything and how to set the iTunes preferences. You'll be an expert iTunes user in no time.

Understanding the iTunes window layout

Figure 11.1 shows the iTunes default interface and points out the multitude of buttons and menus.

11.1 iTunes is your personal entertainment hub.

Table 11.1 describes what some of the buttons and menus can help you do in iTunes. More are covered later in the chapter.

Table 11.1 iTunes Functionality

Item	Description
Library button	This lists all the items available for you to use in iTunes.
Source bar	This lists views and items specific to the library you're currently viewing.
iTunes Store	Click this to access the iTunes Store.
Playlists	This lists the playlists and Smart Playlists that you have created.
MiniPlayer	Click this to switch to MiniPlayer mode.
Full screen	This puts iTunes into Full Screen mode.
Search Library	Type text to help you find items in your iTunes library, such as the name of a song or the artist who sings it.
View options	Choose this to view items grouped together by song title, album title, artist name, or genre.
Status window	This shows the status of songs currently being played, CDs being burned, or items being copied.

Genius
Still can't get used to the new iTunes layout (as of iTunes 11)? Do you deeply miss the Sidebar that iTunes proudly utilized for its first ten iterations? Well, Apple didn't leave folks like you (and me, to be truthful, although the new layout is quickly growing on me) in the cold. You can regain the Sidebar by choosing View ⇨ Show Sidebar from the menu.

Using MiniPlayer

I'm a creature of habit, so I still prefer the standard view in iTunes, but I'm beginning to understand why others tend to like MiniPlayer. MiniPlayer, which is a miniature version of the iTunes window, is a convenient way to access iTunes without taking up all your display's real estate. To enable the MiniPlayer, click the MiniPlayer button in the upper-right corner of the standard iTunes window. When you first launch the MiniPlayer it is indeed quite mini; to see a few more options and a slightly larger player, click the album art on the left side of the MiniPlayer window. Access the full iTunes interface again by clicking the rectangular button in the upper-left corner of the MiniPlayer window, shown in Figure 11.2.

11.2 iTunes in MiniPlayer mode.

MiniPlayer allows you to do much more in Mavericks than in any previous version of iTunes. The playback controls are self-explanatory, but there's more to the MiniPlayer window than you might realize at first glance. Click the Up Next list button to see what songs are next in the queue, click the magnifying glass icon to search your iTunes library, and click the right-pointing arrow button in the upper-right corner of the MiniPlayer window, shown in Figure 11.3, to perform a bevy of actions, including these:

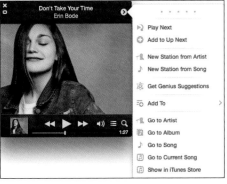

11.3 You can perform several actions from within MiniPlayer.

- Assign a star rating to the song currently playing.

- Play the next song in the Up Next queue, or add the currently playing song to the Up Next queue.

- Create new stations from the artist or the song.

- Get Genius suggestions based on the song currently playing.

- Add the currently playing song to a playlist.

- Go to the artist, album, or song in the standard iTunes interface.

- Show the current song in the iTunes Store.

Genius

You can also open the MiniPlayer in another, much less obvious way: Click the album art in the status window, and the MiniPlayer pops right up!

Setting iTunes Preferences

In the iTunes preferences, you tell iTunes how to interact with you, as well as with items such as iPods, iPads, iPhones, and Apple TV. Let's explore these preferences, because they determine how iTunes functions to best suit your needs. Choose iTunes ⇨ Preferences to get started.

General

The General tab lets you change the name of your library, choose what items are shown in the Source pane (such as Tones (ringtones), Internet Radio, Podcasts, and so on), adjust the size of the text for items in your library when in List view, adjust the background colors for open items, determine how iTunes should react when a CD is inserted, and specify whether to automatically check for updates.

Playback

The Playback preferences, shown in Figure 11.4, determine how iTunes plays your music and videos.

11.4 The Playback preferences allow you to listen to music and watch movies and television shows the way you want.

Genius

Selecting the Sound Check option is a good idea. This prevents you from listening to one song that may have a lower volume level and then having your eardrums blown out by another song with a much higher volume level. Sound Check evens all the volume levels of items in your library so there are no surprise attacks.

Sharing

The Sharing preferences, shown in Figure 11.5, determine how (if at all) you share your libraries with other users. You can share your iTunes library with up to five other computers on your network as long as they are in the same network subnet as your Mac. Although you can listen to music and watch video shared by other computers on your network, you cannot add them to your iTunes library.

You can share your entire library or only selected libraries or playlists.

Select the Require password option to allow others to see your library but not play any items it contains unless they have a password that you assign.

11.5 Share your library with other users on your network.

Select the Home Sharing computers and devices update play counts check box to update the play counts for items in your library when they are played by other devices (such as another Mac, iPhone, iPad, or iPod). After you make your selections, click OK to put them into effect.

Store

You can decide how iTunes handles your purchases.

- **Always check for available downloads.** iTunes informs you if it finds items in the iTunes Store that you've purchased but haven't yet downloaded to your Mac.

- **Download pre-orders when available.** If you select this option, iTunes automatically downloads any items you've preordered as soon as they become available.

- **When downloading High Definition videos, prefer.** Use the pop-up menu to choose your preferred resolution for High Definition videos: 720p or 1080p.

- **Automatic Downloads.** If you enable this feature, you put iTunes in touch with purchases you make on other devices using your Apple ID (such as an iPhone, iPad, iPod touch, or another computer). Purchases made on any of these devices are automatically downloaded to iTunes the next time you launch it.

- **Show iTunes in the Cloud purchases.** Enabling this option allows you to see purchases you've made in the iTunes Store but have not yet downloaded to your devices.

- **Sync playback information across devices.** This option lets every device that is signed in with your Apple ID know the playback position of any media that you pause, helping you to pick up right where you left off with a song, movie, or what have you, regardless of which device you're using at present.

- **Automatically download album artwork.** This option allows iTunes to find and download artwork for your songs and albums.

- **Share details about your library with Apple.** Enable this option to allow Apple to provide you with extras related to items found in your library. For example, Apple may suggest albums and artists that you might enjoy based on the content of your music library.

Parental

Most parents don't like to think of their kids having unfettered access to anything and everything on the Internet, so why should items in iTunes be any different? The Parental preferences, shown in Figure 11.6, let Mom and Dad decide what limits to place on iTunes content for their children.

These options are available:

- **Disable.** Select the check boxes next to the items to which you would rather your prodigies not have access. The Shared Libraries is a big one; you never know what others may be sharing in their libraries, so be cautious.

- **Ratings for.** Many countries use their own rating systems for entertainment. Select the country you need from the pop-up menu, and then select the Show content ratings in library check box to show the ratings right next to the items in your library.

- **Content Restrictions.** Restrict users from accessing items that don't match the ratings you set up in these options. The ratings available here depend on the country you select in the Ratings for option.

After you make your selections, click OK to put them into effect.

Devices

The Devices preferences pane helps determine how iTunes interacts with devices you connect to your Mac.

Parental Control Preferences

General Playback Sharing Store Parental Devices Advanced

Disable: ☐ Podcasts
☐ Internet Radio
☐ iTunes Store
☐ Allow access to iTunes U
☐ Shared Libraries

Ratings for: United States ⇅
☑ Show content ratings in library

Restrict: ☐ Music with explicit content
☐ Movies to PG–13 ⇅
☐ TV shows to TV–14 ⇅
☐ Apps to 12+ ⇅
☐ Books with explicit sexual content

Restrictions apply to sharing, iTunes in the cloud, and the iTunes Store.

Click the lock to prevent further changes.

Cancel   OK

11.6 Take control of what your children can do within iTunes.

- **Device backups.** This is simply a list of iPods, iPads, or iPhones that are backed up on your Mac. You can delete a backup file by selecting it from the list and clicking Delete Backup. Confirm the removal by clicking Delete when prompted, or click Cancel.

- **Prevent iPods, iPhones, and iPads from syncing automatically.** Select this check box to keep your Mac from trying to sync automatically every time one of these devices is connected. This is a good idea if you like to have more manual control over what is synced and what isn't.

- **Allow iTunes audio control from remote speakers.** Selecting this option allows you to control iTunes via a third-party remote that connects to an AirPort Express.

- **Forget All Remotes.** The iPad, iPod touch, and iPhone can act as a remote control using an app called Remote. Click this button to cause iTunes to disconnect from these devices.

Note Consult your iPhone, iPod, or iPad documentation for instructions regarding how to synchronize the device with iTunes and how to use iTunes to change the settings for the device.

Advanced

The Advanced preferences, shown in Figure 11.7, is where you can make the most useful settings in iTunes.

Table 11.2 breaks down some of the major features in each section.

11.7 The Advanced tab of the iTunes preferences.

Table 11.2 iTunes Advanced Preferences

Option	Description
iTunes Media folder location	This option lets you choose to keep your imported media in a location other than the default, which is the Music folder of your user account (your home folder/Music/iTunes). Click Change to move the folder to another location, or click Reset to move it back to the default location.
Keep iTunes Media folder organized	I highly recommend selecting this check box because it allows iTunes to organize its folder, as opposed to just throwing tracks in willy-nilly.

continued

Table 11.2 continued

Option	Description
Copy files to iTunes Media folder when adding to library	This option makes a copy of a file in your iTunes Music folder when adding the track to your library. You can deselect this option if you don't want to have multiple copies of the same file strewn throughout your system. I prefer to make the copy and delete the original.
Reset all dialog warnings	Clicking this reactivates iTunes warnings. For example, if you've told iTunes to stop asking you if you're certain that you want to make a purchase, clicking Reset causes iTunes to start asking again.
Reset iTunes Store cache	Much like a web browser, iTunes keeps the iTunes Store pages you visit in a cache file. If you visit these pages again, iTunes pulls them from the cache, which is much faster than having to download them from the Internet again. If you have problems loading pages, or if the information appears to be out of date, click Reset cache to clear the cache and download the page from scratch.
Keep MiniPlayer on top of all other windows	Select this check box to keep the MiniPlayer from being hidden under other open windows.
Keep movie window on top of all other windows	Select this option to keep movies playing over other open windows.

Organizing and Playing Media

iTunes is a pretty useless application without content. It's also a master at helping you organize that content. This section quickly teaches you how to import your own music from CDs or files and how to use the iTunes Store to find and add new content to your collection.

Setting the viewing options

iTunes lets you decide what information you want to view about your files. As a matter of fact, it provides a huge list of possible columns to help you sort your media, depending on the view or item you've selected in the source bar. For example, to adjust your views when selecting songs from the source bar in your music library, follow these steps:

1. **Choose View Options from the View menu.**

2. **Select the check boxes next to the columns you want to appear in the iTunes window, such as Composer, Date Added, or Year.**

3. **Click OK. Your iTunes window displays the columns you've added to your view.**

Importing music

Bringing your music into iTunes is the first order of business. Apple makes it ridiculously easy to import your CD collection, as well as music files that you have stored on other computers or discs.

Importing from CDs

When you insert a CD into your Mac, you're asked if you want to import its contents into iTunes, as shown in Figure 11.8. Click Yes to automatically import all the content on your CD into iTunes.

Your newly imported content now appears in your library.

11.8 A confirmation dialog appears when you insert a music CD.

Importing individual files

iTunes lets you import music files that exist on other media as well, such as a folder on your hard drive or another computer on your network. To import music files, follow these steps:

1. **Press ⌘+O.**

2. **Browse your Mac or your network for the music file (or files) you want to import from within the Add to Library window.**

3. **Highlight the music files, and click Open.**

The new music is now available in your library.

Creating playlists

You can create playlists using the songs in your library. Playlists are collections of songs that you arrange in the order that you want them to play. Here's how to make a playlist:

1. **Press ⌘+N.** A playlist called (appropriately enough) Playlist appears on the right side of the iTunes window.

2. **Type a name for your new playlist.** I'm creating a playlist for a compilation of songs by Anna Netrebko.

3. **Find the items you want to add to the playlist in your library, and drag and drop them into the new playlist, as shown in Figure 11.9.** You can drag the songs around in your playlist to have them play in your preferred order.

4. **Click Done when you're finished adding songs to your playlist.**

11.9 Adding songs to my new playlist.

Setting up Genius playlists

iTunes can create a playlist of songs that go well together using the songs already in your library. This Genius playlist uses anonymous information from your library to create the playlist. iTunes also uses your Genius playlist to suggest similar songs in the iTunes Store. Follow these steps:

1. **Open the Genius feature, shown in Figure 11.10, by selecting Playlists in the music library source bar and clicking Genius in the Playlists pane that appears to the left side of the iTunes window.**

2. **Click Turn On Genius in the lower right to start the feature.**

3. **Sign in using your iTunes Store account.**

4. **Select a song from your iTunes library.**

5. **Click the action menu (looks like a right-pointing arrow in a small circle) immediately to the right of the song you selected, and choose Create Genius Playlist from the list.** You can view the playlist by clicking Genius under the Playlists heading on the left side of the iTunes window.

11.10 The Genius window explains what Genius playlists are, and it allows you to enable the feature and view suggested songs from the iTunes Store.

Using Smart Playlists

Smart Playlists automatically add songs based on criteria that you set for them. iTunes already comes with a few Smart Playlists, such as Recently Played and Recently Added. To create a new Smart Playlist, follow these steps:

1. **Press ⌘+Option+N.**

2. **Type the criteria the Smart Playlist should use when adding songs.** In Figure 11.11, I'm creating a new Smart Playlist that adds any songs by Dwight Yoakam (yes, you could say my taste in music is fairly eclectic).

11.11 Creating a new Smart Playlist.

3. **Add more criteria by clicking the plus sign (+) on the right side of the window, or click the minus sign (–) to remove criteria.** Select the Live updating check box to have the Smart Playlist check every time you add an item to your library to see if it meets your criteria.

4. **You can limit the number of items to be found and how they are chosen for playback by selecting the Limit to check box.**

5. **Select the Match only checked items check box to have iTunes include only songs that have a check mark next to them in the library.** Feel free to deselect any titles that you don't want added to your Smart Playlist.

Burning CDs

I enjoy a variety of music, and I love having the ability to create my own albums and burn them to CDs. There's nothing to it:

1. **Create a playlist of the music you want to burn to a CD.**

2. **Right-click (or Control-click) the playlist you want to burn, and select Burn Playlist to Disc, as shown in Figure 11.12.**

3. **Select a recording speed from the Preferred Speed pop-up menu.** If you have trouble burning the CD, try recording at a lower speed.

4. **Choose Audio CD as the format of choice.**

5. **If you would like a gap of silence between tracks, choose its duration from the Gap Between Songs pop-up menu.**

6. **Check the Use Sound Check box if you want the volume of each track to be about the same.**

7. **Check the Include CD Text box to burn title and artist information to the CD. Some CD players can show this information about the tracks being played.**

8. **Click Burn, and insert a blank CD into your Mac. iTunes takes care of the rest.**

11.12 Burning a playlist to a CD.

Print Your Music

The old days of handwriting the names of your songs onto those boring blank CD labels are over! iTunes lets you create custom CD jewel case inserts, or song and album lists, in a snap. Follow these steps:

1. **Highlight the playlist, artist, or album about which you want to print information.**

2. **Press ⌘+P to open a print window.**

3. **Choose whether to print a jewel case insert, a song list, or an album list.**

4. **Select one of the available themes.**

5. **Click Print in the lower-right corner.**

6. **Choose the printer to which you want to send the job, adjust any settings you deem necessary, and click Print.**

Managing file information

iTunes allows you to manage the information contained in your tracks, which helps you organize your library and find tracks faster and easier. The Info, Video, Sorting, Options, Lyrics, and Artwork tabs in the information window let you specify items such as the composer of the track, the album to which it belongs, the year it was composed, and more. You can also add lyrics and album artwork to the track.

To edit the information for a file, follow these steps:

1. **Select the audio track in your library.**

2. **Press ⌘+I to open the information window, as shown in Figure 11.13.**

11.13 You can check or modify audio track information in the information window.

3. **Click one of the tabs at the top of the window to edit the information it contains.**

4. **When finished, click OK.**

Adding album artwork

To add the album cover artwork to your music files, choose File ⇨ Library ⇨ Get Album Artwork. iTunes automatically scans your library and adds artwork to your songs. You must have an Apple ID to perform this action, but that's easy enough. If you aren't already logged in, iTunes explains how to log in with an existing Apple ID and how to create a new one. As you probably realize by now, an Apple ID performs several functions within iTunes, including allowing Apple to access your billing and shipping information and unlocking files you purchase from iTunes.

Streaming radio

The Internet is teeming with radio stations for every genre of music and talk radio you can conjure, and iTunes is more than happy to stream many of those stations for your listening pleasure.

Note You must have an Internet connection to use the Radio and Internet features in iTunes.

Follow these steps to start streaming:

1. **Select Internet in the source bar of the music library.**

2. **Choose a music or talk genre from the list, as shown in Figure 11.14, and click the arrow to the left of it to see stations catering to your tastes.**

3. **Double-click a station in a genre to begin streaming its content to your Mac.**

If you don't see the Internet option in the source bar of the music library, open iTunes Preferences (press ⌘+, or go to iTunes ⇨ Preferences in the menu), click the General tab, and check the box next to Internet Radio in the Show section. Click the OK button and you'll see Internet in the source bar.

Genius You can save links to your favorite Internet radio stations so you can easily access them from your library rather than browsing the various categories each time. Simply drag the name of the radio station and drop it onto a playlist; your playlists automatically appear in a pane on the right side of the iTunes window as you begin to drag. When you want to launch the station, just go to the playlist where you saved it and double-click the name.

11.14 There is a veritable cornucopia of options to choose from in Internet radio.

Still another option for those who enjoy their music streamed is to listen to Internet radio stations that focus on certain artists, genres, or songs; you can even customize your own stations. Click the Radio option in the source bar of the music library and scroll through the preconfigured stations at the top of the window, or click the Add Station button at the bottom to create a custom station to your liking, as shown in Figure 11.15.

Backing up your library

Most people amass a huge volume of music and video after using iTunes for a while. No one wants to risk losing all their entertainment and having to start all over from scratch. You can back up your iTunes library in two ways: Copy your iTunes folder to another computer or hard drive, or burn your files to CDs or DVDs.

To copy your iTunes folder, follow these steps:

1. **Open a Finder window, and click the name of your account in the sidebar on the left of the window.**

2. **Select your Music folder.**

3. **Drag the iTunes folder, as shown in Figure 11.16, to another hard drive or computer to begin copying it.**

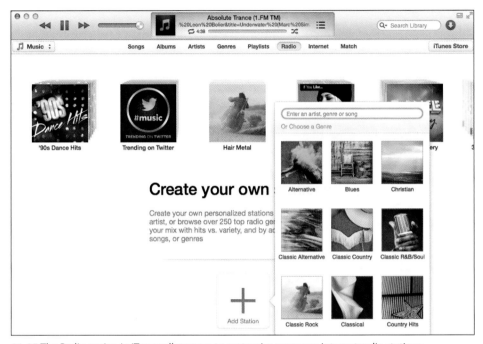

11.15 The Radio option in iTunes allows you to customize your own Internet radio stations.

11.16 The iTunes folder contains the files in your library (unless you've specified a different location).

4. **If something happens to your iTunes library, simply copy the backup iTunes folder to the Music folder in your home directory to restore it.** You may lose files you've added since your last backup, but that's better than losing everything.

Converting audio formats

Sometimes, you may want to use your audio files with another device or share them with someone else. In some cases, the device you or the person with whom you are sharing is using may not be able to use the file because of its file format. You can create copies of your audio files in other formats while retaining the originals. To do so, follow these steps:

1. **Choose iTunes ⇨ Preferences.**

2. **Click the General tab, and click Import Settings to open the Import Settings window, as shown in Figure 11.17.**

3. **Choose a format from the Import Using pop-up menu.**

4. **Determine the quality of the imported files using the options in the Setting pop-up menu.**

11.17 Select a new format for importing audio files into iTunes.

5. **Select the Use error correction when reading Audio CDs option if you have experienced problems with the audio quality of files imported from CDs.**

6. **Click OK, and then click OK again in the General preferences pane.**

7. **Select an audio file, and right-click (or Control-click) it.**

8. **Choose the Create X Version, where X is the file format you selected in Step 3. The new version of the file appears in your iTunes library along with the original.**

Creating ringtones for your iPhone

For some reason, Apple removed the built-in ability to make your own ringtones from iTunes, but where there's a will, there's a way.

Note
Before beginning this process, find a song from which you want to create a ringtone. Next, choose a 30-second (or less) section of it with which to create your ringtone. Be sure to note the seconds at which the section starts and ends in the Status window while playing the song.

Follow these steps to create your ringtone:

1. **Find the song in iTunes that you want to be your ringtone.**

2. **Right-click (or Control-click) the file, and select Get Info.**

3. **Click the Options tab, as shown in Figure 11.18.**

11.18 Find the perfect section of a song to use as an iPhone ringtone.

4. **Select the Start Time and Stop Time check boxes, type the start and end times for the section of the song from which you want to create the ringtone, and click OK.**

5. **Right-click (or Control-click) the song again, and select Create AAC Version. This creates a new version of the song using the time section you specified in the Info window.** (If you see a format other than AAC, go to the General preferences pane, click Import Settings, and change the Import Using option to AAC.)

6. **Right-click (or Control-click) the newly created song in iTunes, and select Show in Finder.** A Finder window opens and shows you the file.

7. **Change the .m4a extension of the file to .m4r. If Finder squawks at you to make sure you really want to change the extension, click Use .m4r.**

8. **Go back into iTunes, find the newly created song, and press the Delete key on your keyboard.**

9. **iTunes asks if you want to delete the file; you do, so click Delete Song.**

10. **iTunes now asks if you want to move the file to the Trash; you DO NOT want to move the file to the Trash, so click Keep File.**

11. **Go back to the Finder, browse to the newly created ringtone file, and double-click it to automatically import it into iTunes. If double-clicking the file doesn't work, simply drag-and-drop it onto the iTunes icon in the Dock to add it to the library. If that fails to work, choose File ⇨ Add to Library in the menu, browse for and select the file to import it.**

12. **Select Tones in the source pane on the left side of the iTunes window. You see your newly created ringtone ready for service on your iPhone.**

Importing items from other iTunes libraries

iTunes includes a neat feature called Home Sharing that lets you import media from up to five other iTunes libraries shared by computers on your network. To use Home Sharing, follow these steps:

Note You must have an Apple ID in order to use Home Sharing, and all computers should be using the latest version of iTunes.

1. **Choose File ⇨ Home Sharing ⇨ Turn On Home Sharing.**

2. **Type your Apple ID username and password when prompted, and click Create Home Share.**

3. **Click Done.**

4. **Repeat Steps 1 through 3 on the other computers on which you want to enable Home Sharing, assuming they're running a version of iTunes 11; earlier versions use a different method, which you can find by perusing Help.** Make sure you use the same Apple ID for each.

5. **To import media from another computer, select its name from the Shared list in the source pane and drag items from its library to yours.**

Using the iTunes Store

The iTunes Store is your one-stop shop for content such as music, movies, television shows, and podcasts of all kinds. New items are added to the iTunes Store all the time. After you try it, you'll be as hooked as I am. To access the iTunes Store, simply click the iTunes Store button in the upper-right corner of the iTunes window, as shown in Figure 11.19.

The categories of items you can get from the iTunes Store are listed at the top of the window. Simply click a category to see a drop-down menu of its subcategories. Table 11.3 lists many of the options offered by Apple.

11.19 The iTunes Store is addictive, so be careful.

Table 11.3 Items Available in the iTunes Store

Item	Description
Music	Download individual songs or entire albums. You can also download music videos and search from the extensive list of music genres.
Movies	You can rent or buy movies to watch.
TV Shows	Watch your shows on your own time instead of the networks's time.
App Store	Find lots of cool applications to use with your iPhone, iPad, or iPod touch.
Books	Download and listen to audiobooks. If you prefer to read them yourself, you can download electronic books to your Mac, iPhone, iPad, or iPod touch.
Podcasts	Podcasts are radio shows or videos to which you can subscribe and download. I swear by my favorite podcasts.
iTunes U	Not only can the iTunes Store entertain, but it can also educate! Here, you can find audio and video from institutions of higher learning to listen to or view on your Mac, iPhone, iPad, or iPod touch.

Signing in to your Apple ID

In order to use the iTunes Store, you must have an Apple ID. If you do not yet have one (how did you get this far in the book without one?), click the Store menu, select Create Apple ID, and follow the instructions.

If you have an account, follow these steps to sign in:

1. **Click Sign In in the upper-left corner of the iTunes Store window.**

2. **Type your Apple ID and password, and click Sign In. If successful, you're whisked away to the iTunes Store home page, and your Apple ID appears in the upper left of the window.**

Authorizing and deauthorizing a computer

iTunes lets you authorize up to five computers to use your purchased content. To authorize a computer, follow these steps:

1. **Choose Store ⇨ Authorize This Computer.**

2. **Type your Apple ID name and password, and click Authorize. If you are successful, iTunes tells you so.**

To deauthorize (I think Apple made this word up) a computer, follow these steps:

1. **Choose Store ⇨ Deauthorize This Computer.**

2. **Type your Apple ID name and password, and click Deauthorize. iTunes lets you know that you successfully deauthorized this computer.**

Finding music

You can browse through the vast collection of iTunes music, or you can do what I prefer to do: Perform a search. When you have an idea what you're looking for, this is the fastest way to go:

1. **At the iTunes Store home page, click the Music button across the top of the window.**

2. **Type any information that may help you find what you're looking for in the Search iTunes Store field in the upper-right corner of the iTunes window, as shown in Figure 11.20.** You can narrow your search further by selecting Songs or Albums on the right side of the iTunes Store window.

3. **Browse the items in the search results to find what you're looking for.**

11.20 A search is the quickest way to find items in the iTunes Store.

Renting or buying movies and TV shows

That trip to the video store just got much shorter because you can use iTunes to rent or buy the latest releases, as well as the classic films of yesteryear. This may not make the video store happy, but your automobile will thank you for the mileage you save. Follow these steps:

1. **Click the Movies link at the top of the iTunes Store home page.**

2. **Browse the top ten lists to find the latest and most popular releases, choose a genre to browse through, or perform a search to find your favorite movie.**

3. **Click the movie title to open its page. You see something similar to Figure 11.21.**

11.21 A typical movie page in the iTunes Store.

4. **Click View Trailer if you want to preview the movie before you rent or buy it.**

5. **Click Rent Movie or Buy Movie.** Some movies can only be rented, and others can only be purchased. You can preorder some items before they are released.

6. **The movie downloads and is available for you to watch in the Movies section of your iTunes library.**

Subscribing to podcasts

Podcasts are audio or video recordings that you can download and play back at your leisure. There are podcasts for almost any taste, ranging from the most popular talk shows to comedy, technology, and more. To subscribe to your favorite podcast, follow these steps:

1. **Click the Podcasts link in the iTunes Store section of the iTunes Store home page.**

2. **Find podcasts by searching in the different categories, performing a search, or browsing the Top Podcasts lists.**

3. **When you find one that strikes your fancy, click the link to go to its page, as I've done in Figure 11.22.**

11.22 A podcast page in the iTunes Store summarizes the content and provides a list of the most recent episodes.

4. **Click Subscribe to have iTunes automatically download the latest episodes.**

5. **Select Podcasts from the music library source bar to view your subscribed podcasts and listen to or view them.**

Genius You can also synchronize podcasts with your iPhone, iPad, iPod, or iPod touch. This enables you to play them back on the go. Consult the documentation that came with your device for information on syncing with iTunes.

Enrolling at iTunes U

You don't have to be enrolled at a prestigious university to take courses there. iTunes U provides online courses from some of the premier institutions in the world, and they are yours to take for free! Follow these steps:

1. **Click iTunes U at the top of the iTunes Store home page.**

2. **Browse the different categories, providers, and Top Downloads section to find content or a particular institution in which you are interested.**

3. **Click the link for the institution (or a course you want to view). A page similar to Figure 11.23 appears.**

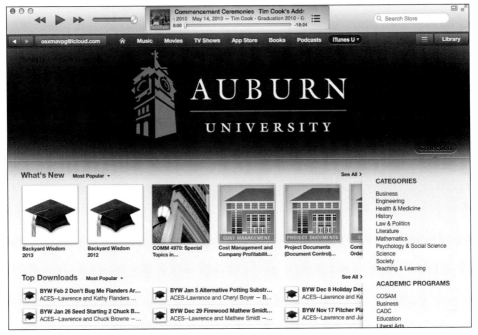

11.23 Some of the finest institutions around, including Apple CEO Tim Cook's alma mater, provide content to iTunes U.

4. **Click Subscribe for the audio or video course you want to take.** The course downloads can be found in the Podcast section of the source pane. You can view or listen to it as you would any other podcast.

Reading or listening to your favorite books

The iTunes Store has already taken over your neighborhood video and music haunts, and now it's time for the traditional bookstore to have a little competition. iTunes is also a full-scale bookstore where you can download either electronic books to read on your devices or audiobooks to listen to on your Mac or on the go. To browse the store shelves, follow these steps:

1. **At the top of the iTunes Store home page, click Books.**

2. **Browse the lists of popular books and latest selections, or perform a search for a particular title or author.**

3. **Click the link for a book to see its information, as shown in Figure 11.24.**

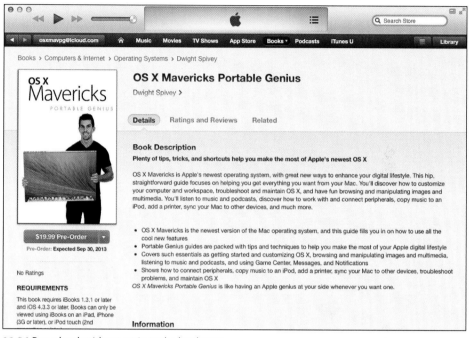

11.24 Buy a book without a trip to the bookstore.

4. **Click Buy Book to purchase one, or click Sample to read a preview.**

5. **iTunes downloads your purchase; you can find it by selecting Books from the Library button.** Sync your iPhone, iPad, or iPod touch so you can read your new purchases on it.

Downloading apps

iTunes is also home to the App Store, as shown in Figure 11.25, for your iPhone, iPad, or iPod touch. This is where you download and sync all those awesome apps you see in the Apple commercials.

To purchase an app, follow these steps:

1. **At the top of the iTunes Store home page, click App Store.**

2. **Browse the categories in the Quick Links section on the right side of the window, as shown in Figure 11.25, check out the Top Charts section for the most popular apps (both free and for purchase), or do a search.**

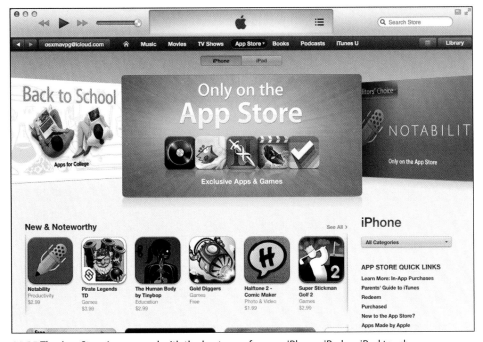

11.25 The App Store is crammed with the best apps for your iPhone, iPad, or iPod touch.

3. **When you find the app you want, select it and click the Buy or Free button to purchase it.** The next time you sync your device, the new app is ready to use.

How Do I Work with Images and Video?

In today's digital age, you most likely use your computer to catalog and share images. Mavericks offers several ways to have fun with digital photography and video. In addition to taking pictures, you can use Photo Booth to record video and add special effects, including your own custom backdrops. Mavericks automatically works with most digital cameras and scanners. Image Capture helps you transfer images to and from your digital camera and import files using your scanner. In this chapter, I also cover viewing images in Preview, taking screenshots, watching movies with QuickTime Player, and using FaceTime for video calls.

Working with Images in Preview

Preview is an application that has been with OS X from the beginning. It is commonly considered to be a jack-of-all-trades when it comes to opening and working with many file types. In this portion of the chapter, I cover how to work with images in Preview, but for more information on what Preview can do, see Chapter 7.

Image file types supported by Preview

Preview can open and export many different image file types. Table 12.1 lists the image file types supported by Preview.

Table 12.1 File Types Supported by Preview

File Extension	File Type/Description
JPG	Joint Photographic Experts Group: A popular image file format used by most digital cameras. Also known as JPEG.
GIF	Graphics Interchange Format: An image file format mainly used on the Internet for small animations.
HDR	High Dynamic Range: An image file format associated with high-end digital cameras.
TIFF	Tagged Image File Format: A popular image file format used primarily by graphic artists.
PSD	Photoshop Document: The Adobe Photoshop default image file format.
OpenEXR	"A high dynamic-range (HDR) image file format…for use in computer imaging applications," developed by George Lucas's Industrial Light & Magic (source: www.openexr.com).
PNG	Portable Network Graphics: An image file format.
BMP	Bitmap: An image file format.
RAW	A file format for an image that has not been processed in any way; mostly used by digital cameras and scanners.
SGI	Silicon Graphics Image: The native raster graphics file format of Silicon Graphics workstations.

Setting the Preview preferences

Preview has its default ways of working with images, but thankfully you can customize it to fit your needs.

The Preview preferences are divided into four categories: General, Images, PDF, and Signatures. I discuss the General and Images preferences in this chapter; the other two are covered in Chapter 7.

To get started, open Preview and press ⌘+, to open the Preview Preferences window.

General

Table 12.2 breaks down the settings in the General tab of the Preview Preferences window.

Table 12.2 General Preferences

Preference	Function
When opening files	Determine how you want Preview to open multiple files: Open all files in one window, open groups of files in the same window, or open each file in its own separate window.
Window background	Change the default background color of the windows you open in Preview by clicking the color box and choosing a new color from the color palette window.

Images

The Images preferences pane has only one set of options: Define 100% scale as. The options available are self-explanatory:

- **1 image pixel equals 1 screen pixel (default setting).** This setting causes the image to appear on-screen at different dimensions, depending on the screen resolution.

- **Size on screen equals size on printout.** Choose this setting to display images at the same size regardless of the screen resolution.

Viewing and editing images in Preview

Preview is more than happy to fill the role of basic image editor if you don't already have one with more frills, such as iPhoto or Adobe Photoshop. Although it cannot manipulate photos and add effects like the two applications I just mentioned, Preview can handle standard resizing, rotating, and a few other nifty tricks. Open an image in Preview to get started.

Get the Inside Scoop on Images

Most people simply want to open, view, and perhaps minimally edit their pictures. However, others (and you know who you are) want the lowdown on every element of the picture, including the camera used, the compression type, the aperture, the Photometric Interpretation, and other information that only a professional photographer could appreciate.

Preview can get all that stuff for you if you simply choose Tools ⇨ Show Inspector or press ⌘+I when your image is open.

Opening and saving images

Preview can open any of the file types mentioned in Table 12.1. To open a file in Preview, do the following:

1. **From within Finder, choose Go ⇨ Applications, and double-click the Preview icon to open it.** You can also look for Preview's icon in the Dock and click to launch it.

2. **Browse your Mac for the file you want to open, click the files icon once to highlight it, and then click Open, as shown in Figure 12.1.**

If you make changes to an image you've opened in Preview, those changes are automatically saved as you work. Even new images are saved automatically as you work with them, but when you're ready to name the image file, press ⌘+S; you can also choose File ⇨ Save. If you've made changes to an image file, but you want to save it under a different name, press ⌘+Shift+S (or choose File ⇨ Export) to open the Export As dialog, as shown in Figure 12.2. Type a new name for the image file, and choose the location to which you want to save it on your Mac. Next, select the format and quality of the image, and click Save.

Note If you can't seem to find the location to which you want to save your file, click the light gray square containing the black arrow (just to the right of the Export As text field). This expands your Export As window, allowing you to browse your entire hard drive.

12.1 Choose the file you want to open in Preview.

Genius If the Preview icon is in your Dock, whether it's already open or because you keep an alias for it there, you can simply drag and drop a file onto it to open it.

12.2 Name your file, choose where to save it, select a format and quality, and click Save.

Importing new images

You can use Preview to import new images from a scanner or camera connected to your Mac via a USB, FireWire, or network (assuming your scanner or camera supports one or all of these connection types).

Importing images from a scanner

To import images into Preview from a scanner, follow these steps:

1. **Choose File, and hold your mouse over Import from Scanner.** Select your scanner from the pop-up menu.

2. **When your scanner window opens, choose the appropriate settings for the type of file you're importing, as shown in Figure 12.3.**

3. **Click Scan to initiate the scanning sequence.**

12.3 Be sure to choose the appropriate settings for the type of file you want to scan into Preview.

4. **Browse your Mac for the location to which you want to save the file, and click Choose Destination.** The file you scanned opens in Preview. You can also save the file to iCloud if you're logged in to your iCloud account.

Importing images from a camera

To import images into Preview from a camera, follow these steps:

1. **Choose File ⇨ Import from *camera name*.**

2. **When the camera window opens, browse to find the pictures you want to import into Preview, as shown in Figure 12.4.** To select multiple pictures, hold down the ⌘ key while clicking each picture.

3. **Click Import to import pictures you've selected.** If you want to import every picture on your camera, click Import All.

4. **Browse your Mac for the location to which you want to save the file, and click Choose Destination.** The pictures you imported open in Preview. You may also save the file to your iCloud account, if you're logged in to it.

Genius
When viewing your pictures in the Import window, you can change the way they display by clicking the List or the Icons button found in the lower-left corner. You can also rotate and delete images from here.

12.4 Choose the pictures you want to import into Preview.

Resizing and rotating images

If a photo or image is just too big dimensionally, Preview can easily squeeze it until it fits the spot in which you want to place it.

To adjust the size of your image, choose Tools ⇨ Adjust Size. The dialog shown in Figure 12.5 opens.

Make the necessary changes to these settings to adjust your image, and click OK when you are finished. Table 12.3 explains the options and how they affect the image.

Preview also lets you rotate images to change their orientation. If you have a picture that was taken by holding the camera sideways (to take a full-length shot of someone, for example), you can rotate it so the subject is standing

12.5 Adjust the size of an image in Preview.

upright (instead of on his or her side) when you open the image in Preview. To rotate an image to the left, press ⌘+L; to rotate it to the right, press ⌘+R.

Table 12.3 Size Adjustments

Option	Function
Fit into	This option lets you choose automatic size settings from the pop-up menu. Use Custom to create a custom size.
Width and Height	This option changes the physical size of the image.
Resolution	This option changes the quality of the image. Increasing this number may have adverse effects on the image.
Scale proportionally	This option keeps the dimensions of the image intact when selected. For example, if you change the width, the height changes proportionally.
Resample image	Deselect this check box if you want to reduce the dimensions of a file without losing image details.

You can also flip an image to make the subject face a different direction, as shown in Figure 12.6. I flipped my image both vertically and horizontally to give you a better idea of what these functions do.

To flip your image horizontally, choose Tools ➪ Flip Horizontal; to go vertical, choose Tools ➪ Flip Vertical.

Adjusting color in images

Sometimes the colors in your pictures just don't look quite right. What is someone who isn't a color specialist to do? Preview has the answer! Preview can handle basic color adjustments very well.

To make color corrections in Preview, choose Tools ➪ Adjust Color, or press ⌘+Option+C. The color adjustment sliders in the Adjust Color window, shown in Figure 12.7, can work wonders on your images.

When you move the sliders, your image is automatically updated to reflect the adjustments.

12.6 My kids are flipping out in this picture!

Genius You can also crop an image in Preview. Notice that the mouse cursor changes to a cross hair when you move it over your image; use this to select the area on your image that you want to crop. Place the cross hair underneath or over the area you want to crop, and then click and drag to draw a box around it. After the area is selected, press ⌘+K, and save your new image (File ➪ Export in the menu).

12.7 Move the sliders to make the necessary color adjustments to your image.

Taking Screenshots

At some point during your Mac adventure, you may need to take a shot of your screen. There are many reasons for taking screenshots. For example, you may want to share information about your system with someone else, or you may want a quick snap of some settings you've made so that you can refer to them later. You can take screenshots manually with just a couple of key presses, or you can gain a little more control over the shots by using the Grab utility that ships as part of Mavericks.

Capturing screenshots manually

The quick and easy way to take screenshots is to incorporate a little manual dexterity:

- **Press ⌘+Shift+3.** Doing this takes a shot of the entire screen.

- **Press ⌘+Shift+4.** Doing this narrows the scope of your screenshot. Your cursor turns into a cross hair, which you then drag over the section of your screen that you want to shoot. As soon as you let go of the mouse or trackpad button, a screenshot is taken of the area you highlighted.

295

Genius You can also take a shot of an individual window. Press ⌘+Shift+4 again, but don't drag the cross hair. Instead, press the spacebar, and the cross hair changes to a camera icon. Position the camera icon over the window you want to shoot, and click your mouse or trackpad button.

Taking screenshots in Preview

You can take a screenshot within Preview in three ways. Choose File ⇨ Take Screen Shot and select one of the following options:

- **From Selection.** When you choose this option, your cursor turns into a cross hair. Click and drag the cross hair over the portion of the screen you want to capture. The screenshot opens in Preview.

- **From Window.** When you choose this option, the cursor turns into a camera icon. Move the camera icon over the window (or the menu) that you want to shoot, and click your mouse or trackpad button to capture it. The screenshot then opens in Preview.

- **From Entire Screen.** When you select this option, Preview displays a countdown to when it will take the shot. This gives you time to position the windows where you need them on-screen or to select an item from a menu before the screenshot is taken. It then displays in Preview.

Using Grab to capture screenshots

Grab is a utility that helps you take screen-shots that include various types of mouse pointers, take timed screenshots, and more. Grab can be found in the /Applications/ Utilities folder. Double-click to open Grab, and use the Capture menu to choose the type of screen capture you want it to perform.

The Grab Preferences, shown in Figure 12.8, let you choose from a variety of mouse pointers.

12.8 Select a pointer to appear on your screen captures.

Discovering QuickTime

QuickTime Player allows you to watch, create, and share movie files in Mavericks. To open QuickTime Player, go to the Applications folder and double-click its icon.

Playing back video and audio files

QuickTime Player can open and play back video and audio of various formats.

These video formats are supported:

- ⦿ QuickTime Movie (.mov extension)
- ⦿ MPEG-4 (.mp4 or .m4v)
- ⦿ MPEG-1
- ⦿ 3GPP
- ⦿ 3GPP2
- ⦿ AVI
- ⦿ DV

These audio formats are supported:

- ⦿ iTunes Audio (.m4a, .m4p, and .m4b)
- ⦿ MP3
- ⦿ AIFF
- ⦿ AU
- ⦿ SD2
- ⦿ Core Audio (.caf)
- ⦿ WAV
- ⦿ SND
- ⦿ AMR

You can open any file using one of the aforementioned formats by simply double-clicking it in the Finder. QuickTime Player automatically launches and affords you the controls necessary to play back your media, as shown in Figure 12.9.

If you move your mouse pointer off the video or audio playback window, the controls disappear. Don't worry; to get them back, just hover the cursor over the playback window.

Note

If the tiny playback window isn't your style, click the Full Screen button (the two diagonal arrows) in the upper-right corner of the controls window.

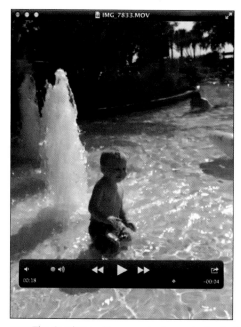

12.9 The QuickTime Player controls are similar to those found on a DVD player.

Creating new video or audio recordings

QuickTime Player isn't just a player; it can take on the role of recorder as well. You can create video from the built-in Mac camera, a digital video camera connected with FireWire, or a USB webcam (if supported by the manufacturer). Audio can be recorded using the microphone built in to your Mac, an external microphone, or a musical instrument connected to your Mac.

To create a new video or audio recording, follow these steps:

1. **Choose File ⇨ New Movie Recording, or File ⇨ New Audio Recording. (You can't choose to do both at the same time, but if you're recording a movie, the audio is automatically recorded anyway.)** A preview window opens.

2. **Make sure you have everything set up correctly and that you are ready to record before clicking the Record button.**

3. **Change the input source, adjust the quality of the recording, or select a folder in which to save the finished file by clicking the arrow in the preview window, as shown in Figure 12.10.**

4. **Click the Stop button when you're finished recording.**

12.10 Make adjustments to the input source and quality of the recording if necessary.

Recording your on-screen movements

If you teach classes or make presentations that often include demonstrations of actions you can take on a computer, you'll love QuickTime Player's ability to record your on-screen movements. To enable this feature, follow these steps:

1. **Choose File ⇨ New Screen Recording.** A preview window opens.

2. **Change the input source, adjust the quality of the recording, choose to show mouse clicks in the recording, or select a folder in which to save the finished file by clicking the arrow in the preview window.**

3. **Make sure you have everything set up correctly, and click the Record button.**

4. **Click the Stop button to finish recording your on-screen movements.**

Sharing your recordings via the Internet

The Internet has become the number one way to share information with friends, family, and colleagues. QuickTime Player allows you to easily share your movies and recordings using several methods.

To do so, open the file you want to share, choose the Share menu, and select one of the following:

● **AirDrop.** This allows you to instantly copy movies and recordings from one Mac to another, assuming both are using AirDrop.

● **Messages.** You must sign in to Messages to use this option. You can share your audio and video with others through instant messaging.

- **YouTube.** Select this option to upload your file (which must be shorter than 15 minutes and smaller than 2GB) to your YouTube account. Give the file a title and description, as shown in Figure 12.11, to become the next YouTube sensation.

- **Vimeo.** If you have a Vimeo account, upload your file there, to share it with others. Be sure to set the option to make the file personal if you want to view it yourself or share it with those you deem privileged.

- **Flickr.** If you have a Flickr account, you can share your Oscar-worthy performances. Simply log in to your Flickr account, set up the appropriate options (name, description, and so on), and upload your file.

12.11 Upload your movies to YouTube so friends, family, and the rest of the world can enjoy them.

- **Facebook.** It's a safe bet that most, if not all, folks with whom you want to share your recordings have Facebook accounts, so this might be a preferable option for some. Simply log in to Facebook and upload your file.

- **Email.** Select this sharing method to open a new e-mail message in Mail that automatically contains a copy of the file as an attachment. You can then type the e-mail addresses of your intended recipients and click Send.

You may also use iTunes to share your movies and recordings. Select iTunes, select a size for your movie or recording, and click Share; a copy of your movie or recording is placed in the iTunes library, where it can be copied to and played on an iPhone, iPod, iPad, or Apple TV.

Using Photo Booth

Apple has moved the old-fashioned photo booths—the kind that we used to cram ourselves into with our friends on Friday nights at the mall—to our Macs. Simple as it is, there are still a few features that could use an explanation. When I purchase something new, I like to read the instructions and learn what all the buttons and gadgets are for, hence my insistence on covering the Photo Booth features shown in Figure 12.12.

12.12 The main Photo Booth window in Snapshot mode.

When you open Photo Booth for the first time, it launches in Full Screen mode. Throughout this section I'll be working in windowed mode, so if you'd like the same view as mine just hold your mouse pointer in the upper-right corner of the window and then click the Full Screen button to exit Full Screen mode. You still can follow along if you prefer to work in full screen.

Taking snapshots

Any kind of picture that you take with Photo Booth is considered a snapshot, whether it's a still picture or a video. You can take three kinds of snapshots: single still picture, four quick snapshots (which are much more fun than you might think), and video. Use the snapshot-type buttons under the bottom-left corner of the viewer window to select the kind that you want to take.

Taking a single snapshot

Single snapshots (or still pictures) are so easy to take that it's ridiculous. Follow these steps:

1. **Click the single still picture button under the bottom-left corner of the Viewer window.**

2. **Position yourself in front of the Mac camera so your image fits inside the Viewer window.**

3. **Click the Camera button.**

4. **Photo Booth begins its countdown from 3, flashes, and takes the picture.** That's it!

Taking four quick snapshots

Taking four quick snapshots lets you create different poses in rapid succession. Follow these steps to try it out:

1. **Click the four quick snapshots button in the middle under the bottom-left corner of the Viewer window.**

2. **Position yourself in front of the Mac camera so your image fits inside the Viewer window.**

3. **Click the Camera button to begin the countdown.** Get into your first pose before the first flash goes off.

4. **After the first flash, immediately change to your next pose and continue to do that through all four pictures.** You have only about a second between snapshots, so you have to move quickly. When all four snapshots are taken, you see a preview of your images, similar to Figure 12.13.

Creating a video snapshot

To create some movie magic in Photo Booth, follow these steps:

1. **Click the video button on the right under the bottom-left corner of the viewer window.**

2. **Position yourself in front of the Mac camera so your image fits inside the viewer window.**

3. **Click the Camera button to begin the countdown.**

4. **Begin your video after the flash goes off.**

5. **When you're finished, click the Stop button.**

Viewing your snapshots

All your snapshots are stored in the Thumbnail bar at the bottom of the Photo Booth window. You can scroll through the list of snapshots by clicking the right and left arrows on either side of the bar.

To view a snapshot, click it in the Thumbnail bar; it displays in the Viewer window. To export a snapshot to another location on your Mac, right-click (or Control-click) the snapshot in the Thumbnail bar and select Export. A Save window opens; browse to the location where you want the file to reside on your Mac, and click Save. Simply click the camera button to return to taking pictures.

12.13 A preview appears in the viewer window so you can see your four-up handiwork.

Genius

You can access your snapshots without opening Photo Booth each time you need them. Photo Booth stores snapshots in the Photo Booth Library package, which resides in the Pictures folder of your home folder (hard drive/Users/your account name/Pictures/). Right-click (or Control-click) the Photo Booth Library package, and select Show Package Contents. When the contents are displayed, browse to the Photos folder to access your pictures.

Using special effects

You've only seen the tip of the Photo Booth iceberg. Photo Booth can do something the old photo booths at the mall could only dream of: add awesome special effects and backdrops!

Adding effects to Snapshots

To use visual effects like filters or distortions for your snapshots, follow these steps:

1. **Position yourself in front of the Mac camera so your image fits inside the Viewer window.**

2. **Click Effects to see the cool filter effects shown in Figure 12.14.**

3. **Click the right arrow next to Effects to see the distortion effects, like those shown in Figure 12.15.**

4. **Select the effect you want to use by clicking it, and then click the Camera button to take the picture.**

12.14 The filter effects available in Photo Booth. You gotta love X-Ray!

Adding a Video backdrop

Video backdrops are really neat to use. They place a moving video of some exotic location behind you so it appears as if you're really there. Impress family and friends by creating a video of yourself in front of the Eiffel Tower, swimming with the fishes, or flying through the clouds!

Here's how to do it:

1. **Position yourself in front of the camera so your image fits inside the Viewer window.**
2. **Click Effects.**
3. **Click the right arrow next to Effects until it brings you to the video backdrops.**
4. **Select the backdrop you want to use.**
5. **Step out of the frame when prompted until you see the backdrop you chose in the Viewer window.**
6. **Move into the frame of the Viewer window, and click the Camera button to make your video, as shown in Figure 12.16.**

12.15 The distortion effects are a blast to play with!

12.16 Their hair isn't even wet!

Adding custom backdrops

My favorite feature of Photo Booth is the ability to use my own photos and videos as backdrops. To create a custom backdrop, follow these steps:

1. **Click Effects, and then click the right arrow next to it until you see the Custom Backdrop window.**

2. **Drag and drop a picture or video from the Finder, iPhoto, or iMovie into one of the Drag Backdrop Here windows.**

3. **Select the new backdrop to use it for your picture or video.**

Using your pictures and videos

What to do with all these great snapshots you've been taking? You can save your snapshots in iPhoto if you like (assuming you have it on your Mac, of course), e-mail them to family and friends, or use them to represent you in an online chat session.

Click the snapshot you want to use in the Thumbnail bar. Notice in Figure 12.17 that when you open the snapshot in preview mode, you now have access to the Sharing button. Click the Sharing button to do one of the following:

- Send an e-mail with the selected picture attached.
- Send an instant message with the picture attached.
- Tweet the photo.
- Add the photo to your Flickr account.
- Post the picture to your Facebook account.
- Add the picture to iPhoto.
- Set the photo as your profile picture.
- Instantly send the photo to another computer that uses AirDrop.

Note

You can print from Photo Booth just as you can from any other application. To print your snapshots, choose File ➪ Print or press ⌘+P. When the Print dialog opens, click Show Details and choose one of the options in the Photo Booth pane. You can print the picture normally, or you can print proof sheets (either several different sizes of the same picture on the same page or eight pictures of the same size).

12.17 Select how to use your snapshot by clicking one of the options under the viewer window.

Working with Image Capture

Image Capture is a great tool that may surprise you with its versatility. You can use it to do any of the following:

- Transfer images from your digital camera.
- Delete images from your digital camera.
- Import images with your scanner.
- Find shared devices on your network.

To open Image Capture, press ⌘+Shift+A from within the Finder. Find Image Capture in the resulting Finder window and double-click its icon. If you don't have a digital camera or scanner attached to your Mac when you start Image Capture, you are notified in the main window that no device is connected. If this is the case, read on to discover how to connect your device.

Note

You may wonder why iPhoto, the amazing Apple photo-organizing and editing program, isn't covered in this book. iPhoto is actually part of the iLife application suite, which Apple sells separately from Mavericks. Because I concentrate on Mavericks in this book, Image Capture gets all the glory.

Connecting your device

If you haven't already done so, attach your device to the Mac with whatever connection its manufacturer recommends; most use USB. If Image Capture is already open, when you attach a camera or scanner, it should automatically display under Devices on the left side of the Image Capture window.

If you have multiple devices attached to your Mac, you can choose the device you want to use by selecting it in the Devices menu.

Note

In addition to pictures, Image Capture is versatile enough to import movies and MP3 files, assuming your camera has the ability to record such files.

Using a digital camera

A digital camera is your window to the world, and it allows you to keep your memories for a lifetime. However, the memory cards that cameras use to store your precious keepsakes have a finite amount of space. Therefore, they need to be emptied of their contents every now and again. This is where Image Capture comes in handy.

Transferring images from your camera

As stated earlier in this chapter, when you connect your camera to your Mac with Image Capture already up and running, a window opens similar to the one shown in Figure 12.18. This gives you access to—and a measure of control over—your camera.

Here are three of the options:

- **Connecting this camera opens.** This pop-up menu lets you choose an application to open automatically when the camera is connected to your Mac.

- **List or Icons buttons.** Click one of these viewing options at the bottom left of the window to change the view.

- **Rotate buttons.** Click these to rotate selected images before downloading them.

12.18 Control your camera with the options in the Image Capture window.

Importing files

Click Import All to do just that: Import all the pictures and files from your camera to your Mac. However, if you want to import only a few files, the Import button is your best option.

To import only certain files from your camera, click those you want to import from within the Image Capture window. To choose multiple files, as shown in Figure 12.19, hold down the ⌘ key while making your selections.

Next, click Import to proceed with the transfer. The files you downloaded can then be found in the Pictures folder of your home directory. You can change the location to which your pictures are imported by clicking the Import To pop-up menu at the bottom of the window.

Deleting images from your camera

Sometimes, you may want to delete some of the images on your digital camera as opposed to all, but deleting individual images can be a chore. Image Capture comes in handy in this situation. To delete individual files from your camera, follow these steps:

1. **Select the files you want to remove from your camera.** Hold down the ⌘ key while clicking to choose multiple files.

2. **Click the Delete button at the bottom of the window.**

309

3. **Click OK to confirm the deletion, or click Cancel to stop it.**

12.19 You can select only the pictures you want to delete rather than deleting them all.

Scanning images

Your Mac happily uses Image Capture to import images and documents from a scanner. Simply connect your scanner to get started.

Note

You need to install the scanner software before connecting the scanner to your Mac. The software probably came on a CD with the scanner, but it's always a good idea to visit the manufacturer's website for any updated drivers it may have released.

Using the Image Capture scanning options

The default scan window that opens offers a few basic options for scanning your documents into your Mac, as shown in Figure 12.20.

To scan an item using these options, follow these steps:

1. **Highlight the scanner under Devices on the left side of the Image Capture window.**

Getting the Red Out

Image Capture is a great application, but if you need to touch up photos, such as removing the red in your subject's eyes or cropping part of the image, you need other software. iPhoto is the perfect application for such common tasks, and it's also great for organizing and sharing images. You can purchase iPhoto from Apple as part of the iLife suite of applications.

Open the Applications folder on your hard drive, double-click the Image Capture icon, and choose the scanner from the list. Place the item you want to scan onto the glass of the scanner (if it is a flatbed scanner) or into the feeder (if it is a document-feed scanner). This is where the fun begins!

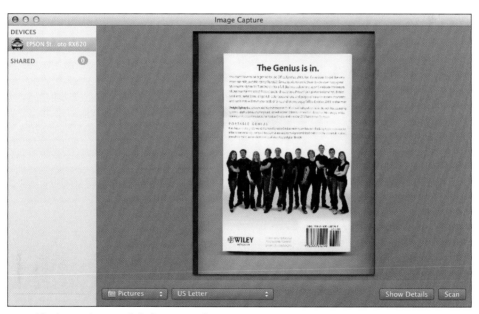

12.20 The Image Capture default scan window.

2. **Choose a location in which to store the scanned file or an application with which to open it, and select the paper size of the original, using the pop-up menus in the lower left of the scan window.**

3. **Click Scan.** After the scan is completed, you can find the document in the location you chose in Step 2.

Using the scanner software options

Your scanner software may offer many options that are not available in the Image Capture standard scan window. To access those features, follow these steps:

1. **Highlight the scanner under Devices on the left side of the Image Capture window,
   and click Show Details in the lower-right corner to see the scanner options, as
   shown in Figure 12.21.** Your options may be different, depending on the driver it uses.

2. **Choose what type of image you are scanning from the Kind drop-down menu.**

3. **Select the Resolution you want to use from its drop-down menu.** Resolution plays a
   major role in the quality of the image. The higher the better, but a higher resolution
   increases your file size.

12.21 You have more control over the quality of your scans when using the software provided by the
scanner manufacturer.

4. **Determine the size and orientation of your image.**

5. **Choose a location on your Mac in which to save the scanned images or an application you want to use to open them by using the Scan To drop-down menu.**

6. **Name the file, and select the format in which you want to save the scanned image.**

7. **If your scanner offers other options, such as Image Correction, Unsharp Mask, and so on, make any corrections you feel are necessary using these options.**

8. **If you are using a document-feed scanner, simply click Scan to begin scanning the pages and skip the rest of the steps.** If using a flatbed or transparency scanner, continue to Step 10.

9. **Click Overview scan to see a preview of the item on the glass.**

10. **Click and drag your mouse over the portion of the preview that you want to scan, and click Scan.**

Using FaceTime

FaceTime is a communication technology from Apple that allows you to make video calls to any-one who has an iPhone 4 or newer, iPad 2 or newer, Mac, or iPod touch. FaceTime uses the built-in cameras on these devices to send a crystal-clear video of you (depending on your network con-nection, of course) to the person you're calling, and you can see the other person talking back to you on your device.

FaceTime requirements

You need all of the following to use FaceTime for making video calls from your Mac:

- **An Internet connection using Ethernet or Wi-Fi.**

- **A Mac running Mac OS X 10.6.6 or later. You have Mavericks, which is 10.9, so you're okay.**

- **A camera, of course, or there won't be much video for your video call.** You can use the built-in Mac camera, an external camera that connects to FireWire, or an external USB camera that supports DV/HDV cameras and the UVC specification.

- **A microphone, or the call will be a quiet one.** Your Mac has a built-in microphone, or you can use an external microphone connected to the audio port. USB and Bluetooth microphones/headsets also work.

- **An Apple ID to sign in to FaceTime.**

- **Contacts in your Address Book.** FaceTime uses phone numbers to call iPhone 4 (and newer) users, and it uses e-mail addresses to call Mac, iPad 2 (and newer), and iPod touch users.

Signing in to FaceTime

When you first open FaceTime, you are asked to sign in using your Apple ID, as shown in Figure 12.22.

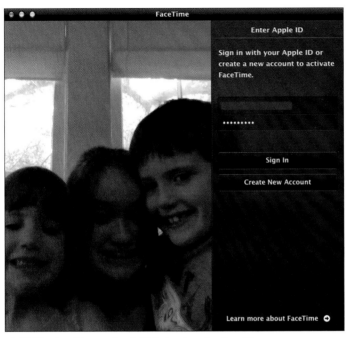

12.22 Sign in with your Apple ID to begin using FaceTime.

To sign in to FaceTime, follow these steps:

1. **If you don't have an Apple ID, click Create New Account, follow the instructions, and then continue to Step 2.** If you do have an Apple ID, continue to Step 2.

2. **Type your Apple ID username and password in the appropriate fields, and click Sign In. If this is not your first time signing in to FaceTime, you may skip the remainder of these steps.**

3. **Type the e-mail address you want other FaceTime users to use to call you, and click Next.**

4. **Apple sends a verification e-mail if this is your first time signing in with your AppleID.** After you receive the e-mail, respond to it by clicking the Verify Now link it contains.

5. **On the web page that opens, sign in with your Apple ID username and password, and click Verify Address.**

6. **When the e-mail address is verified, go back to FaceTime and click Next again.** FaceTime shows that your address is verified.

7. **Press ⌘+K to turn on FaceTime. Your Address Book contacts appear in the FaceTime window.**

Placing a call with FaceTime

After you're signed in, it's time to make some calls. The best thing is that no long-distance fees apply! You can feel free to call folks who are using an iPad 2 (or newer), a Mac running 10.6.6 or later, or an iPod touch (4th generation) or iPhone 4 (or newer) running iOS 4.1 or later.

To place a call, follow these steps:

1. **Find a contact to call in one of three ways:**

    - **Type the contact's name in the search field near the top of the FaceTime window.** Names that match appear as you type.

    - **Add a new contact by clicking the plus sign (+) in the upper-right corner.** Type the contact's name and information, and click Done.

    - **At the bottom right of the FaceTime window, click Favorites, Recents, or Contacts, as shown in Figure 12.23.** Scroll through the list until you find the person you want to call.

2. **Click the contact you want to call. You see the contact information.**

3. **Call the person by clicking the contact information:**

    - **If the person you're calling is using an iPhone 4, click the phone number to initiate the call.**

    - **If the person you're calling is using a Mac, iPad 2 (or newer), or iPod touch, click the e-mail address to place the call.**

315

4. **The person you are calling can then either accept or decline your call.** If the call is accepted, commence the conversation.

12.23 Select a contact to call on FaceTime.

Managing FaceTime calls

When you're on a call, you can manage it in various ways:

- **Enlarge the call window by dragging the lower-right corner of the window outward.** Shrink the window by dragging the lower-right corner inward.

- **Press ⌘+Shift+F to enter Full Screen mode.**

- **Click and drag the picture-in-picture display (the picture of you) to any corner of the window.**

- **Change the orientation of the call window by choosing Video ⇨ Use Portrait or Video ⇨ Use Landscape from the menu.**

- **Mute the sound on a call by choosing Video ⇨ Mute from the menu.**

- **Pause a video call by choosing FaceTime ⇨ Hide FaceTime.**

◉ **Resume a paused video call by clicking the FaceTime icon in the Dock.**

◉ **Click End to end a video call in progress.**

You can block an incoming call by clicking Decline or receive it by clicking Accept.

Share?

 EPSON Stylus Photo RX620

Pause Settings

Scanner

| General | Options | Supply Levels | Utility |

Name: EPSON Stylus Photo RX620

Location: dwight's Mac

Device Name: EPSON_Stylus_Photo_RX620

Driver Version: 9.00

Cancel   OK

OS X is known for its printing prowess, but Mavericks ups the ante when it comes to ease of installation and managing jobs. Because Mac has been the publishing industry's best buddy for more than two decades, Apple ensures that printing with OS X is just as it should be—simple and intuitive—which is exactly how I like it. Also, no other operating system is as friendly with its competitors as Mavericks. Whether your network consists of Windows PCs, Linux computers, or an all-Mac configuration, you can share files, folders, printers, and even your Internet connection.

Setting Up a Printer

Installing a printer in OS X is a snap, provided that everything the Mac needs to communicate with the printer is installed (software and drivers) and the necessary hardware (devices and cables) is functioning as it should.

Before you purchase a printer, make absolutely certain that it is Mac-compatible (the vast majority sold today are, but it's best to be sure). Don't just trust the well-meaning employees at the electronics superstore; check it out yourself by going to the printer manufacturer's website and checking the specifications for the printer.

You can also look for familiar Mac logos on the printer box. Logos to look for would include the large X logo with the Made for OS X tagline and the happy Mac, as shown in Figure 13.1, which also appears on the left side of your Dock as the Finder icon. If you buy your printer directly from Apple, it's a given that the printer is Mac-compatible.

You must take three main steps before you can use your printer with your Mac:

1. **Install the software that came with your printer.**

13.1 Look for the familiar Mac logos on the box of the printer you want to purchase.

2. **Connect your printer to your Mac or network.**

   - If your printer has a USB connection, connect one end of the USB cable to the printer and the other to your Mac.

   - If your printer has a network or Ethernet interface, use an Ethernet (or RJ-45) cable to connect it to the network router or switch.

3. **Use the Printers & Scanners System Preferences pane to create a print queue for the printer (in other words, install the printer).**

Installing printer software

OS X needs special software, called a driver, to be able to communicate effectively with your printer, just as it does to speak to any other device you may connect to it. OS X comes preloaded with some printer drivers from several popular printer manufacturers, so you may not need to install any additional software.

The OS X installer application previously installed several gigabytes of printer drivers by default. Now, it installs drivers as needed when a printer is detected.

For example, if you have a printer connected to your Mac or network during or after installation of OS X Mavericks, the installer detects it and installs the drivers needed by the printer. This process works only with printers by manufacturers who have supplied drivers to Apple. Software Update finds new drivers as they become available, as indicated in Figure 13.2.

13.2 Mavericks can automatically install many printer drivers from preferred manufacturers.

If you want Mavericks to automatically download and install the necessary drivers for your device, click the Install button. Simply follow the prompts to begin and complete the installation.

However, the safest way to go is to install the software the manufacturer provides in the box, typically on a CD or DVD. You can also download the latest software from the manufacturer's support website, which is the way you'll have to go if you have a MacBook Air which doesn't include an optical disc drive. Often, some vendor-specific utilities (such as dedicated scanning programs) are included with software directly from the manufacturer that may not download when using Maverick's automatic feature.

Note Be sure the driver files you download are for the version of OS X you are using. If you're reading this book, the automatic assumption is that you're running Mavericks (OS X 10.9).

Caution It's always a good idea to just go to a printer manufacturer's website and download the drivers right from the beginning. This ensures that you have the latest and greatest software for your printer.

Unfortunately, there's not just one way to install drivers. Printer manufacturers provide drivers and software in a number of ways using different installer applications. So the way you install your HP printer software may be different than the way you install your Brother, Xerox, or Epson printer software.

Some printer manufacturers may install other software in addition to the printer driver, such as utilities that allow you to monitor the printer consumables (such as toners, ink cartridges, and drums), perform maintenance tasks, or run diagnostics for troubleshooting. These utilities are typically installed in the Hard Drive⊱Applications folder. Consult your printer manufacturer if you're not sure what software should be installed to maximize your use of the printer (other than the driver, of course).

Generally, you should follow the installation instructions included with the printer, but this is the typical process used to install printer drivers and software:

1. **Insert the CD that came with your printer or download the software from the printer manufacturer's website.**

2. **Double-click the CD icon to open a window (if one doesn't open automatically) and see its contents, and then double-click the software installer icon.** If you download the driver from the web using Safari, Safari automatically opens and mounts the disk image (if the developer is identified) and displays a window showing the contents. Double-click the installer icon in the disk image window. If you receive a message stating that the installer comes from an unidentified developer, you need to try again. On the second attempt, right-click (or Control-click) the installer icon and select Open. When the message window opens again, click the Open button to begin the installation.

3. **Type your user account login password when prompted during installation.** When the software installation is complete, you see a prompt similar to Figure 13.3.

4. **Click Close to complete the process.**

Your Mac should now have the necessary drivers and utilities to communicate with your printer. You can move on to the second major step in your printer setup: connecting your printer.

Connecting your printer

How you connect your printer is just as important as having the correct driver software installed. Some printers come with only one connection type (usually USB), but others may have multiple connection options. The most common is an Ethernet interface for directly connecting the printer to your network.

USB

Connecting with USB is certainly the easiest way for your Mac to get its print on, and USB is reasonably fast for most printing needs. There's not much to it: Connect one end of the USB cable to the printer, the other to the Mac, and—voila!—the printer is connected.

13.3 Click Close to finish the driver software installation process.

Note

Check the contents of the printer box for a USB cable; most don't include one, and you may have to pick one up before you leave the store. A USB device cable has a standard A plug on one end (the flat, rectangular connector most of us are familiar with) and a standard B plug on the other (a smaller, almost completely square connector). The standard B plug is the end that you connect to your printer.

Network

Connect your printer to your network if you want multiple Macs to be able to print from it. Typically, connecting to a network involves hooking up your printer to a router or network switch through an Ethernet cable. There are other methods of using your printer with a network, such as sharing the printer from a Mac, using print servers (devices designed to connect a printer that doesn't have an Ethernet port to an Ethernet router), or using a wireless network adapter. Sharing a printer is covered later in this chapter.

Using print servers and wireless network adapters to connect your printer to a network achieves the same goal as using an Ethernet cable: They all assign a network or IP (Internet Protocol) address to the printer. Because Ethernet cable is the most common method (this may change one day, but for now it's still the norm), I stick with that as the default network connection.

Here are general instructions for connecting your printer to a network:

1. **With the printer off, insert one end of the Ethernet cable into the Ethernet port on your printer.**

2. **Insert the other end of the Ethernet cable into an available Ethernet port on your network router or switch.**

3. **Turn on the printer.** If your printer is running DHCP (Dynamic Host Configuration Protocol) right out of the box (most do), it is automatically assigned an IP address by the router or a DHCP server on the network. Consult the printer documentation to find out how to determine what IP address is assigned to your printer by your network router.

Note   If you plan on using only Bonjour as the connection protocol to your printer, there's no need to worry about the IP address.

Creating a print queue

The next step on your printer installation odyssey is to create a print queue. Creating a print queue allows you to print to the printer from your Mac, as well as manage print jobs. Later, I show you how to set up a print queue for your printer regardless of the connection type it uses.

Which Network Protocol Should I Use?

Network printers can communicate with your Mac using two protocols: Bonjour (known as Rendezvous in an earlier incarnation) and IP Printing.

- **Bonjour.** This is the latest no-configuration-needed protocol from Apple. Like AppleTalk before it, your Mac simply sees a printer running the Bonjour proto-col, so printer queue installation is a snap. Older printers most likely won't have Bonjour, so AppleTalk will have to suffice.

- **IP (Internet Protocol) Printing.** This is the most difficult to set up because you must know the IP address of the printer being installed. I say it's the most difficult, but the only real difficulty with IP Printing is that it is more time con-suming to set up than Bonjour.

If you're on a small network, Bonjour is your best bet because of its extreme simplicity. Consult your IT administrator if you are on a larger corporate network to find out how he or she prefers you to install the printer. I would use IP Printing only if your IT department prefers it.

If you're a fan of AppleTalk and haven't upgraded your Mac since Leopard (10.5), I'm sorry to disappoint you, but OS X no longer supports that protocol.

Note If you connect your printer with a USB after installing the software, your Mac sometimes automatically creates a print queue; you don't have to lift a finger! To see whether this is the case, choose Apple menu ⇨ System Preferences ⇨ Printers & Scanners. If a print queue has been created, you see it in the Printers list on the left side of the window. Now, get to printing!

Opening the Add Printer window

Now that you have the printer connected, let's get it rolling. Follow these steps:

1. **Choose Apple menu ⇨ System Preferences, or click the System Preferences icon in the Dock.**

2. **Click the Printers & Scanners icon in System Preferences to open the Printers & Scanners preferences pane, shown in Figure 13.4.**

13.4 Click the Printers & Scanners icon to open its preferences pane.

3. **Click the plus sign (+) in the lower-left corner of the pane, shown in Figure 13.5, to add a printer to the list.** To delete a printer from the list, highlight it and click the minus sign (–).

325

13.5 Click the plus sign (+) in the Printers & Scanners window to open the Add window.

When the Add window opens, you can use one of the following methods to create a print queue for your printer.

Installing a printer using USB or Bonjour

If you are installing the printer through USB or Bonjour, do the following:

1. **Click Default in the upper-left corner of the window's toolbar.**

2. **Click the name of the printer in the window.**

3. **The Use pop-up menu should automatically show the name of the printer you are setting up.** If not, click the pop-up menu, choose the Select Printer Software option, and browse the list of installed printer drivers. Select the one you need, click OK, and then click Add in the bottom-right corner.

Installing a printer using IP Printing

If you are using IP Printing as your protocol, do the following:

1. **Click IP in the toolbar.**

2. **Type the printer's IP address in the Address field.**

3. **Select the correct protocol from the Protocol pop-up menu.** Consult your printer manufacturer's documentation, website, or technical support department for more information on which protocol to choose.

4. **Type the printer's queue name into the Queue field.** Again, consult your printer man-ufacturer's documentation for the proper setting.

5. **Edit the Name and Location fields to your liking.**

6. **The Use pop-up menu may show the name of the printer you are setting up.** If not, click the pop-up menu and choose the Select Printer Software option. Browse the list of installed printer drivers, select the one you need, click OK, and then click Add in the bottom-right corner, as shown in Figure 13.6.

13.6 Be sure to type the correct Address and Queue information when using IP Printing.

Your newly installed printer queue is now visible in the printer list of the Printers & Scanners window, similar to the one shown in Figure 13.7.

13.7 My newly installed printer queue is now ready to feed jobs to my printer.

To make certain you can now enjoy the fruits of your labor, you need to try a test print. Follow these steps to do so:

1. **Click the printer name in the printer list to highlight it.**

2. **Click Open Print Queue.**

3. **In the print queue's menu (the name of the print queue is to the right of the Apple menu), choose Printer ⇨ Print Test Page, as shown in Figure 13.8.**

13.8 Print a test page to make sure everything is working properly with your printer.

CUPS

At some point during your printing experience with Mavericks, you may run across the term *CUPS*. CUPS is an acronym that stands for Common UNIX Printing System, which is the print system utilized by OS X. It has no relation to the containers that hold our liquid refreshment, nor is it referring to protective athletic wear. CUPS controls all aspects of printing in OS X, such as creating print queues, creating print jobs using the information provided by the printer driver software, and managing jobs in the print queue.

Printing Documents

Now that you have a printer installed, you can get busy printing those pressing sales figures, your family vacation photos, or that map to Aunt Linda's house.

TextEdit is the application I use to show you how to print documents in Mavericks. From the Finder, choose Go ⇨ Applications (or press ⌘+Shift+A), and double-click the TextEdit icon.

TextEdit automatically opens a new blank document when it first starts. Type something interesting in the document, and print it.

To print from just about any application in OS X, do one of the following:

1. **Choose File ⇨ Page Setup:**

   a. **Select the printer in the Format for pop-up menu, as shown in Figure 13.9.**

   b. **Choose the paper size in the Paper Size pop-up menu, also shown in Figure 13.9.**

   c. **Make adjustments to the Orientation and Scale as you see fit.**

   d. **Click OK.**

2. **Choose File ⇨ Print, or press ⌘+P:**

   a. **The standard Print dialog opens, as shown in Figure 13.10.**

   b. **Click Show Details to expand the Print dialog, as shown in Figure 13.11.**

   c. **Change any print options, if necessary.** See the next section for a description of the available print options.

   d. **Click Print to send your print job to the printer queue, where it is passed on to the printer.**

13.9 The standard Page Setup dialog is used in most OS X applications.

13.10 This is the standard OS X Print dialog used by most applications.

13.11 The expanded Print dialog gives you access to the printer's features.

Genius Some printers—typically PostScript-capable laser printers—can print certain files (such as PDFs, JPEGs, or TIFFs) directly. To do so, you simply drag and drop the file into the print queue; you don't even have to open the file in an application. Check with your printer manufacturer to see whether yours can handle such a cool task.

Discover the Mavericks printing options

Mavericks has many built-in print options that allow you to configure your print jobs in so many ways that it can make your head spin. I cover the most popular options in this section.

Caution Some applications, such as QuarkXPress and Adobe InDesign, use their own print dialogs. This can really throw you for a loop if you're used to the standard OS X way of doing things. Peruse the application documentation to learn how to navigate the myriad options they provide.

The main sheet of the standard Print dialog offers some bare-bones basics as well as application-specific print settings. Refer to Figure 13.11 to see the main sheet of the standard Print dialog when using TextEdit.

Table 13.1 breaks down the basic print options.

Table 13.1 Basic Print Options

Option	Function
Printer	Select a printer from the pop-up menu.
Presets	Choose a preconfigured set of options.
Copies	Enter the number of copies you want to print.
Two-Sided	Select this check box to duplex your print job automatically. This option is available only if you have a duplexer installed on your printer; contact the manufacturer of your printer if you need more information.
Pages	Specify whether you want to print all pages of a document or a specific page range.
Paper Size	Select the size of the paper on which you are printing.
Orientation	You can select Portrait or Landscape.
Options menu	This pop-up menu allows you to select from several option sheets (see Figure 13.12). This menu is typically set to the application-specific settings in the main sheet of the Print dialog. For example, Figure 13.11 shows TextEdit.

To access the other printing options that OS X Mavericks provides, click the options pop-up menu, as shown in Figure 13.12. Note that some of the options that appear here are specific to the printer you're using.

Tables 13.2 through 13.6 list the other printing options and their functions.

13.12 Choose from several option sheets to customize your Mavericks printing experience to the max.

Table 13.2 Layout Options

Option	Function
Pages per Sheet	Use this option to print multiple pages of your document on a single side of your paper.
Layout Direction	Choose how the pages are laid out on the page when printing multiple pages per sheet.
Border	Place a border around the individual pages when printing multiple pages per sheet.
Two-Sided	This option is available only if your printer supports a duplexer option, which allows the printer to print on both sides of the sheet.
Reverse Page Orientation	This option causes the job to print out upside down. This is useful if you have paper, such as letterhead, that needs to be printed in a certain direction but you can't place it on the printer in that direction.
Flip horizontally	Anything on the page flips and prints as if being viewed in a mirror.

Table 13.3 Color Matching Options

Option	Function
ColorSync/In Printer	Choosing ColorSync allows Mavericks to handle color matching, while choosing In Printer lets the printer do all the grunt work.
Profile	This option allows you to associate a color profile with this print job. This option is available only when using the ColorSync option.

Table 13.4 Paper Handling Options

Option	Function
Collate pages	Select this check box to print all pages of the document sequentially before printing the next copy.
Pages to Print	Print all pages, just odd- or even-numbered pages, or a certain page range.
Page Order	Choose from Automatic, Normal, or Reverse page order.
Scale to fit paper size	Select this check box to scale the page contents to fit the size selected in the Destination Paper Size pop-up menu.
Destination Paper Size	This allows the document to be printed on a different paper size than specified in the Page Setup dialog. This option is available only if the Scale to fit paper size check box is selected.
Scale down only	Select this check box to prevent the items on the page from being scaled larger than they presently are.

Table 13.5 Paper Feed Options

Option	Function
All pages from	Select a paper tray from which to print the job. This option is useful only if your printer supports multiple paper trays.
First page from	Print the first page of a document using a particular paper tray. For example, use this option if you want to print the first page of a job on your company's letterhead, which is in one tray on your printer.
Remaining from	Print the remainder of the print job from the paper tray you select. This option is available only when selecting the First page from option. Continuing the example from the First page from option, select the paper tray on your printer that contains plain paper to finish the rest of your job, as opposed to using more letterhead.

Table 13.6 Cover Page Options

Option	Function
Print Cover Page	Select either Before document or After document if you want to print a cover page that differentiates your jobs from those of other people using the printer.
Cover Page Type	Select the type of cover page to print. This option is available only if Before document or After document is selected in the Print Cover Page options.
Billing Info	This information is used to identify you if you are being billed for each job you print.

Why and how to create PostScript files

When you first click Print in the Print dialog, Mavericks immediately creates PDF information for the print job behind the scenes. Sometimes, you may need to generate a PostScript file for a certain job, especially if you work in the publishing industry and outsource your printing, or to troubleshoot a printer or printing issue. Because PDF uses a subset of the PostScript language, it's relatively easy for OS X to convert the PDF data generated when you first click Print into a PostScript file. To create a Postscript file, follow these steps:

1. **Choose File ⇨ Print in your application's menu.**
2. **Click PDF in the lower-left corner of the Print dialog.**
3. **Select Save as PostScript from the pop-up menu.**
4. **Give the document a name, select a location to save it to, and click Save to generate a PostScript file.**

Assigning ICC profiles to a printer

Having spent many years in the printing industry, I know that a frequently asked question is how to use ICC profiles with a printer. An ICC profile is a data file that characterizes how a device handles color. ICC profiles may be generic or specific to a particular device, such as a monitor or printer. Consult the manufacturer of your device to inquire about its support of ICC profiles. These profiles can be assigned to single print jobs using the application that designed the document or to printers on an individual basis. Consult the application documentation to find out how to use ICC profiles with it. Here, I show you how to use the ColorSync Utility to assign profiles to individual printers:

1. **From the Finder, press ⌘+Shift+U to open the Utilities folder.**

2. **Double-click the ColorSync Utility icon.**

3. **Select Devices from the toolbar at the top of the window.**

4. **Click the arrow next to Printers to expand the list.**

5. **Highlight the printer to which you want to assign the profile, as shown in Figure 13.13.**

13.13 Assign color profiles to devices using ColorSync Utility.

6. **Click the arrow to the right of Current Profile, and select Other.**

7. **Browse your Mac for the ICC profile you want to use with the device, select it, and click Open to assign the profile.**

8. **When you print using the printer to which you assigned the profile, turn off any color matching options provided by the manufacturer in the Print dialog to force the printer to use the profile you just created.**

Using the Sharing System Preferences

Sharing System Preferences is where all the action begins. That's where you go to enable and configure sharing of all types. Choose Apple menu ⇨ System Preferences, and click the Sharing icon to open the Sharing preferences window, as shown in Figure 13.14.

First things first: If the Computer Name field is blank at the top of the Sharing pane, type a name for your computer. Other users can see your computer on the network using this name.

Your Mac can share many different items, but some don't demand the same amount of coverage as others. For that reason, Table 13.7 gives a brief overview of each sharing option, and the rest of this chapter is devoted to the areas of sharing that need a bit more attention.

13.14 This is where you tell Mavericks how to share with friends.

Use Bonjour with Windows and Mavericks

Mavericks uses a network protocol called Bonjour that allows almost effortless networking between devices that are running Bonjour. Bonjour requires no configuration of any kind; devices that are using Bonjour simply see one another on the network. Although Bonjour is built in to Mavericks, you might be pleased to know that Apple has developed Bonjour for Windows as well. See how simple networking can be between OS X and Windows by downloading and installing Bonjour for Windows from http://support.apple.com/kb/DL999.

Table 13.7 Sharing Preferences

Sharing Type	Description
DVD or CD Sharing	Select this option to allow other computers to remotely connect to and use the Mac optical drive. This option is helpful if your computer doesn't have a built-in optical drive (like the MacBook Air, for example). With this option, you can share the optical drive from another Mac.
Screen Sharing	This feature allows other users to remotely access your Mac and see your screen on their screens. They can also move and open items, such as folders and applications, on your computer.
File Sharing	Select this option to give other users access to folders that you are sharing from your Mac. There's much more about this later in this chapter.
Printer Sharing	To share printers for which you have created a queue in your Printers & Scanners preferences, select the Printer Sharing check box. See more on this feature later in this chapter.
Remote Login	Select this option to let users on other computers remotely access your Mac through a Secure Shell (SSH) in Terminal. Although you can restrict which users have access, I don't recommend using this option due to security concerns, unless you are otherwise directed by someone in your company's IT department.
Remote Management	If you or your network administrators use Apple Remote Desktop to access your computer remotely, you must enable Remote Management. I discuss this option later in this chapter.
Remote Apple Events	Select this option to allow applications and users on other computers to send Apple Events to your Mac. Apple Events are commands that cause your Mac to perform an action, such as printing or deleting files. I don't recommend using this option unless you know what you're doing and trust other users on your network.
Internet Sharing	You can share your Mac's Internet connection with other computers through Ethernet, AirPort, or FireWire. This comes in handy if only one Mac has access to the physical Internet connection in your home or office. If you enable this option, you must check which of the aforementioned connection types you want to share.
Bluetooth Sharing	Use the Mac Bluetooth connection to communicate with other devices, and then select this check box to share files. I cover more about Bluetooth later in this chapter.

Sharing Files

File sharing is what most people think of when you mention sharing on a computer. Mavericks lets you decide which folders and volumes to share from your Mac and who can access those shared items. Select the File Sharing check box to enable it on your Mac (refer to Figure 13.14).

Adding shared folders and users

The Shared Folders window lists the folders on your hard drive that are set up to share files. To add folders to this list, follow these steps:

1. **Click the plus sign (+) beneath the Shared Folders window.**

2. **Browse your Mac, and select the folder you want to share.**

3. **Click Add to begin sharing items in this folder.**

Next, you need to specify which users can access the folders you are sharing. Follow these steps:

1. **Select the newly shared folder in the Shared Folders window, and click the plus sign (+) under the Users window.**

2. **Select a group of users from the list in the left pane, and choose the user from the right pane with whom you want to share the specified folder, as shown in Figure 13.15.**

13.15 Click the user with whom you want to share your folder.

3. **Click Select to add the user to the list of authorized users.**

4. **Choose the user's name in the list, and assign permissions to him by clicking in the pop-up menu, as shown in Figure 13.16.**

  - **Read & Write.** This allows the user to modify and delete the files in the shared folder, as well as copy new files into it.

  - **Read Only.** This means the user can only see and open the files being shared in the folder.

  - **Write Only (Drop Box).** This allows users only to copy files into the folder; they can't see or open its contents.

13.16 Assign file-sharing permissions for a user.

You can remove folders or users by highlighting them and clicking the minus sign (–) under the appropriate window.

Enabling file-sharing protocols

Mavericks is very advanced in its sharing capabilities and can share using multiple protocols. Click Options on the right side of the File Sharing pane to see which protocols are available, as shown in Figure 13.17. Selecting the check box next to the protocols you want to use enables them, allowing you to share items over your network with other users running the same protocols.

13.17 Select the check boxes next to the protocols you want to use for sharing your files.

Table 13.8 briefly explains the protocols.

Table 13.8 File-sharing Protocols

Protocol	Description
AFP	Apple Filing Protocol is an older network protocol that Mavericks uses for talking to ancient AppleTalk networks.
SMB	Server Message Block (Microsoft Windows Network to former Windows users) allows Mavericks to work seamlessly with a Windows-centric network. Select the check boxes next to the accounts you want to enable for SMB sharing. You must type the password for each account you enable.

Sharing Printers and Scanners

When you share a printer from your Mac, you aren't physically sharing it. You're actually sharing the print queue that you created for the printer in the Printers & Scanners preferences. This means that when you share a printer, the clients who send jobs are sending them to your Mac, not directly to the printer. It's your Mac's responsibility to funnel the job to the printer after it has received it. Select the Printer Sharing check box to enable this feature for Mavericks, as shown in Figure 13.18.

13.18 Share printers you have installed on your Mac using Printer Sharing.

Sharing a printer with OS X users

It's pretty easy to share printers with other OS X users. Simply select the check box next to the printer you want to share in the Printer Sharing pane, and the shared printer is then visible to users when they go to add a printer.

Sharing a printer with Windows users

To share any printer on your Mac with other computers running Windows, follow these steps:

1. **Select the check box next to the printer you want to share in the Printer Sharing pane (refer to Figure 13.18).**

2. **Enable File Sharing by selecting the File Sharing check box in the Service list.**

3. **Click Options in the File Sharing pane.**

4. **Select the Share files and folders using SMB (Windows) check box.**

5. **Choose which accounts can access the printer, and type their passwords.**

To add the printer to a Windows PC, follow these steps:

1. **Open the Printers control panel in Windows.**

2. **Click Add Printer, and install a network printer.** See the Windows documentation for instructions on installing a network printer if you're unfamiliar with the procedure.

3. **Select the generic PostScript printer driver during the installation, even if the printer isn't a PostScript printer.** Anyone who understands printer drivers is probably slapping his forehead at this point, but here's the cool part: When the PC sends a print job, Mavericks automatically translates the PostScript code generated by the PC into a code that the printer understands. This further proves how awesome Mavericks is.

Note   A Windows user must be logged in as an Administrator account on the PC in order to install a shared printer.

Sharing scanners

Mavericks allows you to share scanners that are physically attached to your Mac with other Macs on the network. The Printers & Scanners preferences pane makes this a snap:

1. **Select the scanner you want to share from the device list in the Printers & Scanners preferences pane.** If the scanner is also a printer, click the Scan tab on the right.

2. **Select the Share this scanner on the network box.**

Note   Remember that the Mac connected to a shared printer or scanner must remain on in order for other computers to access them.

Remote Management

When you first select the Remote Management check box, you are prompted to configure what level of access other users can have to your Mac, as shown in Figure 13.19. The options are self-explanatory.

13.19 Decide what users can do after they access your Mac.

After you enable Remote Management, you can add local users to the access list. Follow these steps:

1. **Click the plus sign (+) under the access list.**

2. **Browse the list of available users, click the user you want and then click Select.**

3. **Configure the access options for this user as you did when you first enabled Remote Management.** You can change these options at any time by clicking Options.

Caution Remote Management is used only when Apple Remote Desktop is being used by a technician to access and troubleshoot your computer from a remote location. Enabling it could interfere with Screen Sharing, so Remote Management is a feature you want to enable only if you must utilize Apple Remote Desktop.

Sharing via Bluetooth

The Bluetooth Sharing feature, shown in Figure 13.20, lets you configure how your Mac interacts and shares files with other devices running the Bluetooth protocol.

13.20 Bluetooth Sharing options.

Again, first things first: You must enable Bluetooth on your Mac in order to share files with other devices running the protocol. If Bluetooth is not already on, follow these steps:

1. **Click the Bluetooth Preferences button in the Bluetooth Sharing window to open the Bluetooth preferences pane.**

2. **Select the check boxes next to On and Discoverable.**

3. **Click the Back button in the upper-left corner of the Bluetooth pane to go back to the Sharing pane.**

Table 13.9 briefly explains the options in the Bluetooth Sharing pane.

Table 13.9 Bluetooth Sharing Options

Option	Function
When receiving items	Decide how your Mac reacts when another Bluetooth device sends an item to it.
Folder for accepted items	Set the default folder for files received from other devices.
When other devices browse	Determine how your Mac reacts when another Bluetooth device wants to browse your shared folders.
Folder others can browse	Set the default folder on your Mac that users of other Bluetooth devices can browse.

343

Note

You must pair a device with your Mac in order to exchange files with it.

Using Bluetooth File Exchange

Bluetooth File Exchange is the utility you use to browse and exchange files with other Bluetooth devices. Open Bluetooth File Exchange by pressing ⌘+Shift+U in the Finder, and then double-click the Bluetooth File Exchange icon.

Send a file from your Mac

To send a file from your Mac to another Bluetooth device, follow these steps:

1. **Choose File ⇨ Send File, or press ⌘+O.**

2. **Browse your Mac for the file you want to send, highlight it, and click Send.**

3. **Select the device to which you want to send the file from the list in the Send File window, as shown in Figure 13.21, and click Send.**

13.21 Select the device to which you want to send a file from the list of available devices.

4. **The receiving device may prompt you to allow the incoming traffic from your Mac.**

   The transfer is complete after the receiving device has received all the data from your Mac.

Browse another Bluetooth device

You can browse another Bluetooth device to find files you want to copy or to send files from your Mac to a specific location on that device. Follow these steps:

1. **Choose File ⇨ Browse Device, or press ⌘+Shift+O.**

2. **Select the device you want to browse from the Browse Files list, and click Browse.**

3. **Browse the folders on the device from within the Browsing window, as shown in Figure 13.22.**

4. **If you are sending a file, open the folder on the device in which you want to place the file and click Send.** Browse your Mac for the file you want to send, select it, and click Send.

5. **If you want to get a file from the device, find and select it, and click Get.** Name the file, choose where to save it, and click Save.

6. **You may also delete a file from the remote Bluetooth device by high-lighting it and clicking Delete in the upper-right corner of the Browsing window.**

13.22 Browse the directories and folders on another Bluetooth device from your Mac.

345

How Can I Automate My Mac?

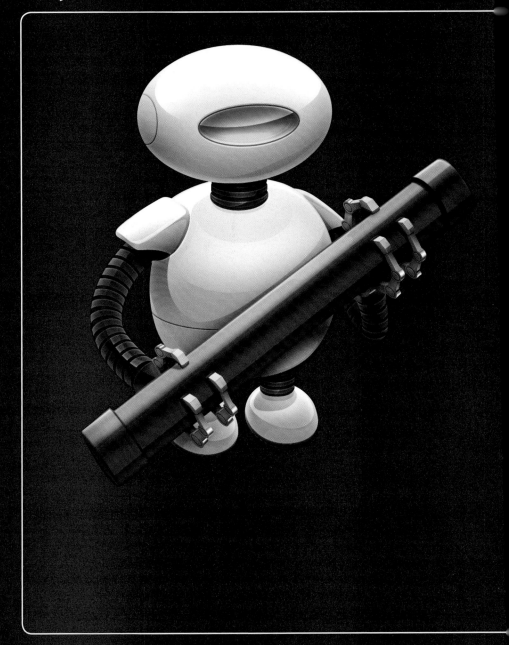

What if your Mac could perform routine (and possibly mundane) tasks for you automatically? Sounds pretty tempting, no? Mavericks is fully equipped to make your Mac life more enjoyable with a handy application called Automator. Automator uses actions (or steps) to create workflows that you can run any time to complete repetitive tasks quickly and easily. Services and AppleScripts can automate repetitive steps even further. Another way Mavericks can help with your Mac housework is with Time Machine, the OS X backup utility. Time Machine literally takes you back in time to retrieve lost data.

Getting Around in Automator

It's most helpful to know your way around Automator before trying to create workflows and actions. Open Automator by pressing ⌘+Shift+A in the Finder and double-clicking the Automator icon. After Automator opens, select a location to save or store your Automator files (this happens the first time you open Automator), and then make a selection in the Choose a type for your document window, as shown in Figure 14.1.

Choose a type for your document:

Workflow   Application   Service   Print Plugin

Folder Action   Calendar Alarm   Image Capture Plugin

Workflow

Workflows can be run from within Automator.

Open an Existing Document...   Close   Choose

14.1 Select an item from the list to move into the main Automator window.

For this example, select Workflow and click Choose. You are now in the main Automator window. Figure 14.2 points out the most important features in Automator.

Table 14.1 gives a brief description of each Automator feature.

Run the current workflow

Stop the currently running workflow

Open the Media Browser

Step through the currently running workflow

Library column

Action column

Record user events

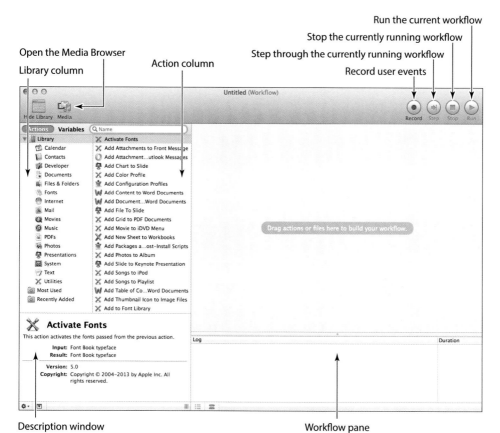

14.2 The main Automator window, where all the action takes place.

Description window

Workflow pane

Table 14.1 The Main Automator Window

Item	Description
Library column	Lists the available applications and other items from which you can choose actions.
Action column	Lists the available actions for each application or item in the Library column.
Workflow pane	Allows you to arrange actions in the order they are to be performed.
Description window	Displays a brief explanation of the selected action.
Media Browser	Lets you browse your Mac for audio, photos, or videos that you may want to include in your workflows.

Using Workflows

Workflows are groups of actions that are combined to help you accomplish a task. When you run a workflow, the actions in it are carried out in sequential order until the last action has been performed. The results, or output, of the first action become the input for the next action, and so on, until the workflow is completed.

Designing a workflow

Building a workflow from scratch is much simpler than you may think. To help you get started with Automator, I've created a new workflow, and I'll walk you through its creation step by step. First, here's what I want to do with my new workflow:

- **I want to rename images that I've saved from my camera to a folder on my desktop called New Pics using Image Capture.** My camera automatically adds IMG to the beginning of every file and then numbers them sequentially. I want to name the files a little more descriptively, and Automator is the perfect tool to accomplish this task.

- **Once renamed, I want to open my files in Preview so that I can check them out.**

- **I want my images to automatically print so that I can have a hard copy of each.**

- **I want to e-mail my new pictures to friends and family.**

As I mentioned, my camera automatically saves files with an IMG prefix, so that's the convention I use in this short tutorial. You may want to adjust the variable in Step 3 here to match the default naming conventions of your camera.

Follow these steps to begin building the workflow:

1. **Tell Automator which files you want to interact with.** Select Files & Folders from the Library column, and then drag and drop Find Finder Items into the Workflow pane, as shown in Figure 14.3.

2. **Choose Other from the Search drop-down menu, and select Desktop on the left side of the resulting window.** Click New Folder, name the folder New Pics, click Create, and then click Choose.

3. **In the criteria section, leave the All pop-up menu alone, change the Any content pop-up menu to Name, leave the contains pop-up menu alone, and finally type IMG in the text field.** This tells Automator that you are looking for files with names that start with IMG.

14.3 Adding actions to my new workflow in Automator.

4. **Tell Automator that you want to rename the items in the New Pics folder.** Select Files & Folders from the Library column, and then drag and drop Rename Finder Items into the Workflow pane beneath the Find Finder Items action. A caution window appears; click Don't Add to proceed.

5. **Choose Make Sequential from the first drop-down menu, select the new name radio button in the Add number to option, and type the name with which you want to begin each of your files in the text field.** I use dwightpix at the beginning of my picture files, as shown in Figure 14.4. This action causes Automator to replace the prefix IMG on all files with dwightpix, followed by a sequential number. However, I'm not quite finished renaming.

6. **Add the date the files were imported to my Mac to the end of the filenames.** Select Files & Folders from the Library column, and then drag and drop Rename Finder Items into the Workflow pane beneath the previous Rename Finder Items action. Click Don't Add to proceed as before. The default criteria, as shown in Figure 14.4, are appropriate for the needs of this example, so nothing needs to be changed.

14.4 Renaming and adding the date to my files in Automator.

7. **I want my renamed images to open in Preview so I can see how they look.** Select
Photos from the Library column, and then drag and drop Open Images in Preview to the
Workflow pane beneath the second Rename Finder Items action. This causes Automator
to start Preview (if it's not already running) and automatically display the new images.

Note You may notice as you drag new actions into the Workflow pane that those already
there move down a bit until the one you are dragging is beneath them. You can easily reposition actions in a workflow by simply dragging and dropping them into the
order you need.

8. **Have Automator print hard copies of the photos automatically.** Select Photos from
the Library column, and then drag and drop Print Images to the Workflow pane beneath
the Open Images in Preview action. Make any additional adjustments that you deem
necessary; for example, I chose to center and scale my images to fit the page, as shown
in Figure 14.5.

9. **Have Automator open Mail and create a new message, automatically attaching the
new images so you can simply type the recipients' addresses and click Send.** Select
Mail from the Library column, and then drag and drop New Mail Message to the

Workflow pane beneath the Print Images action. Type any items that you want automatically added to your new e-mail, such as the e-mail address or a subject, as shown in
Figure 14.5.

10. **Click Run in the upper-right corner, as shown in Figure 14.5, to run the workflow.**
    Automator performs the actions and warns you if there are any problems.

14.5 Automator automatically prints and creates a new Mail message containing the new images.

Saving a workflow

You will certainly want to save your workflows so you don't have to create them every time you
need them, which would defeat the purpose of Automator. You can save your workflows as workflows or applications. Table 14.2 gives a brief explanation of each.

Table 14.2 Different Ways to Save Your Workflows

Save As	Description
Workflow	This saves the actions you brought together as a workflow. You can then open the workflow in Automator to run or edit it.
Application	Saving a workflow as an application makes it a standalone file. Double-click to launch it as you would any other application.

To save your workflow as a new workflow or application, follow these steps:

1. **Press ⌘+S.**

2. **Give the workflow a descriptive name, and choose where to save it.**

3. **Select a format from the File Format pop-up menu.**

4. **Click Save.**

To save an existing workflow that you are modifying, press ⌘+S.

Recording Your Actions

The coolest feature in Automator for Mavericks is the ability to create custom actions based on your keyboard and mouse events. Automator can record your keyboard and mouse events and execute them as part of a workflow.

Genius

Scripters who write their own AppleScripts or developers who create their own applications will be delighted to know that they can develop their own actions specific to their needs. Xcode, which is an API (application programming interface) distributed by Apple with Mavericks, provides all the tools necessary for programmers to make unique actions.

To record your actions, you must give Automator permission to control your computer in the Security & Privacy preferences. To do so, choose Apple menu ➪ System Preferences, select Security & Privacy (unlock if necessary), go to the Privacy tab and click Accessibility from the list on the left, and then check the box next to Automator in the Allow the apps below to control your computer section.

Note

Before you start recording, make sure that your Mac is set up exactly the way it needs to be to perform the necessary actions. For example, if you are using an application as part of your action, you want to have it open before beginning to record.

To get started on your custom action, follow these steps:

1. **Open a workflow, and click Record in the upper-right corner.**

2. **Perform the steps necessary to complete your action.**

3. **Click the Stop button, shown in Figure 14.6, when you are finished.**

4. **Click Run to test your new actions.**

5. **Edit actions in the list by deleting unnecessary actions, changing the timeout setting for each action, or modifying the Playback Speed.**

14.6 Automator records your actions until you click the Stop button.

6. **Save your action as a workflow or application.**

Using Services to Perform Tasks

Services are yet another way that OS X can automate tasks and make your computing life easier. Essentially, services are Automator workflows available for you to use, depending on the type of file or item you have selected in the Finder or in an application. For example, if you right-click (or Control-click) a JPEG image in the Finder, you see services related to JPEGs at the bottom of the contextual pop-up menu, such as Set Desktop Picture or New Email with Attachment. Another example would be highlighting text in Safari; right-click (or Control-click) the highlighted text, and you can select the Add to iTunes as a Spoken Track service.

To see all the preconfigured services at your disposal in Mavericks, open the System Preferences by choosing Apple menu ⇨ System Preferences. Select Keyboard, and click Services under the Shortcuts tab, as shown in Figure 14.7.

Scrolling through the list of services, you are sure to notice that they are divided into types, such as services dedicated to pictures or text. You can enable or disable a service (that is, make it available or unavailable for a particular type of file or item) by selecting the check box next to it in the list.

Genius You can create and edit shortcuts for services. Select Services in the Shortcuts tab of the Keyboard preferences pane. Click to highlight the service for which you want to create or edit a shortcut, and then click to the right of the highlighted area to see a text field. Type the new shortcut (or edit the existing one), and it appears in the text field. Click out of the text field, and close System Preferences.

14.7 Mavericks has an extensive list of preconfigured services ready to be put to work.

Table 14.3 lists the preconfigured services built in to Mavericks. You may see other services if the application you are using provides them.

Table 14.3 Mavericks Preconfigured Services

Service Type	Function
Pictures	Capture Full Screen.
	Capture Screen using Timer.
	Capture Selection from Screen.
	Import Image.
	Set Desktop Picture.
Internet	Add to Reading List.
	Open URL.

Service Type	Function
Files and Folders	Open Selected File in TextEdit.
	New Terminal at Folder.
	New Terminal Tab at Folder.
	Encode Selected Audio Files.
	Encode Selected Video Files.
	Folder Actions Setup.
	Open.
	Reveal in Finder.
	Show Info in Finder.
	Send File to Bluetooth Device. Keyboard shortcut: ⌘+Shift+B.
Messaging	New Email to Address.
	New Email With Selection.
Searching	Look Up in Dictionary.
	Search With %WebSearchProvider@ (uses the Safari default search engine). Keyboard shortcut: ⌘+Shift+L.
	Spotlight. Keyboard shortcut: ⌘+Shift+F.
Text	Add to iTunes as a Spoken Track.
	Convert Text to Full Width.
	Convert Text to Half Width.
	Convert Text to Simplified Chinese.
	Convert Text to Traditional Chinese.
	Create Collection From Text.
	Create Font Library From Text.
	Make New Sticky Note. Keyboard shortcut: ⌘+Shift+Y.
	New TextEdit Window Containing Selection.
	Open man Page in Terminal. Keyboard shortcut: ⌘+Shift+M.
	Search man Page Index in Terminal. Keyboard shortcut: ⌘+Shift+A.
	Show Address in Google Maps.
	Summarize.
	Show Map.
Development	Compare Files.
	Compare to Master.
	Create Service.
	Create Workflow.
	Get Result of AppleScript. Keyboard shortcut: ⌘+*.
	Make New AppleScript.
	Run as AppleScript.

Discovering Time Machine

One of the Mavericks features that Apple is most proud of—and rightly so—is Time Machine. Oh, there have been backup utilities out there made by third-party companies (even a few good ones), but Apple has delivered something above and beyond in terms of simplicity and information retrieval.

Time Machine backs up your system behind the scenes: You can work while it handles its business undetected in the background. The initial backup takes quite a while, because Time Machine backs up everything on the Mac hard drive (again, it all happens in the background, so you can continue to use your Mac). After the initial backup, Time Machine continues to automatically back up your files every hour, but only those items that have changed. Because it is only backing up changed items, these backups are performed much faster.

Why it's important to back up your files

I want to take a small section of this chapter to preach the doctrine of backing up your computer. You have too many precious memories and too many important documents on your Mac to count on it lasting forever (yes, even Macs do eventually have issues, as I cover in Chapter 16). Take a few minutes out of your iLife and, perhaps, spend a few dollars on an external hard drive to get Time Machine up and going. Backing up your data is something you never regret.

Hardware requirements for Time Machine

Time Machine can back up your data to any of these four configurations:

- **A network volume, such as a file or backup server.** This is a good idea for large networks.

- **An external hard drive.** Be certain that the data capacity of the external drive is large enough to save all the data on the hard drive.

- **A USB flash drive.** Be sure the data capacity of the flash drive is large enough to save all your backup data.

- **A partition on the Mac hard drive (if the drive is, indeed, partitioned).** Partitioning a drive is the act of using a disk utility to divide a single hard drive into several sections, fooling the computer into believing that one drive is actually multiple drives. I do not recommend using this sort of configuration because if your hard drive has a problem, you lose all your data in spite of having backed it up.

The AirPort Time Capsule

Apple's AirPort Time Capsule acts as both a wireless network router (like the AirPort Extreme) and a central backup point for all Macs running Time Machine. The AirPort Time Capsule automatically backs up every file from every Mac wirelessly (or wired) and in the background, eliminating the need to connect an external drive to your Mac. This is one serious backup tool, and I highly recommend getting your hands on one. Check it out by visiting www.apple.com/airport-time-capsule/.

Setting Up a Backup Drive

There are a couple of steps necessary to get started with Time Machine: You need to format your backup drive, and then you need to tell Time Machine that it can use this drive for its backups.

Formatting a hard drive

You must format any drive you connect to your Mac before you can use it with Time Machine. To format a drive (please read the Caution before continuing this procedure), follow these steps:

Caution If this is a drive you've used before, be sure that you copy all the data from it before performing a disk format. After the formatting process has started, all data on the drive is lost forever.

1. **From within the Finder, open Disk Utility by pressing ⌘+Shift+U and then double-clicking its icon.**

2. **Connect the drive to your Mac.**

3. **Select the drive in the list on the left of the Disk Utility window.**

4. **Click the Erase tab near the top of the window, as shown in Figure 14.8.**

5. **Set the Format option to Mac OS Extended (Journaled).**

6. **Click Erase, and then click it again in the verification window.**

7. **After the formatting is finished, click Eject in the Disk Utility toolbar at the top, and disconnect the hard drive from the Mac.**

14.8 Click the Erase tab, and select the volume format to get the drive ready for Time Machine.

Configuring a backup drive for Time Machine

When you first connect an external drive (you may have to format it first) to your Mac, Time Machine detects its presence and asks if you want to use it for backups. If you say yes, Time Machine sets everything up automatically, and away you go. In many cases, this is fine; you are never bothered about it again, and Time Machine does its duty.

You may be asking why you would say no to the question, if that were the case. Well, if this is a drive you've used in the past or one that you want to partition, you may not want Time Machine hijacking it for its sole use. To manually set up a drive, follow these steps:

1. **Open the Time Machine preferences, as shown in Figure 14.9, by choosing Apple menu ⇨ System Preferences and clicking the Time Machine icon.**

2. **Click Select Backup Disk.**

3. **Choose a drive, and click Use Disk.**

4. **Time Machine begins a countdown, similar to the one shown in Figure 14.10, for when it will perform the first backup.**

5. If you want Time Machine to automatically begin backing up everything on the system, just sit back and relax. However, if you want to back up only a portion of the hard drive, click the On/Off switch on the left side of the Time Machine preferences pane to toggle the switch to Off. Next, follow the directions in the upcoming section.

14.9 The Time Machine preferences allow you to manually configure how it works.

14.10 Time Machine counting down to its first backup.

Excluding files from a backup

You may have several good reasons why you don't want Time Machine to back up every file on your Mac. For example, perhaps there isn't enough storage space on the backup drive or you simply don't want to back up all the information for each user on the computer. Whatever the reason, you need not fear, because I'm about to show you how to exclude information from your backup sessions. Follow these steps:

1. **Be sure that Time Machine is Off so it doesn't begin a backup process while you choose the files you don't want to back up.** Simply click the On/Off switch to toggle it.

2. **Click Options in the middle of the preferences pane.**

3. **Click the plus sign (+) in the lower-left corner of the Exclude these items from back-ups window.**

4. **Browse your Mac to select the folders and files that you do not want included in the backup, and click Exclude to add them to the list, as shown in Figure 14.11.** Refer to the Estimated size of full backup to see if your backup drive can store that much data.

5. **Click Save when finished.**

14.11 You can exclude files from a Time Machine backup.

Running a Backup

As mentioned, the entire backup process is handled behind the scenes, but that doesn't mean you can't check out what's going on, or even stop and restart a backup that's already in the works. Open the Time Machine preferences pane to see the progress of a backup procedure.

Performing a manual backup

You don't have to wait for Time Machine to get around to backing up your system. In fact, you can start the process right now if you want. Follow these steps:

1. **Choose Apple menu ⇨ System Preferences, and click the Time Machine icon.**

2. **Select the Show Time Machine in menu bar check box.**

3. **Be sure that Time Machine is On.**
   Toggle the On/Off switch, if necessary. If you have a volume already configured for Time Machine, you can skip this step.

4. **Click the Time Machine icon in the menu bar.**

5. **Select Back Up Now, as shown in Figure 14.12.**

14.12 Select Back Up Now to back up your information immediately.

Caution When you manually select files to back up, the preference files and other items necessary for Time Machine to completely restore your Mac if it fails may not be included in the process.

Pausing or resuming a backup

You can stop and start a backup if you need to. To pause a backup, click the Time Machine icon in the menu bar, as shown in Figure 14.12, and select Stop Backing Up. To resume a backup process, click the Time Machine icon in the menu bar, and select Back Up Now. Your backup should begin where it left off. Nothing to it!

Retrieving Information from Time Machine

Now that you know how to back up your system, it's time to learn how to retrieve that information if you ever need to do so. Let's see how to restore individual items and even an entire drive.

Restoring individual files

Time Machine lets you restore individual files and folders that you may have lost or of which you want to get previous versions. To do so, follow these steps:

1. **Open Time Machine by clicking its icon in the Dock or pressing ⌘+Shift+A, and then double-click its icon in the Applications folder.**

2. **Time Machine opens, and you see a Finder window, similar to that shown in Figure 14.13.**

3. **Use the timeline on the right side of the screen (or the arrows next to it) to navigate through time to the date the item you need was backed up.**

4. **Browse the files in the Finder window to find the item you want to retrieve.**

5. **Select the item in the Finder window, and click Restore in the bottom-right corner of the Time Machine window.** The file is zipped forward in time to today, and Time Machine closes. You have to admit that's one of the coolest things you've ever seen on a computer!

14.13 Traveling through time!

Restoring an entire drive

Time Machine lets you restore an entire drive, which, on its own, is worth the price of upgrading to Mavericks. This saves you countless hours because you don't have to reinstall the OS or all the applications you had on your system. To restore a drive, follow these steps:

1. **Connect your backup drive to the Mac.**

2. **Choose Apple menu ⇨ Restart, and then press and hold ⌘+R while your Mac restarts.**

Delete Files from Time Machine Backups

What if you want to delete, instead of restore, a file from your backed-up folders? Simple! Just follow these steps:

1. **Open Time Machine.** Use the Finder window and timeline to find the item you want to delete from the backup.

2. **Select the file or folder you want to delete.**

3. **Click the Action menu (which looks like a gear) in the Finder tool- bar, and select Delete Backup.** To get rid of all references to the item in Time Machine, select Delete All Backups.

3. Select your language from the Language Chooser, and click Continue (the arrow).

4. Perform one of the following, depending on the type of backup drive from which you are restoring your system:

   ○ If restoring from an external drive (hard drive, USB flash, and so on), select it and click Continue.

   ○ If restoring from a network drive, select it and click Connect to Remote Disk.

   ○ If restoring from a Time Capsule, select your AirPort network using the AirPort menu on the menu bar, select your Time Capsule, and click Connect to Remote Disk.

5. Type your name and password to connect to your backup drive if required, and click Connect.

6. Choose the date and time for the backup you want to restore, and follow the instructions from that point to finish the restoration process. This can take a while, but not nearly as long as starting from scratch.

How Do I Install Microsoft's Windows Operating System on My Mac?

Because Macs are equipped with Intel processors, you can install Windows on your Mac just as you would on any other Intel-based PC. If you're switching from a Windows computer to the wonderful world of Mac, having Windows installed can make the transition a little smoother. However, if you're anything like the Windows converts I know, you will find yourself running Windows less and less as you become more familiar with Mavericks.

Understanding the Boot Camp Assistant

Boot Camp is a tool provided with Mavericks that helps walk you through the process of installing Microsoft Windows on your Mac. It's a simple utility but one that performs some very big jobs, such as:

- **Partitioning your hard drive**
- **Booting from the Windows installation disc**
- **Installing drivers in Windows that you need in order to use hardware that comes with Macs, such as the built-in camera (if you have one)**

Benefits of installing Microsoft Windows

If you're a longtime Mac fan, you may be dubious about the title of this section, but former Windows users probably understand the upside of having Windows at their fingertips. Here are a few of the most obvious benefits:

- **Some companies use software that runs only in Windows.** If you work for one of those companies but are one of the smart folks who insist on having a Mac, you can have the best of both worlds.
- **Windows converts probably have lots of Windows-only software—including games—that they don't want to trash because they now have a Mac.** Boot Camp enables them to keep their software.
- **On increasingly rare occasions, you may run across a website that works only with a Windows operating system version.** Those sites are no longer off limits to Mac users.
- **Some new Mac users may have printers that work only with Windows (this is also becoming increasingly rare).** Installing Windows ensures that they won't have to chuck the printer, which can be pretty painful if you have a stockpile of consumables (such as toner and ink) tied up in the device.

What you need to install Windows

The following requirements must be met before installing Windows on your Mac:

- **At least 20GB of available space on the hard drive for the 64-bit version of Windows 7, and at least 30GB for Windows 8.**

368

- **Your Mac must have an Intel processor at least as fast as 1GHz, which is a foregone conclusion because you're running Mavericks.**

- **You must install all available firmware updates for your Mac.** Run Software Update (choose Apple menu ⇨ Software Update), or go to the Apple support website for your particular model to find any updates for your computer.

- **An external hard drive or USB flash drive.** You use one of these to install Windows support software.

- **At least 1GB of memory, which is also a foregone conclusion because you're running Mavericks.**

- **A Windows 64-bit installation disc.** You can install Windows 7 Home Premium, Professional, or Ultimate, or Windows 8 or 8 Pro. This disc must be a full-install version, not an upgrade version.

Using the Boot Camp Assistant to Install Windows

Open the Boot Camp Assistant to get started:

1. **From within the Finder, press ⌘+Shift+U to open the Utilities folder.**

2. **Double-click the icon for Boot Camp Assistant to see a window like the one shown in Figure 15.1.**

3. **Click the Open Boot Camp Help button to open Apple's official Boot Camp Installation & Setup Guide in your default web browser. You can also find a copy in PDF format in the Boot Camp folder of the Windows support files that you'll down-load later in this chapter.** This guide is necessary, believe me, so you need to either print it or gain access to it on another computer.

4. **Click Continue.**

The Select Tasks window gives you the options to install Windows and to download Apple's latest Windows support software. Select the option to install Windows, of course, and to download the support software if you haven't already done so.

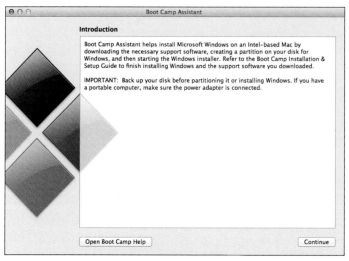

15.1 Boot Camp Assistant standing at attention.

Caution Printing the Boot Camp Help book is necessary in my opinion in order to continue with this chapter. The guide is 19 pages long and chock-full of information that you really need before continuing. To print it, click the printer icon in the upper-right corner of the browser window, select Print Book Boot Camp Help, and then print the book. If you can't print it, run or view it from the Apple support website on another computer (https://help.apple.com/bootcamp/mac/5.0/help/#).

Getting your Mac ready for Windows

Your Windows installation requires special drivers provided by Apple in order for Windows to use Mac hardware, such as the trackpad, mouse, and display. Boot Camp allows you to download the drivers, as shown in Figure 15.2. You can then save them to an external hard drive or USB flash drive (the drive must have at least 900MB of free space). You may want to find something to pass the time while the download occurs; it could take some time. By the way, the drive you're using must be formatted as MS-DOS (FAT); you can format the drive in Disk Utility if it isn't already in MS-DOS (FAT) format.

15.2 You must download special drivers for your Windows installation to successfully utilize Mac hardware.

Follow these steps:

1. **Select the Download the latest Windows support software from Apple option, and click Continue.**

2. **Boot Camp contacts Apple via the Internet and downloads the software.** Downloading the software may take quite some time, depending on the speed of your Internet connection.

3. **After the support software is downloaded, click Continue to move to the next step.**

Partitioning the hard drive

Boot Camp Assistant now wants to help you partition the Mac hard drive. Partitioning the hard drive essentially marks off a section of it and fools Mavericks into thinking your Mac has two hard drives instead of one. This partition is used exclusively for Windows, so keep this in mind when deciding how much space to allocate to it because you cannot recover that space for Mac usage.

Note

If you previously partitioned the Mac hard drive for Windows, you may see a window asking if you want to create or remove a Windows partition or start the Windows installer. To install Windows, choose to start the Windows installer and click Continue.

At this point, you need to decide how much of the Mac hard drive to allocate to Windows. There is no set number that I can recommend to you for the size; it depends entirely on your needs. Keep in mind that you also need additional space to install applications and store files. To divide the drive, click and drag the little dot between the OS X and Windows boxes to the left or right to set the size of each partition. After you've divided the drive, you can't change the partition size. The size is permanent unless you remove the partition.

If you plan to install lots of Windows applications, it might be best to click Divide Equally. This gives half of the hard drive to Windows.

Follow these steps:

1. **Set the size of your Windows partition, and click Partition.** Boot Camp Assistant checks the hard drive for any potential problems and then continues the process.

2. **Insert the Windows installation disc when prompted by Boot Camp Assistant.**

3. **Click Install. Boot Camp completes the partition of the drive, restarts your Mac, and commences the Windows installation.**

Installing Windows and support software

By now, your Mac should have booted into the Windows installer disc, which is where I pick up:

Caution If you mistakenly select the wrong partition on which to install Windows, you could potentially wipe out your OS X Mavericks installation during the steps in the next section. Be careful, particularly in Step 2, or you may run into more problems than you bargained for.

Note If you are using a MacBook Air, you need to install Windows and the Boot Camp drivers by using a compatible external drive connected directly to your computer.

1. **Follow the instructions on your computer for installing Windows.** Be sure to follow along with the Boot Camp Installation & Setup Guide you printed earlier, as well as any other documentation you may have from Microsoft.

2. **At a certain point, you are asked on which partition to install Windows.** Be certain to choose the one labeled BOOTCAMP! This is the key to your success or failure.

3. **Click the Drive options (advanced) option on the lower-right side of the window to reformat the Boot Camp partition.**

4. **Click Format, and then click OK. Click Next, and the Boot Camp partition is correctly formatted.**

5. **Continue through the on-screen prompts.** After Windows is installed, your Mac reboots into Windows.

6. **Configure Windows as you normally would, using the Windows setup options.**

7. **The Boot Camp installer program may automatically run after Windows is fully booted. If not, navigate to the drive to which you downloaded the support software and double-click the setup.exe file.** Follow the instructions on your screen, and never cancel any part of the installation! Remember to read the guide. Your Mac restarts when the installation is completed, and you can begin using Windows on your Mac (the thought still gives me a bit of a queasy feeling, I must admit).

Note If you are prompted by a message saying the software hasn't passed Windows Logo testing, click Continue Anyway.

Note When you first boot your Mac into Windows following the Boot Camp installation, you see the Boot Camp Help window. Use this resource! It has invaluable information on how to use your Mac and its hardware, such as the keyboard, with Windows software. There are some differences when using a Mac compared to using PC hardware, but nothing that you can't easily overcome by reading through a Help window.

Choosing a Startup Disk

Now that you have a Mac with two operating systems, you need to decide which one will be its default: Mavericks or Windows. You can easily select either of the two disks to be your default startup disk, and you can just as easily switch between the two.

From Windows

To select a startup disk from within Windows, follow these steps:

1. **Click the Start menu, and select Control Panel.**

2. **Double-click the Boot Camp icon.**

3. **Under the Startup Disk tab shown in Figure 15.3, select the operating system to which you want to boot by default, and then click OK.** Click Restart if you want to reboot right now.

15.4 The Boot Camp Control Panel in Windows.

From Mavericks

To select a startup disk from within Mavericks, follow these steps:

1. **Choose Apple menu ⇨ System Preferences.**

2. **Click the Startup Disk icon.**

3. **Select the operating system that you want to be your default from the list, as shown in Figure 15.4.** Close the System Preferences unless you want to reboot the Mac now—in which case, click Restart.

15.4 Select the disk partition to which you want your Mac to boot by default.

Removing Windows from Your Mac

If you get tired of Microsoft's operating system taking up a large chunk of your hard drive, you may want to safely remove it. Easy enough:

1. **Open the Boot Camp Assistant by pressing ⌘+Shift+U from within the Finder and double-clicking its icon.**

2. **Click Continue.**

3. **Select Remove Windows, and then click Continue.**

4. **Click Restore to completely wipe out your Windows partition, and restore the Mac hard drive to a single partition.**

Caution   When you wipe out your Windows partition, all your Windows content is permanently lost. If you have important files or documents on the Windows side, back these up before restoring the Mac hard drive.

Alternative Methods for Running Windows on Your Mac

You may be happy to know that you can install and run Windows (and other operating systems) on your Mac in a way that doesn't require partitioning a section of the hard drive. My biggest beef with the Boot Camp method is that the partition you create for Windows has a fixed size; it doesn't increase or decrease, which can waste lots of space if you don't use the entire partition. On the other hand, it may not be large enough to contain all your data. My second beef is that I'm limited to installing Windows and not alternative operating systems like Linux. Thankfully for folks like me, there is another way: virtualization.

Virtualization is a method that allows you to install multiple Intel-capable operating systems on your Mac at the same time (as many as your hard or external drive can hold) and run them simultaneously within OS X. Several software packages can help you achieve this dream, some of which I mention here. These applications help you create virtual machines on which you can install operating systems. These virtual machines access the computer hardware and run at almost native speeds. Another great upside to virtual machines is that they can be made to expand or contract based on the amount of data they contain, which prevents you from wasting hard drive space.

Note I do not endorse any one of the upcoming software titles over another. All three have their pros and cons, and one may suit me better than it suits you. The two titles that you have to buy offer free trials you can download. The third option is completely free to try and use, so there's no reason not to give each one a go and determine which you like best.

Parallels Desktop for Mac

Parallels Desktop for Mac from Parallels was the first viable virtualization option for Macs with Intel processors. The latest release (as of this writing), version 8, introduced many new and powerful features, such as improved battery life for laptops, up to 1GB of video memory, faster startup and shutdown for Windows, improved data security, better compatibility for Linux systems, enhanced 3D performance, and support for Surround Sound 7.1. All this allows you to simultaneously run multiple virtual machines even more efficiently than before, as shown in Figure 15.5.

For more information or to download a trial copy of Parallels Desktop for Mac, visit www.parallels. com/products/desktop.

15.5 Parallels Desktop for Mac in action.

VMWare Fusion

VMWare Fusion, shown in Figure 15.6, is the brainchild of VMWare, one of the most trusted virtual- ization applications in the PC and Linux markets for years. In 2007, VMWare decided it was time to apply its knowledge of virtualization to the Mac platform, and a wonderful competition (from the consumer's standpoint) began with Parallels. This resulted in both companies trying to outdo each other by making great leaps in software capabilities. This competition caused VMWare to gain a significant chunk of ground technology-wise between versions 1 and 2, and to go even further with versions 3, 4, and 5 (the latest version as of this writing).

Features such as Unity View (the ability to run Windows programs as if they were native Mac applications) and Data Sharing (you can drag and drop files between operating system windows) make VMWare a viable option for anyone who needs to run multiple operating systems on her Mac. To learn more about VMWare Fusion or to download a trial copy, visit http://vmware.com/products/fusion.

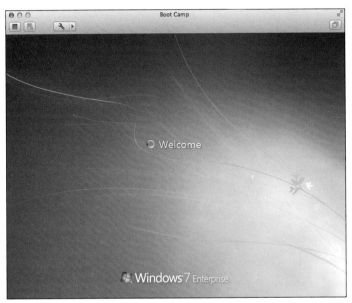

15.6 VMWare Fusion booting Windows 7 within OS X.

VirtualBox

If you want to use Parallels Desktop for Mac or VMWare Fusion, you have to shell out some cash. Don't have any to spare? Don't worry; you're not completely without options. As a matter of fact, Oracle has provided you with a very nice option that not only supports multiple operating systems but is also free: VirtualBox, shown in Figure 15.7. VirtualBox doesn't have all the bells and whistles that accompany the previously mentioned apps, but if you simply need the ability to run Windows, Linux, or another Intel-based operating system within OS X, VirtualBox can get the job done. Check it out at http://www.virtualbox.org.

15.7 VirtualBox running Windows 7 within OS X.

Do You Have Any Troubleshooting Tips?

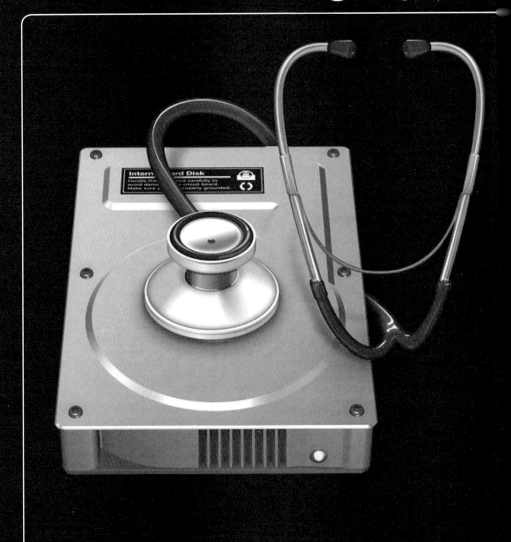

Macs have a well-earned reputation for being as rock-solid reliable as it gets in the tech realm, but nothing, not even Cupertino engineering, lasts forever. Things happen, and the information in this chapter can point you to the help you need, if not lend a hand in resolving the issue altogether.

Start Problem Solving

I realize that if you're reading this book, you are most likely a savvy computer user and that you may already be beyond the basics. However, by nature, any troubleshooting chapter must begin with the basics, so let's dive right in.

Restarting your Mac

Most issues with a Mac are fairly simple to resolve. As a matter of fact, the resolution to most problems is to simply restart your Mac.

Restarting is something that most computer users have to do at some point, and it's always the first recourse when you notice quirky things beginning to happen. To restart your Mac, choose Apple menu ⇨ Restart. Mavericks asks if you're sure you want to restart, as shown in Figure 16.1. Click Restart to reboot the computer.

16.1 Click Restart to perform the oldest troubleshooting trick in the book.

I hope that your woes are gone after your Mac boots back up; if not, the rest of this chapter should help you get to the heart of the matter.

Backing up your Mac

Before continuing any further, I cannot stress enough the importance of backing up your information. Maintaining a backup of your files prevents you from losing them if something catastrophic happens to your Mac, not to mention the peace of mind it fosters. I learned the hard way, by losing items that were precious to me, that files should always be backed up. I hope in the following section to prevent you from experiencing the same nightmare I did.

Chapter 14 covers the use of Time Machine for keeping an external hard drive continuously updated with backed-up files. Although Time Machine is an easy way to keep your backups current, it's not the only way you can back up your Mac. You can also do one of the following to keep things current:

- **Purchase backup software.** Why lay down your hard-earned cash for a backup application when you have Time Machine as part of Mavericks? Time Machine is a great utility, but it may not be enough (or offer enough control) for some users. That's where third-party applications come in. Here are a few I've personally used:

- **Carbon Copy Cloner by Bombich Software.** This one has been a tried-and-true app for a very long time on the Mac platform. Carbon Copy Cloner can even create a bootable backup of your system, which is quite a keen feature. Learn more about CCC at www.bombich.com/index.html.

- **Retrospect.** This is another backup stalwart that I remember using as far back as Mac OS 8. Download a trial, and even find a comparison to Time Machine, at www.retrospect.com/en/products/mac.

- **MacKeeper.** MacKeeper is a system utility that also provides a great backup utility as part of its total package. This app is the newest of the three I mention here, but it's already garnering wide attention and support for its capabilities. You can download MacKeeper for a 15-day free trial. Give it a look at http://mackeeper.zeobit.com.

- **Back up manually (the old-fashioned way).** Simply attach an external hard drive, install an internal drive (if you have a Mac Pro this is a cinch), use a flash drive, or connect to another computer (directly or via a wired or wireless network), and then drag and drop your files to that device.

Make Sure You Are Up to Date

A bug in your operating system or application software could be causing your problems. Check to be sure that you are using the latest versions of Mac firmware and Mavericks by running Software Update. To do so, choose Apple menu ⇨ Software Update. If Software Update finds new versions of your firmware or software, install them and see if this resolves your issues.

If the problems you are experiencing are related to a particular application, visit the website of the application developer to see if any updates to the software are available or if there are any known issues with it. Table 16.1 lists the web addresses of some of the most popular Apple software vendors and a list of their more popular products.

Table 16.1 Third-Party Apple Software Vendors

Company	Popular Applications	Website
Adobe	Photoshop, InDesign, Illustrator, Acrobat	http://helpx.adobe.com/support/
Quark	QuarkXPress	http://support.quark.com
Microsoft	Word, Excel, PowerPoint, Outlook	www.microsoft.com/mac/
Mozilla	Firefox, Thunderbird	http://support.mozilla.org/en-US/home
Evernote	Evernote	http://evernote.com/contact/support/

continued

Table 16.1 continued

Company	Popular Applications	Website
Intego	VirusBarrier, FileGuard	http://support.intego.com/home
Intuit	TurboTax, Quicken, QuickBooks	http://smallbusiness.intuit.com/small-business/support/index.jsp
FileMaker	FileMaker Pro, Bento	www.filemaker.com/support/index.html
Roxio	Toast, Popcorn	http://corel.force.com/roxio?lang=en

Startup Issues

When your Mac won't start, it's pretty scary. I won't insult your intelligence by telling you not to worry, but most of the time this can be solved with a few quick-and-easy steps. If you told me you had startup issues, the first question I would ask is if the Mac literally won't power up, or if it is getting hung up in the boot process. Let's take it from there.

Your Mac won't power up

Here are a few questions and tips to try if your Mac simply won't power up:

- **Is the power cable connected?**

- **Does the power outlet you are connected to work with other devices?**

- **If you are using a laptop, is the power adapter connected or are you running off the battery?** If so, is the battery charged? Does the Mac work with the power adapter connected?

- **Is the Mac powering up, but the display won't come on?** If so, you could have a bad display. Try connecting another display to your Mac to determine if that is the issue. If a new display doesn't work, or if your display works with another computer, the problem could be your Mac's video card.

- **Have you added any devices (such as an external hard drive) or parts (such as memory) to your Mac, either internally or externally?** If so, remove or reconnect the device or part, and try to reboot. You may have a defective device, cable, or part.

- **If all else fails, try to reset the System Management Controller (SMC).** You can reset the SMC in three ways, depending on the model of your Mac:

  - **Mac Pro, iMac, and Mac mini.** Shut down the computer and remove all its cables (mouse, keyboard, power cord, and so on). After waiting at least 15 seconds, reconnect only the power cable, mouse, and keyboard (in that order), and then push the power button.

- **MacBook (excluding the Late 2009 model) and MacBook Pro (excluding the Early 2009 model).** Remove the battery and unplug the power adapter if it is connected. Hold the power button down for at least 5 seconds and release. Install the battery, connect the power adapter, and then press the power button.

- **MacBook Air, MacBook (Late 2009 model only), and MacBook Pro (Early 2009 model only).** Connect the power adapter to the computer. While holding down the Shift, Option, and Control keys on the left side of the keyboard, press the power button once. Wait at least 5 seconds before pushing the power button again to turn on the computer.

Genius You may be wondering how to determine the model of Mac that you're using, and you can find out in a couple of simple ways. If you still have the original packaging for your Mac, you can use the information at this site to help you determine your model: http://support.apple.com/kb/HT1758. You can also check the model by typing your Mac's serial number into the field provided at https://selfsolve.apple.com/agreementWarrantyDynamic.do (you'll also see a link there to help you find your serial number, if needed).

Your Mac hangs at startup

It can be even more maddening if you're able to start up your Mac but unable to boot into OS X. All sorts of things may occur: You may see a folder with a blinking question mark, the screen may be stuck at the gray Apple logo with the spinning gear, a blue screen may appear but nothing happens past that point, and so on. These issues may be resolved by one of the following steps:

- **Force your Mac to restart.** Hold down the power button for several seconds until the Mac turns off. Restart and see if it boots normally.

- **Reset the parameter RAM (PRAM).** This is also known as zapping the PRAM. Mavericks stores information about your Mac in the PRAM, such as speaker volume levels, time zone and display settings, and so on. Restart your Mac and immediately press ⌘+Option+P+R simultaneously. Continue to hold down all four keys until you hear the Mac startup sound at least twice (wait for three, just for good measure). Release the keys after the second or third startup sound, and hopefully you can start up normally. You may need to set your settings back to what they were before resetting the PRAM.

- **Boot your Mac in Safe Mode.** Hold down the Shift key immediately after the startup sound. Don't let go until you see the gray Apple logo. Booting in Safe Mode (this takes a long time, so don't worry if you have to wait a while) causes your Mac to delete several cache files that may be corrupt, causing problems with your Mac. Reboot normally to see if this resolves your issues.

- **Boot your Mac into recovery mode.** Restart the Mac, immediately begin holding down the ⌘ and R keys, and let go of the keys after you see the white screen with the gray Apple logo. After the Mac is booted up, select Disk Utility from the Utilities menu, click your hard drive icon in the left column of the list, and click Repair Disk in the lower-right corner of the window. After the repair is completed, reboot your Mac to see if it starts normally.

If you still can't start up your Mac at this point, it's time to take some drastic measures. Contact Apple technical support, because your Mac may need a bit more hands-on expertise.

Handy startup keyboard shortcuts

Apple has developed a toolbox of keyboard shortcuts that allow you not only to boot up your Mac but also to perform specific tasks, such as choosing a different startup drive. Table 16.2 lists the shortcut key combinations and the tasks they facilitate.

Table 16.2 Startup Keyboard Shortcuts

Task	Shortcut
Start up from a disc	Insert the disc into the Mac optical drive, and press C until the disc begins to boot.
Choose a startup drive	Press and hold Option as soon as you hear the startup sound. Release the button after you see available startup drives. Select the drive from which you want to boot.
Start in Safe Mode	Press the Shift key as soon as you hear the startup sound. Release it after you see the spinning gear under the gray Apple logo.
Start up in Target Disk mode	Press and hold T immediately after the startup sound. Release it when you see the FireWire logo on your screen.
Zap the PRAM	Press and hold ⌘+Option+P+R immediately at startup before you hear the startup sound. Release the keys after you hear the third startup sound.
Start in Single User mode	Press ⌘+S immediately after the startup sound. You may release the keys after you see the command-line screen.
Start in verbose mode	Press and hold ⌘+V immediately after the startup sound to see detailed messages during the boot process.
Eject a disc at startup	Hold down the mouse button or the eject button on your keyboard at startup. This is particularly useful if you have an optical disc that just won't eject via conventional means.

Isolating Software Trouble

Let's say you're typing away in your favorite word processor and you suddenly see the wait cursor, known fondly as the Spinning Wheel of Death. The application crashes, and you lose about an hour's worth of work because you forgot to save your document. Or perhaps you are making a bank transaction in your favorite web browser when it freezes and you find out that your transaction was lost in the process. What do you do if you have an application that just won't behave? Here are some questions and tips for troubleshooting a software issue:

- **Have you installed the latest updates for your software?** If not, visit the website of the application developer and see if updates are available.

- **Did the issue occur only after you installed an update (either for an application or OS X)?** Check with the application developer for any known issues with the update or to explain the issue you're experiencing.

- **Do you experience problems with only one document?** There may be an element in that particular document, such as a font or graphic, that is corrupted and causing the issue. Try creating a new document, copy and paste elements from the old document into the new one, and see if the issue is resolved.

- **Do you get a specific error message?** If so, consult the application documentation or the manufacturer's website for help interpreting the message.

- **Is the issue related to a software/hardware combination (such as a certain scanner or camera) with a particular application?** For example, if you have a problem with Image Capture crashing when you try to import images from your camera, check to see if you can import images with a different application. If other applications also have this issue, see if another camera works. If other applications do not exhibit the problem, it's quite likely that the single misbehaving application is the culprit.

- **Discard the application's preferences files.** Consult the application documentation or contact the manufacturer to find out where the application stores its preferences in Mavericks. When you restart the application, new preference files are created. You may need to check your preferences to make sure they are set the way you want them to be. If you need to go to the Library folder, press the Option key, click the Go menu, and select Library to open a Finder window in the Library folder.

- **Is the application frozen?** If so, force it to quit by pressing ⌘+Option+Esc. Select the offending application from the list in the Force Quit Applications window, and click Force Quit.

Unfortunately, if the issue isn't cleared up by now, you may need to reinstall the application. Again, be sure to contact the manufacturer or read the documentation included with the application to see if you need to follow any special instructions to properly reinstall it.

Utilizing the root account

Sometimes the problem is that something has become corrupted in your user account. To find out, log in to a different account and see if the issue persists. I prefer to use the root account, which gives you complete control over the Mac. Follow these steps:

1. **Open Directory Utility, which is found in the System/Library/CoreServices folder.**

2. **Click the Services icon in the upper-left corner, and then click the lock icon in the lower-left corner, as shown in Figure 16.2.** Type your username and password when prompted, and click the Modify Configuration button.

16.2 Click the lock to make changes to the Directory Utility.

3. **Choose Edit ➪ Enable Root User to enable the root account.**

4. **Type the root account password twice to confirm it.** Do not forget this password!

5. **Quit Directory Utility.**

6. **Log out of the account you are currently using.**

7. **In the login window, click Other.**

8. **Type** root **for the username and then type the password you assigned to the root account in Step 4.**

9. **Press the Return key to log in to the root account.**

10. **Test your issue while logged in as root.** If the symptom persists, it is a system-wide problem. If the issue does not present itself while logged in as root, you've isolated the problem to the account you were previously using.

11. **For security, go back into the Directory Utility and disable the root account when your testing is complete.**

Deleting preference files

Most applications installed on a Mac create preference files somewhere on the system. These files tell the application how it should behave, what customizations have been made, what passwords may be necessary for someone to use it, and lots of other information it may need to function properly. If these preference files (there may be more than one, depending on the application) have been corrupted, your application may engage in some very odd behavior. In fact, it may not start up at all. If this is the case:

1. **Contact the developer of the application to find out what preference files are used by the app and where you can find them on your Mac.**

2. **Find the preference files and delete them.**

3. **Reopen the offending application, and the preference file(s) will be correctly rebuilt.**

Killing a process

If your Mac is super-sluggish, an errant application may be hogging all the memory. When this happens, you could restart your Mac to effectively kill all processes and start over. If you have other tasks running that you need to leave alone, Apple has made Activity Monitor for just such occasions.

To find and stop a memory-hogging process via Activity Monitor, follow these steps:

1. **From the Finder, press ⌘+Shift+U to open the Utilities folder.**

2. **Double-click the icon for Activity Monitor.**

3. **Browse through the processes list, as shown in Figure 16.3, and see whether any processes are using a large percentage of the computer's cycles.** To see the percentage being used by each process, look under the % CPU heading. You can click the % CPU heading to arrange the processes by the highest percentages.

4. **Highlight the offending process, and click the Force a process to quit button (looks like a stop sign and is found in the upper-left corner of the window) to stop it in its tracks.**

16.3 Activity Monitor keeps up with all the processes running on your Mac.

Correcting permissions issues

Every file in OS X has a set of permissions assigned to it. These tell Mavericks exactly who can access the file and how he can use it. Sometimes these permissions can get a little out of sorts and need to be repaired in order for your Mac to function in its normally spectacular way. Here are some symptoms to look for:

- **You are unable to empty a file from the Trash.**
- **An application can be launched only by one user account even though it is installed for use on all accounts.**
- **You cannot open a document that you know you should be able to open.**
- **The Finder restarts when you are trying to change permissions for a file.**

- You are unable to open folders on your Mac (or the network) to which you are supposed to have access.

- An application crashes when you try to print from it.

Several other issues may be related to permissions problems as well, but these are the most common. Repairing permissions is, thankfully, an easy task to accomplish. Follow these steps:

1. **In the Finder, open Disk Utility by pressing ⌘+Shift+U and double-clicking its icon.**

2. **Select the drive that contains the files with the permissions issues.**

3. **Click Repair Disk Permissions in the lower-left corner of the First Aid tab.** The process of repairing the permissions begins, as shown in Figure 16.4.

16.4 Restore permissions to their proper states.

Note You can also run Disk Utility from within Mavericks's recovery mode. To boot a Mac into recovery mode, restart the Mac, immediately begin holding down the ⌘ and R keys, and release the keys after you see the white screen with the gray Apple logo. Once in recovery mode, choose Utilities ⇨ Disk Utility and run the repair as described in the previous steps.

When All Else Fails—Reinstall

If you've tried everything suggested in this chapter (and you may have dug further into the issues than this book does) and your Mac still doesn't work properly, it's time to completely back up and reinstall Mavericks. See Chapter 14 for help on backing up your system and Chapter 1 for instructions on installing Mavericks over an existing copy of OS X.

Note If you aren't comfortable reinstalling Mavericks without taking a few more stabs at resolving the issue (and you live in the United States), give Apple Technical Support a call at 1-800-APL-CARE (1-800-275-2273). If you live outside the United States, visit the Apple Technical Support contacts website to find support numbers for your country: www.apple.com/support/contact/.

Appendix A

Mac Online Resources

The Internet is an awesome tool for finding more information regarding OS X and all other things Mac. The plethora of sites dedicated to Macs can keep you up to date with the latest Mac news, software updates, issues experienced by other users, help with troubleshooting, and the most recent rumors, as well as the latest, greatest tips and tricks for squeezing all the juicy goodness you can get out of OS X.

Official Apple Sites

The Apple site should be the first stop for any self-respecting Mac user on his or her quest for more information. Here are some helpful links to the most important sections of the site:

www.apple.com/mac/

This is the portal to all things Mac-related on the Apple site. From here, you can check out the latest hardware and software Apple has to offer.

www.apple.com/osx/

This is the Apple OS X site, solely dedicated to the best operating system on earth.

www.apple.com/downloads/

Visit this site to find all the latest software downloads from Apple and the Mac community.

www.apple.com/support/

The Mother of Mac Support Sites; this is where you should go first when troubleshooting an issue with your Mac.

www.apple.com/itunes/

Need to get your groove on? This site takes you to iTunes and iPod nirvana.

https://discussions.apple.com

This site is where you can connect with other Mac users about issues, tips, and all the neatest tricks regarding your Apple hardware or software.

www.apple.com/usergroups/

Would you like to join up with other local Mac users to discuss all things Mac? If so, then a Mac User Group is right up your alley. Go here to find the Mac User Group in your area and get involved.

http://store.apple.com/

This is your one-stop Apple shop, where you can buy all things Apple and many others that are Apple related.

www.apple.com/why-mac/compare

Are you having a difficult time deciding which new Mac you want to use with Mavericks? If so, this site gives a very nice head-to-head comparison of Apple's latest personal computer offerings.

http://support.apple.com/specs/

This is, hands down, the best site for finding specifications for almost any Apple product.

www.apple.com/findouthow/mac/

OS X Mavericks Portable Genius is the first place you should go for help and information regarding OS X. However, if you find yourself without this preferred resource, you can go to this site for help with Mac basics.

www.apple.com/icloud/

Apple's iCloud site explains what iCloud is and how you can use it to simplify the synchronization of your information across multiple devices.

www.apple.com/compare-wifi-models/

Because you are running Mavericks on your Mac, it no doubt has an AirPort card installed, allowing you to connect to a network wirelessly. If you need to buy a wireless router, you might consider one from Apple. This site gives you the information you need to decide which product may be best for your needs.

http://training.apple.com/#certification

If you find you want to delve even more deeply into the whole Mac experience, certification by Apple may just fit the bill. This site lists the kinds of certification available, what courses you can take to achieve your goals, and where to find classes.

More Mac Sites

The web is packed with third-party sites catering to the needs of Mac users. Here are a few of my favorites, in no particular order.

www.macworld.com

You can find all sorts of Mac stuff here, from how-to articles to reviews of the newest products. It is the premier Mac news and reviews site.

www.appleinsider.com

Rumors are a part of life for many Mac fans, and this site relays all the online gossip regarding Apple's latest and greatest offerings.

www.macintouch.com

One of my favorites since the 1990s (I'm dating myself a bit), this is a great source for Mac news and reader reviews.

www.macnn.com

News, podcasts, reviews, blogs, and forums can be found on this Mac news site.

http://hints.macworld.com

Formerly www.macosxhints.com, this site is great for OS X tips and tricks, from the simplest to the most difficult to implement.

www.microsoft.com/mac

Find all the latest updates for your Microsoft Office applications and learn how to better use those with which you currently work.

http://mactimeline.com/

A great history of Apple updates and when they were offered to users, this site benefits the nerdiest of Mac users (obviously, including myself), but I've included it for all Mac nerds-to-be as well.

http://macscripter.net/

Everything you want to know about scripting for your Mac, and more! AppleScript and Automator are favored topics on this forum.

http://reviews.cnet.com/macfixit

This is a great site for learning about Mac hardware, how to solve hardware issues, and where to find tutorials about how things work.

http://macrumors.com

Another of the great rumor sites, this one has been in my bookmarks since the days of Mac OS 8.

http://download.cnet.com/mac

Find the latest versions of your favorite third-party software, as well as offerings from the best Mac developers around.

http://db.tidbits.com

This is another tried-and-true (and old) site that faithfully caters to the news and tips needs of Mac users.

Appendix B

Mac Shortcut Keys

The keyboard can be quite an efficient tool for quickly executing tasks on your Mac, and this section lists some of the more common keyboard shortcuts. Keyboard shortcuts can save your mouse or trackpad oodles of mileage, as well as speeding up nearly every job you'll tackle on your trusty Mac.

Finder Shortcuts

Use the shortcuts in Table B.1 to switch Finder window views, open a new Finder window, eject a disc, duplicate files and folders, maneuver through the Finder sidebar, and manage your Trash.

Table B.1 Finder Shortcuts

Shortcut	Description
⌘+A	Select all items in the current window.
⌘+D	Duplicate the selected item.
⌘+E	Eject the current disc.
⌘+F	Display the Find dialog.
⌘+I	Open the Get Info window for the selected item.
⌘+J	Show the View options.
⌘+L	Create an alias for the selected item.
⌘+N	Open a new Finder window.
⌘+O	Open the selected item.
⌘+R	Show the original item for the current alias.
⌘+T	Open a new Finder tab.

continued

Table B.1 continued

Web site	Description
⌘+W	Close the current Finder window.
Shift+⌘+W	Close the current Finder window (when using tabs).
⌘+Delete	Move the selected item to the Trash.
⌘+1	Switch the active window to Icons view.
⌘+2	Switch the active window to List Flow view.
⌘+3	Switch the active window to Columns view.
⌘+4	Switch the active window to Cover Flow view.
Shift+⌘+A	Go to the Applications folder.
Shift+⌘+C	Go to the Computer folder.
Shift+⌘+D	Go to the Desktop folder.
Shift+⌘+G	Display the Go to Folder dialog.
Shift+⌘+H	Go to the Home folder.
Shift+⌘+K	Go to the Network folder.
Shift+⌘+N	Create a new folder in the current Finder window.
Shift+⌘+U	Go to the Utilities folder.
Shift+⌘+Delete	Empty the Trash (with the confirmation dialog).
Option+Shift+⌘+Delete	Empty the Trash (without the confirmation dialog).
Option+⌘+N	Create a new Smart Folder in the current Finder window.
Option+⌘+W	Close all open Finder windows.

Application Shortcuts

Table B.2 shows you how to cycle through the current application's icons, how to open an application's preferences, and how to maneuver through windows without resorting to your mouse.

Table B.2 Application Shortcuts

Shortcut	Description
⌘+Tab	Cycle forward through active application icons with each press of the Tab key; release ⌘ to switch to the selected application.
⌘+,	Open the current application's preferences.

Shortcut	Description
⌘+H	Hide the current application.
⌘+`	Cycle forward through the current application's open windows.
Shift+⌘+`	Cycle backward through the current application's open windows.
Shift+⌘+Tab	Cycle backward through active application icons with each press of the Tab key; release Shift and ⌘ to switch to the selected application.
⌘+M	Minimize the current window to the Dock.
⌘+Q	Quit the current application.
Option+⌘+H	Hide all applications except the current one.
Option+⌘+M	Minimize all windows in the active application to the Dock.
Option+⌘+Esc	Display the Force Quit Applications window.

Startup Shortcuts

Table B.3 details shortcuts you can use for alternate booting techniques.

Table B.3 Startup Shortcuts

Shortcut	Description
C	Press and hold to boot from the inserted CD or DVD.
T	Press and hold to invoke FireWire Target Disk mode.
N	Press and hold to start up from the default NetBoot disk image.
Option	Press and hold to display the Startup Manager where you can select a startup drive.
⌘+.	Open the optical drive when you are in the Startup Manager.
Mouse button	Press and hold to eject any removable discs.
⌘+Option+P+R	Press and hold to reset your Mac's parameter RAM.
⌘+S	Press and hold to start up in single user mode.
⌘+V	Press and hold to see detailed status messages during the boot process.
Left Shift key	Hold down as soon as you see the progress indicator (which looks like a spinning gear) to prevent automatic login.
Shift	Press and hold as soon as you hear the startup sound and release as soon as you see the progress indicator to boot into Safe Mode.
Shift	Press and hold immediately after clicking the Log In button to keep Finder windows and login items from opening when you log in.

Restart and Shutdown Shortcuts

Table B.4 gives you some different options for the various dialogs you see when you restart or shut down your Mac.

Table B.4 Restart and Shutdown Shortcuts

Shortcut	Description
Control+Eject	Display the Restart/Sleep/Shut Down confirmation dialog.
Power	Press and hold to display the Restart/Sleep/Shut Down confirmation dialog, or quickly press to blank the screen and lock the account you're logged in to.
Shift+⌘+Q	Log out (with confirmation dialog).
Option+Shift+⌘+Q	Log out (without confirmation dialog).
Option+⌘+Eject	Put your Mac into Sleep mode (without confirmation dialog).
Control+⌘+Eject	Restart your Mac (without confirmation dialog) with the option to save changes in open documents.
Control+Option+⌘+Eject	Shut down your Mac (without confirmation dialog) with the option to save changes in open documents).
Control+⌘+Power	Force your Mac to restart (without confirmation dialog) without the option to save changes in open documents.
Power	Press and hold to force your Mac to shut down (without confirmation dialog) without the option to save changes in open documents.

Safari Shortcuts

Table B.5 details the shortcuts you can use to maneuver through Safari windows, manage your bookmarks, send e-mail messages, and perform Google searches.

Table B.5 Safari Shortcuts

Shortcut	Description
⌘+I	E-mail the contents of the current page.
⌘+L	Select the Address bar text.
⌘+N	Open a new window.
⌘+O	Display the Open dialog for opening a file.
⌘+R	Reload the current page.
⌘+T	Open a new tab.
⌘+W	Close the current tab if using tabbed browsing, or close the current window if not using tabs.

Shortcut	Description
Option+⌘+W	Close all windows when not using tabs.
Option+Shift+⌘+W	Close all windows when using tabs.
Shift+⌘+W	Close the currently active window when using tabs.
Option+⌘+B	Open the Bookmark dialog.
⌘+n	Open the nth item (where n is a number between 1 and 9) on the Bookmarks bar.
⌘+}	Select the next tab.
⌘+{	Select the previous tab.
⌘+.	Stop loading the current page.
⌘++	Make the text bigger on the current page.
⌘+0	Make the text normal size on the current page.
⌘+-	Make the text smaller on the current page.
⌘+[	Navigate backward.
⌘+]	Navigate forward.
Shift+⌘+H	Navigate to the home page.
Shift+⌘+T	Toggle the Tab bar on and off (works only if you have one tab open).
Shift+⌘+W	Close the current window.
Shift+⌘+I	E-mail a link to the current page.
Shift+⌘+F	Run a Google search on the selected text.
⌘+Return	Open the Address bar URL in a background tab (you must select the URL in the Address bar for this command to work).
Shift+⌘+Return	Open the Address bar URL in a foreground tab (you must select the URL in the Address bar for this command to work).
Shift+⌘	Click a link to open it in a foreground tab.
⌘	Click a link to open it in a background tab.
Option+⌘	Click a link to open it in a background window.
Shift+Option+⌘	Click a link to open it in a foreground window.
Shift+⌘+D	Add the current page to Bookmarks (without the Bookmark dialog).
Option+⌘+B	Display the Bookmarks window.
Option+⌘+L	Display the Downloads window if there are downloads in the list.
Option+⌘+A	Open the Activity window (the Develop menu must be enabled to use this shortcut).
Option+⌘+Return	Open the Address bar URL in a background window.
Shift+Option+⌘+Return	Open the Address bar URL in a foreground window.

Miscellaneous Shortcuts

Use the shortcuts in Table B.6 to cut, copy, paste, undo recent actions, manage the dock, and capture screenshots.

Table B.6 Miscellaneous Shortcuts

Shortcut	Description
⌘+X	Cut the selected objects or data.
⌘+C	Copy the selected objects or data.
⌘+V	Paste the most recently cut or copied objects or data.
⌘+Z	Undo the most recent action.
F12 or Eject	Press and hold to eject an inserted disc (which button to use depends on your keyboard).
Fn+Control+F2	Give keyboard control to the menu bar.
Fn+Control+F3	Give keyboard control to the Dock.
Option+⌘+D	Toggle Dock hiding on and off.
Option+Volume up/down/ mute	Display the Sound preferences.
Option+Brightness up/down	Display the Display preferences.
Shift+⌘+3	Capture an image of the screen.
Shift+⌘+4	Drag the mouse to capture an image of the selected area of the screen.
Shift+⌘+4	Press spacebar and then click an object to capture an image of it.

Glossary

access point A network device that allows two or more Macs to connect over a wireless network.

Contacts Application for maintaining lists of personal contacts and their pertinent information, such as phone numbers, e-mail and street addresses, and relevant web pages.

administrator A powerful user account that has the ability to make permanent changes to the Mac operating system, including (but not limited to) creating and deleting other users or administrators, installing software for system-wide use, installing device drivers, and so on.

AFP (Apple Filing Protocol) A network protocol used to share files and network services among Mac computers.

AirDrop A feature that allows incredibly simple drag-and-drop file sharing with other Macs running AirDrop. Click the AirDrop icon in a Finder window sidebar, find the computer with which you want to share your files, and then drag and drop your file onto the computer name or icon. The file is automatically copied to the recipient's Downloads folder.

AirPort Apple's range of wireless networking products. AirPort uses the industry standard 802.11 protocol.

Apple menu Home to a few key commands, such as Software Update and System Preferences. This menu also includes Sleep, Restart, Shut Down, and Log Out commands. See also *application menu, menu bar, menu extras.*

AppleTalk An easy-to-use networking protocol developed by Apple for communication among computers, servers, printers, and other devices running the protocol.

application Software designed with a specific purpose in mind (such as word processors, web browsers, e-mail clients, page layout, and so on) that you can install on your Mac.

application menu The part of the menu bar between the Apple menu icon and the menu extras. It displays the menus associated with the current application. See also *Apple menu, menu bar, menu extras.*

application preferences The options and settings that you can configure for a particular application via the Preferences command. See also *system preferences.*

back up The process of creating copies of your data.

Bluetooth A wireless networking technology that allows two devices to communicate when they are within range of each other.

Bonjour A service discovery protocol implemented in OS X. Formerly known as Rendezvous, it allows for the automatic discovery of other devices running the protocol, which can then share services. For example, a Mac running Bonjour can discover and print to a printer that's also running Bonjour, without having to know the printer's IP address.

bookmark An Internet site saved in a web browser so that it can be quickly accessed in future browsing sessions.

BSD (Berkeley Software Distribution) A UNIX-based operating system developed by the University of California, Berkeley. OS X runs on a derivative of BSD called Darwin. See also *Darwin.*

Calendar OS X's default scheduling application.

cloud A network-based or Internet-based data storage service that allows you to access data from anywhere you have a connection to the network or Internet.

ColorSync The Apple color management technology. It uses other industry-standard technologies, such as ICC profiles, to keep color consistent among applications, your Mac, and input (scanners and cameras) and output (displays and printers) devices.

command key (⌘) Located next to the space bar on the keyboard. This key can be used in conjunction with other keys to perform certain tasks. For example, pressing ⌘+P causes an application to open its Print dialog.

command-line interface (CLI) A text-only interface used to display information for the user and to send commands to the computer.

compression The process of making a file, or a folder containing many files, smaller in data size.

Cover Flow A Finder view that shows a split screen with a List view of the contents on the bottom and a preview of the current item on the top.

CUPS The printing system used by most UNIX-based operating systems, including OS X.

Darwin The name of the flavor of BSD UNIX on which OS X is based. Darwin is developed by Apple and is the core of the Mac operating system services, such as networking and file systems. See also *BSD.*

Dashboard An application that runs other mini-applications called widgets. Dashboard can be accessed by swiping from left to right on your trackpad or Magic Mouse. See also *widget.*

device driver Software developed by a hardware device's manufacturer that allows the operating system to interact with that hardware.

DHCP (Dynamic Host Configuration Protocol) A protocol used to automatically assign IP addresses to client computers in a network environment.

disk image A file created by Disk Utility that acts exactly like a physical drive in that files can be saved to it the same as they can in any other directory. Many application installers that you download from the Internet use disk images to transport their data.

discoverable Describes a device that has its Bluetooth feature enabled so other Bluetooth devices can connect to it.

Dock Located at the bottom of the screen by default, the Dock stores links to the items or applications used most frequently.

drop box A directory in the home folder that others on your network can use to share files with you.

Eject key The key used to eject a previously inserted CD or DVD. On some Macs, you must hold it down for a second or two.

Ethernet The most common network standard in use today. It links computers together via a system of cables and hubs, or routers. Data transmission speed can range from 10 to as fast as 10,000 megabits (10 Gigabits) per second, depending on the cabling and hardware used.

event An appointment or meeting scheduled in Calendar.

fast user switching A Mac feature that allows more than one user to be logged in at once. It leaves programs running when a user logs out and reinstates them just as they were when the same user logs back in.

file system A technology used by the operating system to keep track of the files stored on a drive, such as a hard drive.

Finder The one application that is always running on a Mac. It's used to navigate the Mac hard drive for files, folders, applications, other volumes, and so on. See also *Spotlight*.

firewall Software that protects a computer or network from outside intrusion.

FireWire A high-speed serial bus standard developed by Apple for the speedy transmission of large amounts of data. Also known as IEEE 1394, it is cross-platform and can transmit between 400 and 800 megabits per second, depending on which version is supported by the Mac hardware.

font A complete set of characters for a particular typeface that defines how the typeface appears on the Mac display and printed documents.

FTP File Transfer Protocol An IP protocol used for transferring, creating, and deleting files and folders located on an FTP server.

group A collection of Address Book contacts. See also *Smart Group*.

405

guest operating system An operating system that runs inside a virtual machine using virtualization software.

HFS+ (Hierarchical File System) The default file system for OS X, which uses a hierarchical system for storing and organizing files and folders.

home directory (or folder) The directory that contains all of a user's personal documents and files. Every user account created on a Mac is assigned a home directory located in the User's folder at the root of the hard drive.

HTML (HyperText Markup Language) The programming language used to render the graphics and text of a web page.

HTTP (HyperText Transfer Protocol) A protocol responsible for linking and exchanging files on the Internet.

iBooks An application designed for reading and organizing electronic books.

iCloud Apple-based cloud storage and computing service that allows you to store and synchronize information with multiple devices, such as a Mac, an iPad, and an iPhone.

iLife A suite of applications that can be installed on a Mac. iLife includes programs such as iDVD, iPhoto, and iWeb.

Image Capture The Mac application that you use to connect to a device (such as a digital camera, scanner, or digital camcorder) and download photos or videos from that device to your Mac.

iTunes The Mac default media player application.

iWork A productivity suite that consists of three programs: Pages, a word processor; Numbers, a spreadsheet program; and Keynote, a presentation program.

Java Cross-platform software development environment used on most computer operating systems and many handheld devices. It also is often used to display dynamic information on web pages.

JPEG (Joint Photographic Experts Group) Perhaps the most common format for pictures on computers and the Internet. JPEG can compress the data size of the image while still retaining reasonable image quality.

LAN (Local Area Network) A network that is confined to one particular area, such as a small office or home business.

Launchpad Provides instant access to applications through an iOS-like interface.

login items The applications, files, folders, network shares, and other items that start automatically when a user logs in to her account.

LPD (Line Printer Daemon) An industry-standard protocol for printing via TCP/IP over a network.

Mail The OS X default e-mail application. Mail can handle multiple e-mail accounts of varying protocols, such as IMAP, POP, and Exchange.

Maps An application designed to help you find geographic locations, get driving directions to those locations, find information for local points of interest, and more.

menu bar The strip that runs across the top of the Mac screen. See also *Apple menu, application menu, menu extras.*

menu extras Icons that appear on the right side of the *menu bar* and show the status of certain Mac features, such as the wireless network connection. These icons also allow the configuration of other features, such as the volume and Bluetooth functionality. See also *Apple menu, application menu, menu bar.*

Messages A Mac application used to converse with other people in real time by sending each other online text messages.

Mission Control Provides an organized overview of every open item in OS X, such as all the windows associated with an application, Dashboard, and full-screen applications.

modifier key Pressed in conjunction with one or more other keys to launch some action. Most Mac keyboard shortcuts involve the Command key (⌘).

Notes An application that you can use to jot down ideas and notes, and then share them with others. Notes uses iCloud to sync your notes with other devices, such as an iPad or iPhone.

open source The software development method that allows for free access to source code, as well as the modification and redistribution of the code.

OpenGL A cross-platform application programming interface (API) developed by Silicon Graphics to produce two- and three-dimensional graphics.

pair To connect one Bluetooth device with another by typing a passkey.

partition A portion of hard drive space that has been separated from the rest of the drive. A Mac views each partition as a separate hard drive that can be used for anything, including installing Windows or storing particular types of files.

permissions Access rights given to the owner and other users of a Mac. Without the right permissions, a user cannot view or access files or folders owned by another user. See also *user account.*

Photo Booth A standard OS X application for taking pictures with the built-in Mac camera and adding special effects.

preference files A document that stores options and other data entered using an application's Preferences command.

Preview An application for viewing PDF files and images that ships with OS X. Preview can open more than 25 file formats, including most of the popular image formats.

printer queue Stores print jobs and data for the printer. If there is a problem, the print data is stored here until printing can resume.

protocol A set of standards or rules that govern the communication of information between two computers.

Quartz A graphics service in OS X responsible for rendering two-dimensional graphics.

QuickTime The Apple default multimedia framework designed for the creation and handling of various video, sound, and animation digital media formats.

QuickTime Player The Mac default digital video player.

Reminders An application that literally reminds you of tasks that need to be done, as well as upcoming events. Reminders can use iCloud to sync items with other devices, such as an iPad or iPhone.

Safari The Mac default web browser.

Safe Boot To start a Mac in Safe Mode. See also *Safe Mode*.

Safe Mode A startup mode in which a Mac doesn't load most of its behind-the-scenes components. See also *Safe Boot*.

sidebar The pane on the left side of any Finder window that offers a number of shortcuts to objects such as devices, network shares, and local folders.

sleep mode A low-power state in which a Mac uses only marginally more electricity than if it were powered off altogether, while still preserving all running applications, windows, and documents.

Smart Folder A kind of virtual folder where the contents depend on the criteria specified by the user. Mac adjusts the contents automatically as the files change.

Smart Group A collection of Address Book contacts in which members have one or more things in common. Address Book automatically updates a Smart Group as contacts are added, edited, or deleted. See also *group*.

Smart Mailbox A Mail folder that consolidates all messages that meet one or more conditions.

SMB (Server Message Block) Protocol used primarily by Windows computers for accessing shared files, printers, and other network services. OS X has the built-in ability to communicate with Windows-based PCs through SMB.

SMTP (Simple Mail Transfer Protocol) Protocol used mainly for sending e-mail, but rarely for receiving e-mail.

Spaces An application that allows a user to work with multiple desktops on which he can run applications and view documents.

Spotlight A Mac feature used to search for files, folders, applications, Mail messages, images, and other data. See also *Finder*.

synchronization A process that ensures that data (such as contacts, e-mail accounts, and events) on a Mac is the same as the data on other devices, such as cell phones, other computers, and PDAs.

System Folder Located at the root of the hard drive and containing the core components needed to boot a Mac system and run it efficiently. A Mac does not boot correctly if this folder is tampered with (such as by changing its name), so it's best to steer totally clear of it.

system preferences The options, settings, and other data that a user configures for her Mac via the System Preferences application. See also *application preferences*.

tags A Finder convention that helps you to organize files based on specific keywords.

TCP/IP (Transfer Control Protocol/Internet Protocol) Set of industry-standard protocols used for communications via the Internet. TCP's job is to keep up with the packets of data being sent, while IP is the actual vehicle for delivering the packets.

Terminal A program used for accessing the command-line interface of OS X.

TextEdit The Mac default word processor.

Time Machine A Mac application used to create and access file backups.

user account Required for every person who uses a Mac to access personal files and folders. See also *permissions*.

utility Specialty software application dedicated to managing and tuning Mac software and, to some degree, hardware.

virtual machine Software files that virtualization applications recognize and utilize as if they were separate computers. A virtual machine runs within OS X, allowing a user to work with OS X and the OS on the virtual machine at the same time. See also *virtualization*.

virtualization Running a guest operating system (such as Windows on a Mac) in a virtual machine. See also *virtual machine*.

widget Mini-applications launched with Dashboard. Typically, widgets concentrate on one particular task, such as local weather, movie show times, sports scores, and so on. See also *Dashboard*.

Index